MAKING SENSE OF THE BIBLE

KEVIN SIMINGTON

© Copyright 2019 Kevin Simington

SMART FAITH PRESS

 A catalogue record for this book is available from the National Library of Australia

All rights reserved. No part of this publication may be reproduced, stored in a retrieval system or transmitted in any form by any means electronic, mechanical, photocopying, recording or otherwise, without the prior written permission of the author.

Unless otherwise specified, Scripture quotations are from the New International Version Bible, copyright © 1973. 1978, 1984, 2011, Zondervan, Grand Rapids, Michigan, USA.

Cataloguing in Publication Data:
TITLE: Making Sense of the Bible
ISBN: 978-0-6484945-0-8
AUTHOR: Kevin Simington
EDITORS: Sandra Simington, John Crooks
COVER DESIGN: Tatiana Villa, viladesign.net

To my wonderful wife, Sandy,

Thank you for your love, prayers, patience and support.

ACKNOWLEDGMENTS

This book would be a much poorer version of itself without the amazing help of my two editors:

- My wife, Sandy, who reads the first draft and makes many corrections and suggestions.

- John Crooks, who scrutinises the second draft, meticulously checks references and makes further suggestions.

Both Sandy and John, through many long hours of tedious editing, have helped to make this book a more polished, consistent literary work. I cannot thank both of you enough!

Table of Contents

Glossary of Terms viii
Preface ix

PART I - THE JOURNEY FROM TEXTS TO TRANSLATIONS

Chapter 1: Are There Mistakes in The Bible? 3
Chapter 2: Manuscripts and Variants 19
Chapter 3: Internal Inconsistencies in the Bible.................... 47
Chapter 4: Bible Translations 65

PART II - GETTING THE BIG PICTURE

Chapter 5: Challenges in Interpreting the Bible 87
Chapter 6: The Two Covenants 101
Chapter 7: Understanding the Old Testament 117
Chapter 8: The Old Testament as Pre-Christian 131
Chapter 9: Progressive Revelation in the Bible 155
Chapter 10: Progressive Revelation in the New Testament 185
Chapter 11: Reading the Old Testament Christologically 195

PART III - PRINCIPLES OF BIBLICAL INTERPRETATION

Chapter 12: Hermeneutics 215
Chapter 13: Literary Genre 221
Chapter 14: Historical and Cultural Context 247
Chapter 15: Literary and Lexical Context 259
Chapter 16: Interpreting Scripture with Scripture 271
Chapter 17: Case Study: The Role of Women in the Church 289
Chapter 18: Reading the Bible with Discernment 307
Author Bio 317
Other Titles by Kevin Simington 319
Connect With Kevin Simington 321
Topical Index 323

Glossary of Terms

Term	Meaning
Autograph	The original ancient document.
Ecclesiology	Doctrines concerning the formal structures and practices of the church.
Eisegesis	Reading your own presuppositions, agendas, or biases *into* a text.
Didactic	Instructional, cognitive teaching.
Exegesis	Deriving the meaning of a text from the text itself.
Genre	A style or category of art, music, or literature.
Hermeneutics	Accepted principles of interpretation, especially of the Bible or literary texts.
Lexical	Pertaining to the precise meaning of words.
Metanarrative	The "Big Picture". An overarching story or belief which acts as a lens through which everything else is interpreted.
Normal	Not unusual.
Normative	Universal and essential.
Praxis	The accepted, definitive practice of something.
Temporal	Relating to time.
Precipitating Circumstances	Specific issues that prompted the writing of a New Testament letter

PREFACE

After more than four decades as a Christian, and having pastored four different churches, I have reached a disturbing conclusion; many Christians have an inadequate understanding of the Bible – not only of what it *says*, but also of what it *is*. Despite the fact that evangelicals base their faith upon the Bible, very few ever move beyond the most superficial understanding of its nature and origin. For the vast majority of Christians, the inspiration and inerrancy of the Bible are beliefs that are held almost unthinkingly, without coming to terms with the many textual challenges and anomalies of this ancient literary work.

"Making Sense of the Bible" will take you on a fascinating journey of discovery. But be warned; the journey will not always be an easy or a comfortable one. It will not allow you to cling to a simplistic view of the Bible's inspiration. It will force you to grapple with issues that you may never have considered, such as:

- The hundreds of historical and numerical discrepancies that exist within the Bible.

- The imperfect transmission of the Bible over the centuries, resulting in thousands of textual variants.

- Textual uncertainty (uncertainty regarding the exact original words) in approximately 2% of the Bible's text.

- Lexical uncertainty (uncertainty regarding the precise *meaning* of the original words) when attempting to translate the ancient languages of the Bible.

Most Christians have never been confronted with these issues. These are not concepts that are commonly addressed from the pulpit. In some cases, this is because preachers with limited theological training are unaware of these issues themselves. Other preachers who have had the privilege of a more comprehensive theological education, may be aware of these challenges, but usually refrain from speaking about them, for fear of confusing or confounding the faith of their congregations.

I am convinced, however, that all Christians need to come to terms with the true nature of the Bible. We must move beyond the simplistic views of our early faith and develop a more complex, robust view of the Bible's inspiration; one that comfortably embraces its textual anomalies.

This book is in three parts:

Part I, *"The Journey from Texts to Translations"*, examines the remarkable journey undertaken by ancient parchments and papyri to eventually become the book that we call "the Bible" today. It describes the complex challenges facing textual critics and translators in producing a finished work that is as close as possible to the autographic (original) text.

Part II, *"Getting the Big Picture"*, examines some fundamental concepts that are essential for correctly understanding the Bible:

- The significant difference between the old and new covenants, including an understanding of the complete obsolescence of the old covenant.

- The concept of progressive revelation: That God's truth was revealed progressively throughout the Bible, so that the doctrines and morals in the Old Testament are the starting point, rather than God's definitive and final declaration.

- The pre-Christian nature of the Old Testament: That God had to deal with the Israelites as unregenerate, spiritual infants, by instituting a system of tangible, immediate rewards and punishments that are no longer relevant for those who have been born again under the new covenant of Christ.

- The Christological metanarrative of the Bible: That the whole of the Bible points to Christ and is, ultimately, his story. Learning to read the Bible through the lens of this metanarrative will significantly impact our interpretation of its message at certain points.

These are vital concepts for correctly interpreting the Bible, particularly the Old Testament, yet they are poorly understood by most Christians. Coming to a clearer understanding of these concepts will enable us to read the Bible with discernment and accurately apply its message to our lives.

Part III, "Hermeneutics: *Principles of Interpretation",* examines some foundational principles that can help ordinary Bible readers avoid the common interpretive errors that often result in misguided application. It explores the importance of interpreting Bible passages in the light of their genre, their historical context, their cultural context, their literary context and their lexical context (the precise meaning of the original words). Each of these principles will be illustrated by very practical examples as we examine commonly misinterpreted passages and show how the implementation of proper interpretive principles results in a more accurate understanding of the Bible's message.

As well as the standard Table of Contents, you will also notice a Topical Index at the back of the book. This index provides a topical reference for the location of key biblical doctrines throughout the book, which are discussed as practical examples of the various principles of interpretation.

"Making Sense of the Bible" is for Christians who want to move beyond a simplistic understanding of the Scriptures. It is for those who desire to grow in their knowledge of God's Word and develop a mature ability to accurately interpret and apply its message. It is my hope and prayer that this book will help you to *"correctly handle the Word of God" (2 Timothy 2:15).*

PREFACE

PART I

THE JOURNEY FROM TEXTS TO TRANSLATIONS

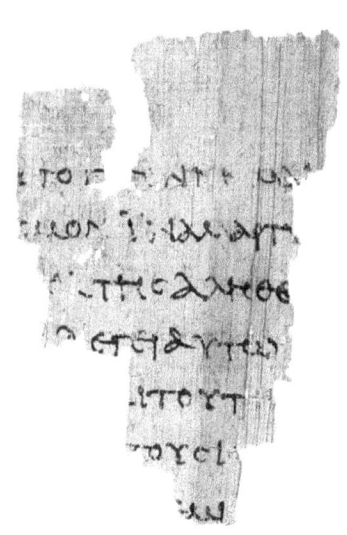

MISTAKES IN THE BIBLE?

CHAPTER 1

ARE THERE MISTAKES IN THE BIBLE?

Are you sitting comfortably? Perhaps in your favourite chair, with a cup of coffee and something tasty to nibble? Have you settled down to have a nice relaxing read? Then I apologise, because I need you to stand up and go and get a Bible. You see, I need to do a little experiment with you! And please make sure it is a modern translation, rather than the King James Version (although, if you have the KJV handy, please bring that as well). Oh, and it needs to be a physical Bible, rather than an electronic copy.

Off you go! I'll make a cup of coffee for myself while I'm waiting.

MISTAKES IN THE BIBLE?

Oh good, you're back. Is that a modern translation you've got in your hand? Excellent. Now please look up Matthew 17:21. I'll have another sip of coffee while you're looking it up.

How did you go? What's that you're saying? You can't find it? It's not there? It goes from verse 20 to verse 22 and there is no verse 21? Well, that's puzzling isn't it? Perhaps it's just a typo. Let's try another verse in the next chapter. Please look up Matthew 18:11. I'll have another sip while you do.

How did you go? You can't find that one either? This is getting ridiculous! I'll tell you what: I'll get you to look up a few more verses, and while you're doing it, I'll go and get a piece of cake to have with my coffee. Please look up any of the following verses:

Matthew 23-14	Mark 7:16	Mark 9:44	Mark 9:46	Mark 11:26
Mark 15:28	Luke 17:36	Luke 23:17	John 5:4	
Acts 15:34	Acts 24:7	Acts 28:29	Romans 16:24	

MISTAKES IN THE BIBLE?

Still no luck? It wasn't a piece of cake was it!

By now, you will have realised that all of those verses are *missing* from most modern translations. Interestingly, they can be found in older translations, such as the King James Version, but modern translations have chosen to omit them.

Do you have any idea why? Most Christians aren't even aware of these missing verses and, even if they are, very few would be able to articulate a clear explanation. In a recent seminar that I conducted on the inspiration and inerrancy of the Bible, I commenced by doing this same experiment with the attendees. Of the 65 people present, all were completely puzzled, and no one was able to offer a reasonable explanation.

The reason for these missing verses is a somewhat complicated. It involves transcription errors in the copying of the biblical manuscripts throughout the centuries, and the resulting textual variants that can be found in different ancient manuscript copies of the same passage. For the moment, these concepts will be a little unfamiliar to you, (although they will soon be explained), and you may already be wondering whether I am going to suggest a view of the Bible that undermines its inspired nature and dilutes its authority. That is not the case.

But I want to suggest that the nature and extent of the Bible's inspiration is much more complex than the simplistic view that most Christians hold. If you are to develop a robust, mature faith, you will need to move

MISTAKES IN THE BIBLE?

beyond the superficial, Sunday-school type of understanding of the Bible's nature that many Christians have. That is the purpose of this book.

So settle back, have another sip of coffee, and let's begin!

THE CLAIM OF DIVINE INSPIRATION

As the Apostle Paul neared the end of his life, he found himself imprisoned for a second time in Rome, under the Emperor Nero. In contrast to his first imprisonment, when he had lived in a private house and was well cared for, he was now locked away in a cold dungeon, chained to a wall like a common criminal. His supporters had difficulty locating him, and his health was deteriorating. Realising that his life was nearing its end, he wrote one final letter, giving encouragement and instructions to a struggling young pastor in the church at Ephesus. Mid-way through that letter, as he sought to exhort Timothy to persevere through various difficulties, Paul reflected on the many ordeals he had suffered in his own service for Christ, and reaffirmed his absolute faith in the inspired nature of Holy Scripture:

> *"You, however, know all about my teaching, my way of life, my purpose, faith, patience, love, endurance, persecutions, sufferings – what kinds of things happened to me in Antioch, Iconium and Lystra, the persecutions I endured. Yet the Lord rescued me from them all…. As for you, continue in what you have learned and have become convinced of, because you know those from whom you learned it, and how from infancy you have known the <u>Holy Scriptures</u>, which are able to make you wise for salvation through faith in Christ Jesus. <u>All Scripture is God-breathed</u> and is useful for teaching, rebuking, correcting and training in righteousness, so that all God's people may be thoroughly equipped for every good work." (2 Timothy 3:10-17).*

To his dying day, to his final breath, the Apostle Paul was convinced that the book we now call "the Bible" is God's inspired, authoritative message

MISTAKES IN THE BIBLE?

to mankind. His assertion that it is *"Holy"* and *"God-breathed"* could not be clearer.

EVIDENCE FOR THE DIVINE INSPIRATION OF THE BIBLE

As an evangelical, Bible-believing Christian, I uphold a high view of Holy Scripture. This collection of ancient writings does not represent the mere speculations of flawed human beings; it bears the stamp of God's Spirit. It is alive with the breath of God. My belief in the divinely inspired nature of the Bible, however, does not rest upon mere blind faith. My confidence regarding its inspiration rests upon some very convincing evidence; both objective and subjective. Objectively, there are two primary areas of convincing evidence [see Footnote 1 at the end of this chapter]:

Firstly; its internal consistency. The Bible was written over a period of approximately 1,600 years, by over 40 different authors from a diversity of cultures and backgrounds. Yet despite this, it exhibits an internal consistency that is beyond remarkable – it is miraculous! During my teaching years, I often said to my Biblical Studies classes that if I sent them to watch a football match and each student had to write a report of the match, the resulting collage of reports would almost certainly contain discrepancies, inconsistencies and contradictions. Such is our fallible human nature. But the Bible contains no such gross inconsistencies. Despite the diversity of authorship and time periods, the Bible speaks with a cohesive, unified voice. This is only possible because of the miraculous inspiration of the Holy Spirit as he guided the writers to record God's message to mankind.

Secondly; fulfilled prophecy within the Bible. In his *"Encyclopedia of Biblical Prophecy"* [2], J. Barton Payne lists 1,817 predictive prophecies in the Bible. While some of these are still awaiting fulfilment, as they are predictions regarding the final events of human history, the rest were fulfilled in precise detail, often centuries after the prediction. 191 of these prophecies are messianic, foretelling specific details of the long-

MISTAKES IN THE BIBLE?

awaited messiah. They predicted the precise nature of Christ's birth, ministry, death and resurrection. For example:

- 700 years before Christ, Isaiah made the seemingly outrageous prediction that the Messiah would be born to a virgin (Isa 7:14).

- Micah predicted that the Messiah would be born in Bethlehem (Mic 5:2).

- Moses, writing 1,500 years before Christ, predicted that he would be from the tribe of Judah (Gen 49:10).

- Isaiah predicted the messiah's rejection and death at the hands of the Jewish leaders (Isa 53).

- Even more remarkably, Psalm 22 predicted Christ's death by crucifixion, including the piercing of his hands and feet, yet this was written centuries before the Romans had even invented crucifixion!

Other extraordinary predictions include:

- The piercing of the Messiah's side with a spear (Zech 12:10).

- The casting of lots for his clothing (Psa 22:18).

- The 30 pieces of silver paid to Judas to betray the Messiah (Zech 11:12-13).

- The fact that Jesus would be beaten and spat upon (Mic 5:1 and Isa 50:6)

- That Jesus would be given wine vinegar to drink as he died (Psa 69:21).

MISTAKES IN THE BIBLE?

- That Jesus would be buried in a rich man's tomb (Isa 53:9).

These are just a small selection of the many hundreds of extraordinarily precise predictions in the Bible, made centuries before their fulfilment. The probability of all these prophecies being fulfilled by random chance is a statistical impossibility. These fulfilled predictive prophecies of the Bible provide powerful evidence for the Bible's supernatural inspiration. They declare that this is no ordinary book.

Subjectively, I am also convinced of the Bible's divinely inspired nature because, as I read it, I encounter God. His Spirit energises the words on each page and his voice whispers words of truth and life into my heart. My own daily, subjective experience affirms Paul's ancient assertion that this book truly is *"God-breathed"*. Millions of Christians similarly testify to regularly, and, at times, powerfully encountering God through his written Word. Minds are renewed, lives are transformed, and destinies are irrevocably and eternally altered through the life-changing power of the Bible.

Liberal Scepticism

There exists a whole branch of Christianity, however, that would strongly dispute most of what I have written thus far. They regard evangelical belief in the Bible's inspiration as naïve and simplistic. Liberal Christians approach the Bible with two presuppositions regarding both its inspiration and inerrancy (lack of errors*)*:

> 1. Liberals claim that Bible, as it was originally written, was not perfectly inspired by God. They say that some writers of the Bible wrote more closely to God's heart than others. Consequently, as well as containing some noble and timeless truths, the Bible also supposedly contains many teachings which are either flawed, outdated or completely erroneous. According to this view, the Bible simply represents mankind's stumbling, imprecise attempt to understand God and to perceive spiritual truth.

MISTAKES IN THE BIBLE?

2. Liberals also claim that the Bible's transmission through the ages has been so corrupted by transcription errors, deliberate editorial changes, and interpolations (insertions by subsequent copyists), that we cannot trust today's text, because it probably bears little resemblance to the original text.

In support of these two critical assertions, Liberal Christians point to a large number of supposed internal contradictions within the Bible. These contradictions fall into three main categories; doctrinal, moral and historical contradictions. In this next section, I have listed a few commonly cited examples of each of these categories of supposed contradictions:

APPARENT DOCTRINAL CONTRADICTIONS

Children Punished for the Sins of their Parents?

- *"Prepare a place to slaughter his children for the sins of their ancestors, for they are not to inherit the land …."* (Isa 14:21)

- *"The fathers shall not be put to death for the children, neither shall the children be put to death for the fathers: every man shall be put to death for his own sin."* (Deut 24:16)

No One Righteous?

- *Noah & Job were righteous. (Gen 7:1; Job 1:1,8; 2:3)*

- *No one is righteous. (Rom 3:10; 3:23; 1 Jn 1:8-10)*

MISTAKES IN THE BIBLE?

Revenge or Forgiveness?

- *"A life for a life, an eye for an eye"* etc. *(Exod 21:23-25; Lev 24:20; Deut 19:21)*

- *"Turn the other cheek…. Love your enemies". (Matt 5:38-44; Luke 6:27-29)*

Divorce

- A man can divorce his wife simply because she displeases him, and both he and his wife can remarry. *(Deut 24:1-5)*

- Divorce is wrong, on any grounds. *(Mk 10:2-12)*

Salvation

- *"Not everyone who calls on the name of the Lord will be saved" (Matt 7:21)*

- *"Whoever calls on the name of the Lord will be saved" (Acts 2:21; Rom 10:13)*

APPARENT MORAL CONTRADICTIONS

Punishment or Mercy?

- *"I will smash them one against the other, fathers and sons alike, declares the Lord. I will allow no pity or mercy or compassion to keep me from destroying them" (Jer 13:14)*

- *"The Lord is full of mercy and compassion" (Jas 5:11). "The Lord is good to all, and he has compassion on all he has made" (Psa 145:9)*

MISTAKES IN THE BIBLE?

Kill or Love?

- God commands the Israelites to *"utterly destroy"* their enemies and show *"no mercy" (Deut 7:2)*. *"In the cities of the nations the Lord is giving you as an inheritance, do not leave alive anything that breathes." (Deut 20:16)*

- *"Love your enemies and pray for those who persecute you." (Matt 5:44)*

Treatment of Slaves

- *"When a man strikes his slave with a rod so hard that the slave dies, he shall be punished. But if the slave survives for a day or two, he is not to be punished, since the slave is his own property." (Exod 21:20-21)*

- *"Masters, treat your slaves with respect. Do not threaten them ..." (Eph 6:9)*

Polygamy or Monogamy?

- David and Solomon had many wives and concubines with God's permission (Solomon had 700 wives & 300 concubines!) *(2 Sam 5:13; 1 Kings 11:3)*. The Old Testament contains many other references to God permitting polygamy, including instructions for the fair treatment of multiple wives *(Deut 21:16)*. Jacob married both Leah and Rachel (sisters), with God's blessing *(Gen 30)*. Yet, not long after this, God commands, *"Do not take your wife's sister as a second wife" (Lev 18:18)*, inferring that polygamy is allowable, except if the women are sisters.

- On the other hand, _monogamy_ is commanded of leaders in the New Testament church *(1 Tim 3:2; Tit 1:6)*.

MISTAKES IN THE BIBLE?

APPARENT HISTORICAL CONTRADICTIONS

Matthew incorrectly attributes a quote by Zechariah to Jeremiah:

- *"Then what was spoken by the prophet Jeremiah was fulfilled: 'They took the 30 silver coins' …" (Matt 27:9)*

- The above quote in Matthew 27:9, however, is from Zechariah, not Jeremiah (Zech 11:11-13). There is nothing like this in Jeremiah!

Josiah's Successor:

- 2 Chronicles states that Jehoahaz was Josiah's successor (2 Chron 36:1)

- Jeremiah states that Shallum was Josiah's successor (Jer 22:11)

David's Bodyguard:

- 1 Chronicles states that David's bodyguard was "Sibbecai" (1 Chron 11:29)

- 2 Samuel states that David's bodyguard was "Mebunnai" (2 Sam 23:27)

How many died in the plague at Shittim?

- Numbers states that 24,000 died in the plague. (Num 25:9)

- 1 Corinthians states that 23,000 died in the plague. (1 Cor 10:8)

MISTAKES IN THE BIBLE?

Solomon's Horses:

- Solomon had 40,000 stalls for horses and chariots (1 Kings 4:26)

- Solomon had 4,000 stalls for horses and chariots (2 Chron 9:25)

Solomon's Supervisors:

- Solomon had 3,300 supervisors. (1 Kings 5:16)

- Solomon had 3,600 supervisors. (2 Chron 2:2)

The Temple Pillars:

- The two pillars of the temple were 18 cubits high. (1 Kings 7:15-22)

- The two pillars of the temple were 35 cubits high. (2 Chron 3:15-17)

How Much Gold?

- 420 talents of gold was brought back from Ophir. (1 Kings 9:28)

- 450 talents of gold was brought back from Ophir. (2 Chron 8:18)

Baasha's Death:

- Baasha died in the 26th year of King Asa's reign. (1 Kings 16:6-8)

- Baasha built a city in the 36th year of King Asa's reign. (2 Chron 16:1)

MISTAKES IN THE BIBLE?

Ahaziah's Age:

- Ahaziah was 22 years old when he began his reign. (2 Kings 8:25-26)

- Ahaziah was 42 years old when he began his reign. (2 Chron 22:2)

MISTAKES IN THE BIBLE?

In *"Alleged Discrepancies Of The Bible'* [3], John W. Haley deals with all three types of contradictions (doctrinal, ethical and historical), and he lists over 2,000 of these alleged contradictions. John W. Haley is an evangelical Christian who writes to defend the Bible in the face of these apparent contradictions, but the answers he gives are not simple, nor will they satisfy people looking for a nice neat theology of biblical inspiration.

Dr. Samuel Davidson, his book *"Introduction To The Old Testament"* [4], lists 114 contradictions in names in just the first 11 chapters of Chronicles when those passages are compared with corresponding narratives in other parts of the Bible. Let me reiterate that: 114 contradictions in just 11 chapters!

Some important questions need to be asked: What do we mean when we say that the Bible is inspired? What do we mean when we say that the Bible is inerrant (without error)? How do we answer these kinds of accusations by sceptics? More to the point, how do we reconcile these kinds of apparent inconsistencies in the Bible with our own belief in the inspired, inerrant nature of the Bible?

THE NEED FOR A MATURE FAITH

There are answers to these challenging issues, but they involve moving beyond a simplistic, Sunday School type of faith. They involve coming to a mature understanding of the nature of inspiration, and the extent and

MISTAKES IN THE BIBLE?

meaning of inerrancy. They also require that we develop a clear understanding of the relationship between the old and new covenants; the misunderstanding of which is a major source of the apparent doctrinal and moral contradictions that are commonly cited.

Most Christians would struggle to come to terms with the kinds of contradictions and issues that I have already outlined. Even mature Christians with a sound knowledge of the Bible and a solid grounding in doctrine often don't have a very clear understanding of the nature and extent of the Bible's inspiration and the inter-relationship of its parts. In fact, often the first time a Christian comes face to face with these kinds of issues at any depth is when they commence theological studies. For these people, their first year in Theological College can be a difficult time, because these issues have never been adequately addressed in their church life.

Of course, not every Christian has the opportunity to formally study theology. But I am convinced that, at some stage, *every* Christian needs to grapple with these issues, in order to move beyond their simplistic view of the Bible and arrive at a mature understanding of God's Word. This requires, not that we discard our previous simple faith, but that we *add* to it, in order that it might become more knowledgeable and mature. The Apostle Peter urges us, *"Make every effort to add to your faith ... knowledge" (2 Pet 1:5).*

Paul, in his final letter to Timothy, writing from his cold, dark prison cell in Rome, awaiting his imminent demise, urges both Timothy and us to *"Do your best to present yourself to God as one approved, a workman who does not need to be ashamed and who correctly handles the Word of Truth" (2 Tim 2:15).* In *"Making Sense of the Bible"*, you will find helpful, indeed, *essential* information that will assist you to reach a more robust, mature understanding of God's Word, so that you, too, will become one who *"correctly handles the Word of Truth".*

For those who can't wait for the answers to the issues that I have raised, or whose faith I have just battered by highlighting these apparent

MISTAKES IN THE BIBLE?

contradictions, let me pre-empt what is to come with some reassuring words. There are no doctrinal or moral contradictions in the Bible. All the commonly cited alleged contradictions result from a lack of understanding of the relationships between the two covenants and the nature of progressive revelation. These concepts will be examined in detail in Part Two of this book.

There are, however, many historical inconsistencies in the Bible regarding names and numbers. These are the result of transcription errors and manuscript variations, which will be explained more fully in the next chapter. If we are to properly understand how these inconsistencies came about, and reconcile them with our view of inerrancy, we must go back to the very beginning. We must examine the incredible journey that the Bible has undertaken and the processes that have occurred in order for us to hold this amazing book in our hands today. This will be the focus of our first area of our study.

Chapter Footnotes

1. I have written extensively of the objective evidence for the inspiration of the Bible on my website, SmartFaith.net. This includes an analysis of archaeological verification of biblical events as a further evidence of the Bible's veracity.

2. J. Barton Payne, *Encyclopedia of Biblical Prophecy*, 1996, Harper & Row

3. John W. Haley, *Alleged Discrepancies of The Bible*, 1992, Whitaker House

4. Samuel Davidson, *Introduction to The Old Testament,* 2010, Nabu Press

Reflection Questions 1

1. How has this chapter challenged your view of the Bible?

2. *What, if anything, surprised you as you read this chapter? How do you respond to some of the inconsistencies mentioned in this chapter?

3. What is your understanding of the inspiration and inerrancy (lack of errors) of the Bible?

4. What do you hope to learn as you continue reading this book?

5. Read 2 Timothy 3:16. What do you think this really means? To what extent do you think the Bible is inspired?

6. Read 2 Timothy 2:15. Firstly, what does it mean to "do your best to present yourself to God as one approved"? What does this mean in practice? Secondly, what does it mean to be "a worker who does not need to be ashamed"? Thirdly, what does it mean to be one who "correctly handles the word of truth"?

CHAPTER 2

MANUSCRIPTS and VARIANTS

Before we even start to read and interpret the Bible, textual critics and translators have already had to make a lot of interpretations and, at times, even guesses, in order to produce our English text. The Bible was written thousands of years ago in ancient languages that are no longer used - Hebrew, Greek and Aramaic. The task of translating from these dead languages into a living one is incredibly complex and difficult. Translators need to understand languages that have not been spoken aloud for thousands of years, including coming to grips with obscure words and puzzling cultural references. But before they can even start to do that, textual critics have had the even more difficult task of trying to determine the exact wording of the original text.

The problem is that we don't have the original manuscripts (autographs) for any book of the Bible; all we have are thousands of subsequent copies, each of them with slightly different wording. For instance, there was once an original manuscript of John's Gospel – the actual papyrus that John (and his scribe) wrote on with quill and ink. But that has long since perished. All we have are copies, and copies of copies, and copies of copies of copies ... etc. For most books of the Bible, the earliest surviving manuscripts are dated decades or even centuries after the original. Many of these manuscripts, when compared with each other, have slight variations in the exact wording, mainly due to transcription errors - mistakes made in the copying process over the centuries. I will explain more about this shortly, and discuss how this impacts the text of the Bible that we read today. But, for now, a little more information is required regarding the manuscript lineage of the Bible.

Throughout the New Testament era, the biblical documents were written on papyrus manuscripts, the ancient precursor to modern paper. As with paper, these papyrus manuscripts were susceptible to decay, particularly in the presence of water or humidity. Consequently, extant manuscripts (manuscripts that still exist today) are usually only found in dry, desert regions like the Middle East, or in airtight containers of some kind (such as sealed pottery, as in the case of the Dead Sea Scrolls).

In terms of the New Testament there are over 5,600 extant Greek manuscripts, and thousands more manuscripts in Latin, Coptic and other languages. Some are mere fragments, while others are complete books of up to 200 pages. These precious manuscripts are safely stored in universities and museums all over the world, and this collection is continually being added to as a result of ongoing archaeological excavations and discoveries.

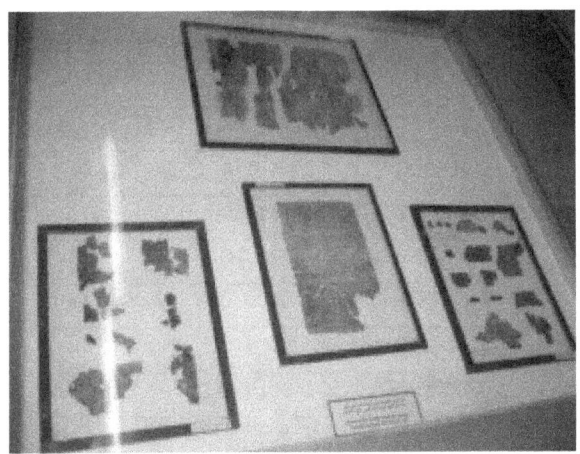

Compared to other books of antiquity, no other literary work comes close to approaching the New Testament in terms of manuscript evidence and time span between the autograph (the original document) and the earliest extant (surviving) copies. The following table shows the New Testament's extraordinary manuscript attestation when compared to the number of copies of other ancient texts, and reveals the extremely short time span from the original manuscripts to the earliest surviving copies.

Comparison of Ancient Texts				
Author	Date Written	Earliest Copy	Time Span in years between original & copy	No. of copies
Pliny	61-113 A.D.	850 A.D.	750	7
Plato	427-347 B.C.	900 A.D.	1,200	7
Demosthenes	4th Cent. B.C.	1,110 A.D.	800	8
Herodotus	480-425 B.C.	900 A.D.	1,300	8
Suetonius	75-160 B.C.	950 A.D.	800	8
Thucydides	460-400 B.C.	900 A.D.	1,300	8
Euripides	480-406 B.C	1,110 A.D.	1,300	9
Aristophanes	450-385 B.C.	900 A.D.	1,200	10
Caesar	100-44 B.C.	900 A.D.	1,000	10
Tacitus	100 A.D.	1,110 A.D.	1,000	20
Aristotle	384-322 B.C.	1,110 A.D.	1,400	49
Sophocles	496-406 B.C.	1,000 A.D.	1,400	193
Homer (Iliad)	900 B.C.	400 B.C.	500	643
New Testament	50-100 A.D.	C 115- 135 A.D.	15-40 (P52)	5,000

This extraordinary manuscript attestation of the New Testament, together with the temporal proximity of surviving manuscripts to the autographs, is unparalleled in ancient literature. Generally speaking, as we go back in time (in terms of manuscript evidence) and the closer we get to the autograph, the less manuscripts there are that have survived and the more fragmentary they are.

EARLIEST MANUSCRIPTS

The earliest manuscript fragment that we have of the New Testament is the John Rylands Papyrus (named after the person who found it). It is a small fragment of John's Gospel, 9cm x 6cm, containing 5 verses from John 18. It is dated about 100-135 AD, which is exceptionally close to the original (c. 95 AD). As it is dated to within 15-40 years of the original, it is possible that this is a 1st or 2nd generation copy.

THE JOHN RYLANDS PAPYRI (front and back)

Dated 115 – 135 A.D.

Another very early manuscript is the Chester Beatty Papyri. This is a group of 11 papyri discovered in 1932, dated about 150 AD, and containing most of Pauls letters, from Romans to 1 Thessalonians, and including Hebrews. Paul's letters were written in the 70's, so that is a gap of only 80 years.

THE CHESTER BEATTY PAPYRI

(2 Cor 11:33 – 12:9)

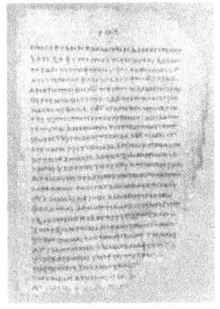

The table below lists some other important early manuscripts, and provides details of their content and their approximate date.

Earliest NT Manuscripts

(p = papyrus, and the number is its identifying number)

Date	Name	Contents
100-115 A.D.	P52	John 18:31-33, reverse: John 18:37-38
100-150 A.D.	P104	Matthew 21:34-37, 43, 45 (5 verses)
c. 125 A.D.	P87	Philemon 13-15 &24
81-96 A.D.	P46	70% of Paul's letters & Hebrews
100-150 A.D.	P66	92% of john's Gospel
150-175 A.D.	P64 and p67	19 verses from Matthew
c. 175 A.D.	P75	1,166 verses from Luke and John (50%)
150-200 A.D.	P77 and p103	16 verses from Matthew
150-200 A.D.	P32	Titus 1:1-15, 2:3-8 (21 verses)
180-200 A.D.	Uncial 0189	Acts 5:3-21 (earliest parchment of N.T.)
200-225 A.D.	P45	Much of Acts and the Gospels
250-300 A.D.	P47	Rev 9:10-11:3; 11:5-16:15; 16;17-17:2
3rd century	P69	Luke 22:40, 45-48, 58-61.
EARLIEST WHOLE N.T. MANUSCRIPTS		
330 A.D.	Codex Sinaiticus	Earliest complete N.T. + some O.T.
325-350 A.D.	Codex Vaticanus	N.T. up to Hebrews 9:15 + most of O.T.
400 A.D.	Codex Alexandrinus	Most of N.T.

TRANSCRIPTION ERRORS

Obviously, the earlier a manuscript is dated, the closer it is to the original, and the less likely it is to have transcription errors (copyist errors). As with any process where copying is done by hand, and there are copies of copies of copies of copies, minor errors, known as transcription errors creep in. Transcription errors were very common in the ancient world, and the Bible was not immune to them.

For example, when a church received a letter from Paul it was often divided up into small sections and circulated amongst the various households. Each household would copy that section for themselves and pass it on. In this way a household would eventually have their own copy of Paul's letter. Copies made from the autograph (the original manuscript) are called first generation copies. Within a short time period, copies of copies of copies had been made and were being circulated around the known world. Because most first century Christians could not afford to pay a scribe for a professionally produced copy, many of the copies were made by ordinary people, with a wide variety of standards of reading and writing. As a result, transcription errors were introduced into the document chains, which were perpetuated in subsequent copies in that document lineage.

(Image courtesy of ebibleteacher.com)

Common transcription errors were:

- Missing words

- Missing sentences

- Misspelt words

- Changes to the wording

Transcription errors were the product of:

- Illegible or poor writing in the manuscript being copied

- Tiredness of the copyist

- Poor lighting

- Jumping a line or misreading the original

VARIANTS

Once an error had been made, all next-generation copies based upon that manuscript would perpetuate that error. Thus, slight differences exist between surviving manuscripts of the same Bible passage. These manuscript differences are known as variants. There are thousands of textual variants among surviving Bible manuscripts. These variants are particularly prevalent in the New Testament manuscripts, as very few of these were produced by professional scribes. The Old Testament documents have significantly fewer variants, as the ancient Israelites entrusted the copying of their Scriptures to professional scribes, who had to follow extremely rigorous procedures including the counting of letters on each page to ensure that the copy was an exact replica of the original.

INTERPOLATIONS

Not all variants are simple mistakes (transcription errors). Some variants are the result of *deliberate* changes to the text by later copyists. Usually these take the form of additional textual insertions, known as interpolations. Take, for example, John 7:39, *"for the Spirit was not yet"* (οὔπω γὰρ ἦν πνεῦμα). This is probably the original text, but there are many interpolations that were added to this by later copyists, in an attempt to interpret John's enigmatic statement. The different resulting variants, found in different manuscripts of the same passage, are:

*"for the **Holy** Spirit was not yet"*

*"for the Spirit had not yet **been given**"*

*"for the **Holy** Spirit had not yet **been given**"*

*"for the Spirit was not yet **upon them**"*

*"for the **Holy** Spirit was not yet **upon them**"*

The second of the above variants is the one printed in the New International Version (NIV) and Today's New International Version (TNIV). It is one of the few interpolations that is published in modern translations, because scholars believe that it captures John's intended meaning.

The following verses are known interpolations and are omitted from most modern translations:

Matthew 23-14	Mark 7:16	Mark 9:44	Mark 9:46	Mark 11:26
Mark 15:28	Luke 17:36	Luke 23:17	John 5:4	
Acts 15:34	Acts 24:7	Acts 28:29	Romans 16:24	

The above are whole verses that were inserted by later copyists. These verses are printed in the King James Version (KJV) but not in most modern translations. The reason for this is an interesting piece of history! It is now known that these verses were added in the 8th and 9th century by monks who were copying the Scriptures and who wanted to embellish the meaning of the text. Bible scholars became aware of this because these verses only appear in some 8th and 9th century manuscripts, the Masoretic Text or "Textus Recepticus", but are not found in any earlier manuscripts, such as the more reliable 4th Century Sinaiticus, Vaticanus and Alexandrinus Texts. However, when the King James Version was produced, in 1611, the translators only had access to the less reliable 8th and 9th century manuscripts and assumed that these verses were part of the original text, and so assigned them verse numbers. More modern translators have had access to the much earlier, more reliable manuscripts, and they were able to determine that the verses in question were interpolations, and were not in the original text. Consequently, modern translations omit them from the text, although they still retain a verse number so that the verse numbering in modern Bibles still aligns with that of the King James Version. If you attempted my little experiment at the beginning of Chapter 1, this explains why you were unable to locate these verses in a modern translation but could find them in the KJV!

THE FREQUENCY OF VARIANTS

There are about 5,600 Greek manuscripts of the New Testament. These manuscripts, of varying age and from different locations, reveal variations in the text due to transcription errors and interpolations. No two manuscripts of the same book of the New Testament are identical. None!

Manuscript P51

P51 is a papyrus fragment (hence the letter "P") containing partial verses from Galatians chapter 1. When this manuscript is compared with other extant (surviving) manuscripts of the same passage, the number of variants becomes apparent. The table below compares P51 with 11 other early manuscripts of the same passage, revealing the textual variants between P51 and each of the others. For example, when manuscript P51 is compared to manuscript P46, and when the same verses are compared side by side, there are 3 variants (textual differences; differences in wording) between the two manuscripts.

Papyrus P51 (Galatians 1:2-10, 13, 16-20)	
Other Manuscripts	Variants
P46	3
A	3
B	7
C	2
D	2
G	2
K	2
L	3
81	4
330	2
365	5

There are an estimated 200,000 variants in the Greek manuscripts. The majority are due to transcription errors (mistakes in copying); the remainder are interpolations (deliberate insertions by copyists). While this seems a staggering amount, it might help to get a little perspective. The 200,000 variants represent 10,000 textual locations (a verse or a word in a verse). For instance, if a word is misspelt in 100 manuscripts, that error is counted as 100 variants, yet it is only 1 textual location.

MINOR VARIANTS

Of these 10,000 textual locations, about 9,600 are minor variants; slight differences in wording with no change of meaning. For example:

- Differences in spelling

- Differences in word order (e.g. *"Christ Jesus"* and *"Jesus Christ"*)

- One or more words missing from some texts (e.g. *"God's only Son"* and *"God's Son"*)

Some Examples of Minor Variants:

Listed below are some examples of minor variants. These are verses where there are minor differences in wording among surviving manuscripts of the same passage. In each of these cases, the variant that is believed to be the original wording (and which has consequently been published in our Bibles) is the first in the list:

In Ephesians 5:31 there are four variants:

- "For this reason, a man leaves father and mother and clings to his wife"

- "For this reason, a man leaves father and mother and clings to the wife"

- "For this reason, a man leaves father and mother and joins the wife"

- "For this reason, a man leaves father and mother".

In Mark 1:2 there are two variants:

- "in Isaiah the prophet"

- "in the prophets"

In Romans 6:11 there are two variants:

- "in Christ Jesus"
- "in Christ Jesus our Lord"

In Romans 1:4 there are two variants:

- "was declared with power to be the Son of God"
- "was appointed to be the Son of God with power"

There are thousands of minor variants like this. In each of these cases, none of the variants has the slightest impact on doctrine. Any of these variants could be published in our Bibles without altering Christian doctrine in the slightest.

MAJOR VARIANTS

The remaining 400 variants represent major variants; moderate to significant differences in wording and/or differences in meaning. These include:

- Whole verses or passages which are in some manuscripts but not others
- Whole verses or passages which are different in different manuscripts

TEXTUAL CRITICISM

Textual scholars undertake rigorous scrutiny of these ancient texts in order to ascertain the exact wording of the autographic (original) text. In most cases, scholars are able to easily rule out the non-original variations and arrive at consensus regarding the original wording. This is accomplished, to within a high degree of probability, using textual criticism. Textual criticism is the science of comparing and dating ancient manuscripts to determine the earliest and most reliable manuscripts, in order to reconstruct the exact wording of the autograph (original writing).

Variants are increasingly prolific in later manuscripts. The later the manuscript, the more variants it usually contains. The reverse is also true. The earlier the manuscript, the less variants it will contain. By comparing earlier manuscripts with later manuscripts of the same passage, textual scholars can accurately determine when variants appeared in the copying chain. As scholars examine earlier and earlier manuscripts of the same text, the majority of variants "disappear". As they arrive at the very earliest manuscripts of a particular passage, there might only be a few minor variations remaining (often involving only slight variations in spelling or word order). In the vast majority of cases scholars can determine the original wording by taking into account the location of the manuscript and its membership of particular families of document chains. (For example, documents produced in certain cities were known to be more reliable copies than those produced in other locations).

In the case of verses or passages that are in some manuscripts and not in others, textual scholars must try to determine whether these variants represent verses that were in the original text but have been accidentally omitted in later copies, or were not part of the original text and were deliberately inserted by later copyists. As we have already discussed, these later additions are known as interpolations.

In 300 of the 400 major variants, Bible scholars can determine, with a reasonable degree of confidence, what the original text probably was. The most likely version of the original text is printed in our English Bibles, and the variant is often footnoted at the bottom of that page of the Bible. If you have a decent, modern translation of the Bible, particularly a study Bible, you will see variants published in the footnote section, with the word "or ..." preceding them. This provides serious Bible readers with the opportunity of reading the alternate version of that verse in those cases where the translators were not completely certain which version was the original and which was the variant.

Some Examples of Major Variants Where Translators <u>Are</u> Confident of The Original Text:

Acts 8:36-38. *"As they travelled along the road, they came to some water and the eunuch said, "Look, here is water. Why shouldn't I be baptised?" (37). <u>Phillip said, "If you believe with all your heart, you may". The eunuch answered, "I believe that Jesus Christ is the Son of God</u>". (38) And he gave orders to stop the chariot ..."* Verse 37 (underlined) is not in the earliest, most reliable manuscripts, therefore it is not published in most modern translations and is only footnoted. It was published in the KJV and so it retains a verse number.

John 7:53 – 8:11. Textual evidence reveals that this section was added in the 5th century, by the copyist who produced the Byzantium Manuscript. These verses were published in the KJV, so it is included in modern Bibles with an accompanying waiver. It also has a grammatical style and vocabulary which is very different to the rest of John's Gospel.

Mark 16:9-20. Textual evidence reveals that these verses were added in the 5th century Byzantium Manuscript. It was published in the KJV, so it is included in modern Bibles with an accompanying waiver. This also has a different style and vocabulary to the rest of Mark's Gospel. Most modern scholars agree that Mark either wrote a different ending which was lost in transmission (and so a later scribe made up another one), or he did not get to finish his Gospel, and so a later scribe wrote a suitable ending. Either way, the majority of scholars agree that this was not Mark's ending.

Romans 8:1. *"Therefore there is now no condemnation for those who are in Christ Jesus, <u>who do not live according to the sinful nature but according to the Spirit</u>, because through Christ Jesus the law of the Spirit who gives life has set you free"* The middle section is an interpolation, occurring only in later manuscripts, and is footnoted rather than published in most translations.

1 John 5:7-8. *"And there are three that testify <u>in heaven: the Father, the Word and the Holy Spirit, and these three are one. And there are three that testify on earth:</u> the Spirit, the water and the blood."* The middle, underlined section is an interpolation, occurring only in later manuscripts, and is footnoted rather than published.

In these instances, and many others, the interpolation is obvious and is discounted from the original text.

In about 100 cases, however, scholars cannot decide which variant is more reliable or more likely, so the variant with the most manuscript evidence is published, and the other variant is footnoted. In some cases, it is almost a coin-toss as to which variant gets published and which gets footnoted.

Some Examples of Major Variants Where Scholars <u>Cannot</u> Unequivocally Decide the Original Text:

Romans 1:17, *"a righteousness that is by faith, from first to last"*, OR *"a righteousness that is from faith to faith"*. (Slight difference in wording; slight difference in meaning).

John 16:31, *"You believe at last!"* OR *"Do you now believe?"* (Slight difference in wording; slight difference in meaning).

Romans 3:25, *"God presented him as a sacrifice of atonement"* OR *"God presented him as the one who would turn aside his wrath, taking away sin"*. (Significant difference in wording; moderate difference in meaning because it introduces an additional concept – God's wrath).

Romans 8:28, *"And we know that in all things God works for the good of those who love him"* OR *"And we know that in all things God works together with those who love him to bring about good"*. (Slight difference in wording and moderate difference in meaning: Is God working in me for *my* good, or in partnership with me for the good of the *world*?)

John 13:1, *"he now showed them the full extent of his love"* OR *"he loved them to the last"*. (Significant difference in wording; moderate difference in meaning: How much he loved them or how long he loved them?).

John 10:29, *"My Father, who has given them to me, is greater than all"* OR *"What my Father has given me is greater than all"*. (Slight difference in wording; significant difference in meaning: Is it the Father who is greater than all or what the Father has given Jesus that is greater than all?)

John 8:38, *"I am telling you what I have seen in the Father's presence, and you do what you have heard from your father."* OR *"I am telling you what I have seen in the Father's presence. Therefore, do what you have heard from the Father."* (Slight difference in wording, major difference in meaning: Is he talking about God or the devil in his second reference to "the Father"?)

John 3:16, *"For God so loved the world that he gave his one and only Son"* OR *"For God so loved the world that he gave his only begotten Son"*. (Slight difference in wording, but a significantly different theological concept. Both meanings are true, but they are quite different statements).

While all this might sound troubling, it must be stressed that in no case does a single variant affect a single doctrine of the Christian faith. Even in the cases where scholars don't really know which variant is the original text, both variants are theologically true, and either one could be published without contradicting Scripture elsewhere.

FOOTNOTES IN THE BIBLICAL TEXT

As explained earlier, in those rare cases where scholars have difficulty deciding which variant to publish in the official biblical text, one variant is published in the main body and the other is published in the footnotes. It can be quite helpful to take note of these alternate readings in the footnotes of your Bible in order to consider possible alternate meanings of the text. Some Bibles don't publish the footnotes and variants. If you are engaging in serious Bible study, it is always helpful to use a Bible which includes footnotes.

VARIANTS AND BIBLICAL CERTAINTY

A discussion of variants, transmission errors and interpolations can overwhelm ordinary Christians and leave them with a feeling of new-found uncertainty with regard to the Bible. What once seemed so simple and certain is now clouded with confusion and doubt. The complexity of the issues and the plethora of divergent texts can seem overwhelming to the lay person.

Scholars who study ancient literature, however, are used to dealing with these issues. Furthermore, biblical scholars who have the task of publishing the accepted original text of the Bible have a huge advantage over scholars who study other ancient texts. The extraordinary number of extant (surviving) manuscripts for the Bible allow scholars to reach a level of certainty regarding the exact wording of the original text that is unprecedented and unreplicated in any other ancient document. Textual scholars are certain of an estimated 97.3% of all New Testament words.

The table on the following page provides a book-by-book summary of the level of textual certainty of the New Testament:

TEXTUAL CERTAINTY OF THE NEW TESTAMENT				
Book	Total words	In doubt	% doubt	% certain
Matthew	18,111	531	2.9%	97.1%
Mark	11,217	567	5.1%	94.9%
Luke	19,581	494	2.5%	97.5%
John	15,604	481	3.1%	96.9%
Acts	18,460	487	2.6%	97.4%
Romans	7,030	253	3.6%	96.4%
1 Corinthians	6,799	104	1.5%	98.5%
2 Corinthians	1,495	55	3.7%	96.3%
Galatians	2,233	38	1.7%	98.3%
Ephesians	2,385	51	2.1%	97.9%
Philippians	1,621	37	2.3%	97.7%
Colossians	1,570	33	2.1%	97.9%
1 Thessalonians	1,477	26	1.8%	98.2%
2 Thessalonians	826	12	1.5%	98.5%
1 Timothy	1,592	22	1.4%	98.6%
2 Timothy	1,336	13	1.0%	99.0%
Titus	657	5	0.8%	99.2%
Philemon	329	6	1.8%	98.2%
Hebrews	4,888	82	1.7%	98.3%
James	1,735	26	1.5%	98.5%
1 Peter	1,648	63	3.8%	96.2%
2 Peter	937	35	3.7%	96.3%
1 John	2,103	30	1.4%	98.6%
2 John	245	7	2.9%	97.1%
3 John	219	3	1.4%	98.6%
Jude	459	7	1.5%	98.5%
Revelation	9,667	127	1.3%	98.7%
Totals	133,892	3,600	2.7%	97.3%

The current certainty regarding the wording of the New Testament will continue to increase as more manuscripts are discovered and as scholars improve their understanding of the family trees of these documents.

Why didn't God protect the Bible from these kinds of errors?

At this point many Christians might ask why God did not protect the Bible from these kinds of errors. Surely an all-powerful God could intervene to ensure that these kinds of variants did not develop? The answer is that God didn't intervene in the past for the same reason he still doesn't intervene to protect the Bible from transcription errors today. Even with today's modern printing presses, when new Bible translations are first published, they sometimes contain printing errors - words accidentally misspelt or omitted - which must be corrected in the second printing run. To say that God must protect every copy of every book of the Bible that is ever written would be to expect God to be constantly, miraculously over-riding our human fallibility. It would require God to watch over every printing press in the modern world, every typist entering text at a computer keyboard, every Bible editor working with a word processor and publishing software. Clearly, God has not chosen to do so because that is not the way he works. God chooses to work *with* our frailty, not constantly over-ride it.

Of course, this is not a nice, neat answer for us. It may not tie in with our theology or our desire for a perfectly ordered universe. It would be nice if God delivered the Bible to us directly from heaven, error-free. But the reality is a little messier than that. The same process of human error that happens today with the printing of our modern Bibles, happened in the ancient world as the Bible was copied by hand. However, this does not mean that God has not been active in the transmission of the Bible through the ages. The miracle of the Bible, and perhaps where we see the greatest evidence of God's protective hand, is that not one of the variants in the biblical text has even the slightest impact on any single doctrine.

What impact does this have on our view of the inspiration and inerrancy of the Bible?

In October 1978, the world's leading Bible scholars met in Chicago, USA, to decide this very issue. How is our view of the Bible's inspiration and inerrancy impacted by the fact that the exact wording of 2.7% of the biblical text remains uncertain? The conference in Chicago concluded with a clear, final statement. The Chicago Statement on Biblical Inerrancy (October 1978) states:

> *"We affirm that inspiration and inerrancy, strictly speaking, apply only to the autographic text of Scripture."*

I will revisit this concept in the next chapter, because there are more complicating factors than just transcription errors. But at this early stage, what we can affirm is that God, in his sovereignty, has ensured that no doctrine of the Bible has had any doubt cast upon it by any variant. Not a single tenet of spiritual truth is uncertain, altered or compromised by the existence of variants.

The other important thing to stress, is that the Word of God is more than mere words on a page. It is a living Word - a living message with spiritual power that still changes lives today. The God of the universe who inspired the original writers is more than able to ensure that the message that has come down to us today is still his divinely inspired, life-changing Word, and no variant has diminished that power or compromised that truth.

GOD'S MIRACULOUS PROTECTION OF MANUSCRIPTS

The proliferation of transcription errors, interpolations and variants could create the impression that God has been curiously absent from the whole process of the Bible's transmission. But that is certainly not the case. God has often miraculously protected biblical manuscripts, so that they are not lost to us. Here are some wonderful examples:

THE BODMER PAPYRI

This is a group of 22 papyri found in the desert near Cairo, in 1952, by an Egyptian shepherd while shepherding his sheep. Wondering if they were valuable, he took them into town and tried to swap some of the papyri for some cigarettes from his mates! His friends weren't interested, so he returned home and started using the papyri to light his fire of an evening! An antique dealer in Cairo, Martin Bodmer, heard about his find and drove out to see if the papyri were of value. He rescued them from the fire, literally! They include the earliest complete copy of John's Gospel, 1 and 2 Peter, and Jude that we have in existence (dated about 200 AD)! They also include other very old portions of the Old and New Testaments. They have made a significant contribution to our understanding of the original texts, and are now stored in a museum in Cologny, Switzerland.

CODEX SINAITICUS

The Codex Sinaiticus is the earliest complete copy of the whole of the New Testament, dated about 330 AD. It also includes some portions of the Old Testament. It is velum (parchment; animal skin) rather than papyri. The Codex (book) was discovered in 1875 by world renowned biblical scholar, Constantin von Tishendorf, in the Monastery of St. Catherine, at the foot of Mt Sinai.

The Monastery of St Catherine, Sinai

Tischendorf had suspected that the monastery might house some ancient biblical documents, and he travelled there, with sponsorship from Prince Frederick of Saxony, to investigate. After talking his way into the monastery (the only way in was via a wicker basket lowered down from the ramparts and lifted back up by monks pulling on a rope!), he searched their libraries and vaults for two days with no success. In Tischendorf's 1865 book, *"When Were Our Gospels Written?"*, he recounts his discovery of the Codex Sinaiticus on the third day. He describes how he found his way into the basement where there was a furnace for heating the monastery. An adjoining wall had been recently demolished as part of ongoing renovations, and behind the wall a large collection of old parchments and papyri had been found by the monks undertaking the renovations. As Tischendorf entered the basement an elderly monk was feeding these documents into the furnace, believing them to be of no value! Tischendorf, cried out for them to stop, and he took possession of the documents. Among the documents that Tischendorf managed to rescue was the Codex Sinaiticus – the earliest copy of the complete Bible that we have in existence today! It was literally rescued from the flames! Such is the providence of God that if Tischendorf had been an hour later that day, this precious book would have been burned.

The Codex Sinaiticus now resides in the British Library in London, and has made a major contribution to our understanding of the original text of the Bible.

THE DEAD SEA SCROLLS

Most people have heard of the Dead Sea Scrolls, but are not aware of their full significance. They are a collection of approximately 1,000 documents, in Hebrew, Aramaic and Greek, discovered between 1947 and 1979 in caves near Qumran on the shores of the Dead Sea, 18km east of Jerusalem and 500m below sea level.

The first manuscripts were found by a shepherd who threw a rock into a cave to chase out a goat that had wandered into it. When he did so, he heard the sound of breaking pottery, and climbed up into the cave to investigate. The cave contained a collection of sealed, pottery jars. Inside the jars were ancient documents, wrapped in linen to preserve them.

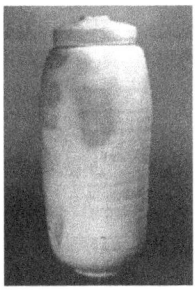

Subsequent exploration by archaeologists discovered 11 caves in total. Most historians believe that the caves were the monastic retreat of a Jewish Essene community (a Jewish sect) who had apparently retreated there during or shortly before the Roman purge of Israel around 70 AD. The majority of documents in the caves were parchment (animal skin) with a few papyrus documents as well. These documents represent the library of that Essene community.

Cave 4, where 80% of the manuscripts were found, contained approximately 15,000 fragments (some of them very small) from 500 documents.

CAVE 4

The documents range in date from 200 BC to about 68 A.D., and include biblical and non- biblical books. The non-biblical books include commentaries on the Old Testament, hymns, liturgies, accounts, monastic rules and procedures. The biblical books comprise copies of about half the books in the Old Testament, including a copy of Isaiah which is 1000 years older than any previously discovered copy! In fact, the Dead Sea Scrolls are, to this day, the oldest collection of Old Testament books ever found.

Some Fragments from Cave 4

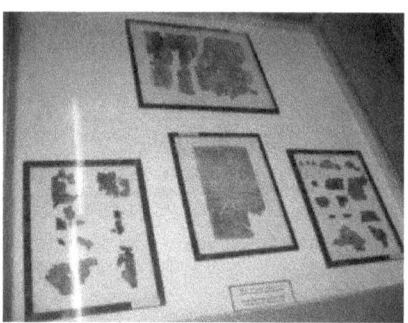

The Dead Sea Scrolls are important because:

- They bring us hundreds of years closer to the Old Testament autographs.

- They show how little the Old Testament documents have changed over time - displaying only minor variations in spelling and grammar between themselves and texts hundreds of years later.

The Dead Sea Scrolls have been hailed by even non-Christian historians as the greatest archaeological discovery of the 20th century. For Christians, they have provided incontestable, objective proof of the textual reliability of the Old Testament and the accuracy of the transmission process over millennia. The scrolls continue to be studied by scholars from around the world, and have made a valuable contribution to the formulation of the accepted text of the Old Testament.

Reflection Questions 2

1. How has this chapter challenged your view of the Bible?

2. What, if anything, surprised you as you read this chapter?

3. Why do you think didn't God protect the transmission of the Bible through the ages?

4. What has encouraged you from reading this chapter?

5. Read 2 Timothy 3:16. What does this say about the Bible, and how can you reconcile this with the kinds of issues that this chapter has identified?

6. Read 2 Peter 1:5. The exhortation to add to our faith "knowledge" is an important one. What do you think this means?

7. Read Philippians 1:9. Paul's desire is that as we grow in Christian maturity, we will grow in "knowledge". How does this apply to our study of the nature of the Bible?

MANUSCRIPTS AND VARIANTS

CHAPTER 3

INTERNAL INCONSISTENCIES IN THE BIBLE

If we are to arrive at a mature and informed understanding of the Bible's inspiration and inerrancy, we will, at some point, have to confront the many glaring internal inconsistencies in the Bible's historical narratives. The vast majority of Christians are not aware of these inconsistencies, and if they were ever asked, *"Does the Bible ever contradict itself?"*, would deny such a possibility vigorously. Yet these internal contradictions exist. Hundreds of them! They fall under 3 main categories: Numbers, Names and Events.

A significant percentage of these inconsistencies occur between the two parallel historical narratives in the Old Testament. Just as there are parallel Gospel accounts of the life of Christ in the New Testament, there are two parallel accounts in the Old Testament which primarily focus on the historical period of the kings of Israel and Judah, as well as the prophetic ministries of Elisha and Elijah. The primary historical narrative flows through the books of 1 & 2 Samuel and 1 & 2 Kings. The secondary, parallel narrative is found in 1 & 2 Chronicles, which describes the same events from a slightly different perspective.

The Parallel Historical Accounts:

1 Samuel 2 Samuel 1 Kings 2 Kings	1 Chronicles 2 Chronicles

The problem arises, however, when the two parallel accounts of the same event are compared. Names are do not correspond. Places are different. Numbers are contradictory. What are we to make of these inconsistencies? How did these differing accounts arise? Which one is correct and how does this affect our view of the Bible?

NUMERICAL CONTRADICTIONS

In Chapter 1, *"Are There Mistakes In The Bible?"*, I gave examples of some numerical inconsistencies in the Bible and foreshadowed our need to discuss them. Here is a further small sample of the many numerical contradictions in the Bible:

1 KINGS 4:26 Solomon had 40,000 stalls for his horses.

2 CHRON 9:25 Solomon had 4,000 stalls for his horses.

1 KINGS 5:16 Solomon had 3,300 supervisors.
2 CHRON 2:2 Solomon had 3,600 supervisors.

1 KINGS 7:15-22 The two pillars of the temple were 18 cubits high.
2 CHRON 3:15-17 The two pillars of the temple were 35 cubits high.

1 KINGS 9:28 420 talents of gold were brought back from Ophir.
2 CHRON 8:18 450 talents of gold were brought back from Ophir.

1 KINGS 16:6-8 Baasha died in the 26th year of King Asa's reign.
2 CHRON 16:1 Baasha built a city in the 36th year of King Asa's reign.

2 KINGS 8:25-26 Ahaziah was 22 years old when he began his reign.
2 CHRON 22:2 Ahaziah was 42 years old when he began his reign.

NUM 25:9 24,000 died in the plague at Shittim.
1 COR 10:8 23,000 died in the plague at Shittim.

In "Alleged Discrepancies Of The Bible" [1], John W. Haley lists about 80 of these numerical contradictions, mainly in the Old Testament. What are we to make of these? Before we can understand how these kinds of inconsistencies can arise, it is helpful to have a basic understanding of the transmission process of the Old Testament.

THE TRANSMISSION OF THE OLD TESTAMENT

The Old Testament was copied by hand, as was the New Testament. The difference, however, was that the New Testament was primarily copied by ordinary people of mixed literary ability, whereas the Old Testament was meticulously copied by professional scribes. When a new copy of an Old Testament book was required, either because the old copy was worn out or a new copy had been ordered by a priest or someone of stature, a scribe was employed to carry out the work. The copying the of the Scriptures was considered to be a sacred duty that had to be performed under the strictest of protocols. Part of these protocols involved the most rigorous cross-checking system of any literary culture in human history.

A scribe copying an Old Testament book would produce the new copy one line at a time. At the end of each line he would put down his quill and pick up a pointer (yad). He would then count the number of letters, jots and tittles (Hebrew grammatical accents) in the new line and then count the number of letters, jots and tittles in the corresponding line in the original document, to ensure that they were identical. He would repeat this process, line by line, until the end of the page. When the final line on a page had been copied and successfully corroborated, an additional cross-check was then carried out. The scribe would use the yad to count the total number of letters, jots an tittles on the original page and the total number of letters, jots and tittles on the new copy. Only after a page had been verified in this manner could it be glued to the scroll and the copying of the next page could be commenced. If a mistake was made at any point in the copying of a page, the entire page had to be burnt and a new copy commenced. Copying books in this meticulous manner meant that a new copy of a book of the Old Testament often took months to complete.

Because of this extremely rigorous process, the Old Testament documents are widely regarded by historians as having the highest transmission integrity of any literary work from antiquity. Unlike the New testament, which exhibits thousands of variants, errors in the transcription of the Old Testament were extremely rare.

IF THEY TOOK THAT MUCH CARE IN COPTYING, HOW DID ERRORS OCCUR?

Despite this meticulous attention to detail, errors were still ocassionally made. How did this occur? The simple explanation is that it was possible for a scribe to write an incorrect number in the new copy, while the letter count could still be correct (just as the words "four" and "five" in English are different numbers but have the same letter count). The situation was exacerbated by two further factors.

1. Sometimes the original document that scribes were working from may have been in poor condition.

An Ancient Manuscript in Poor Condition:

For example, 2 Kings 22 describes the ascension to the throne of a new king of Israel; Josiah. In the 18th year of his reign, he ordered that the temple be repaired and that worship of God be recommenced. It had been about 80 years since the temple had been used, and God's laws had largely been forgotten. As the temple was repaired, a scroll of Deuteronomy was discovered. King Josiah read it and repented. He then led the entire nation in repentance and rededication to the Lord, resulting in a national revival. God's laws had been completely forgotten and this book of the Law had lain in dust for 80 years. Josiah ordered that his scribes make a copy of the scroll because it was in such disrepair. It would have been difficult to read and difficult to copy accurately, and parts of it may have looked something like the picture above, or perhaps even worse. A scribe attempting to copy such a document could easily have mis-transcribed a word or a number. Difficulty reading a manuscript in poor condition was a factor leading to occasional textual variants in Old Testament documents.

2. A second major factor was the Hebrew alphabet itself.

The Old Testament was written in Hebrew. The ancient Israelites used letters of their Hebrew alphabet to represent numbers, in the same way that we sometimes use Roman Numerals: (eg: I = 1, V = 5, X = 10, L = 50, C = 100, D = 500, M = 1,000). Even when the original document was in good condition, Hebrew letters are very similar, and often got substituted for each other during the copying process. Here is the Hebrew alphabet:

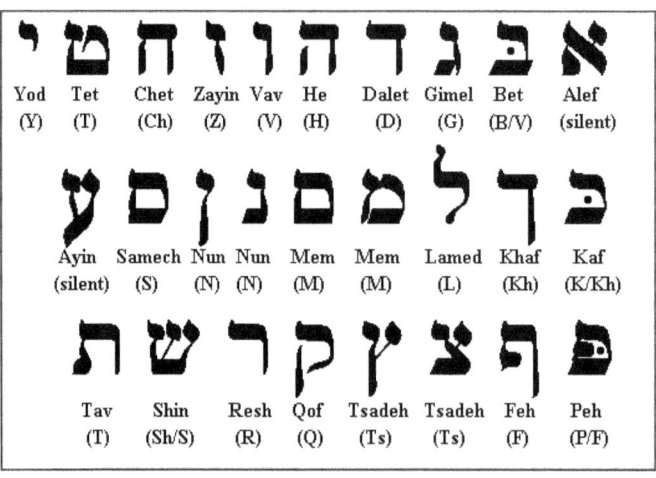

Consider the following Hebrew letters, arranged in similarity clusters:

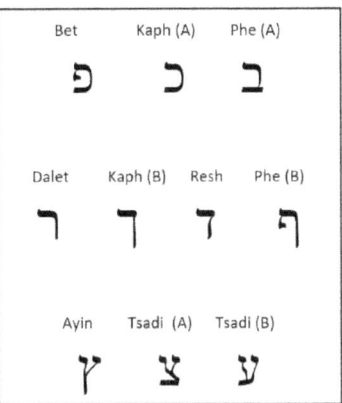

Some of these Hebrew letters vary from each other in the subtlest of ways. It is easy to conceive how, in the copying process, one letter could be mistaken for another, particularly if the original document was in poor condition.

The Hebrew Numbering System:

Letter	Value	Letter	Value
א	1	ל	30
ב	2	מ	40
ג	3	נ	50
ד	4	ס	60
ה	5	ע	70
ו	6	פ	80
ז	7	צ	90
ח	8	ק	100
ט	9	ר	200
י	10	ש	300
כ	20	ת	400

Consider the Hebrew numbering system, in the table on the previous page. This is how numbers were recorded in the Hebrew text of the Old Testament, using letters to represent different numbers. Note how similar some of the letters are to each other. For example, note the similarities between 4 and 200, between 5, 8 and 400, and between 2, 3, and 50. You can see how it would be extremely easy to misread one letter and substitute a different letter in the copied manuscript. This is how numerical inconsistencies occurred between two parallel biblical accounts of the same event:

- Both parallel accounts would have originally had the same number.

- At some point in the copying process a letter (representing a number) was misread and transcribed incorrectly in one of the documents.

- The error was passed on to all subsequent copies, thereby permanently altering the text in that document chain.

So, the questions we are left with are:

- Did Solomon have 3,300 supervisors (1 Kings 4:26) or 3,600 supervisors (2 Chron 2:2)?

- Were the temple columns 18 cubits high (1 Kings 7:15f) or 35 cubits high (2 Chron 3:15f)?

- Was Ahaziah 22 years old when he began his reign (2 Kings 8:25) or 42 years old (2 Chron 22:2)?

The answer is that we simply don't know. But these small inconsistencies do not change a single point of doctrine. The Bible's spiritual truth is unaffected. Of course, God could easily have intervened to protect the Bible from these kinds of textual variants. The fact that he didn't, tells us that he does not deem it important that we know exactly how many supervisors Solomon had! His gaze is fixed on matters of far weightier significance.

CONTRADICTIONS REGARDING NAMES

John W. Haley, in "Alleged Discrepancies Of The Bible" [2], lists about 220 examples of name contradictions, resulting from transcription errors in the Old Testament. For example, in 1 Chronicles 11:29 "Sibbecai" is named in the list of David's 30 mighty warriors, while in 2 Samuel 23:27, the same person is called "Mebunnai". At first glance it might seem hard to believe how these two very different sounding names could result from a transcription error. But in Hebrew these names are extremely similar:

Because of the similarity of many Hebrew letters, it was extremely easy to make such transcription errors, particularly if the original writing was of poor quality, or very small, or if the scribe was tired, rushed or working in poor light. Other examples of names with transcription errors are:

Can you spot the differences in the above names? These minute differences often resulted in the wrong name being written into the newly copied manuscript. As with numerical inconsistencies, conflicting accounts between the parallel historical narratives arose from transcription errors in one of the narratives at some point in the distant past. Both narratives would originally have agreed with each other, but a mistake was made at some point in the document chain in one narrative, and that error was perpetuated in all subsequent copies.

It is important to note, however, that none of the 220 contradictions in names within the Bible change a single point of doctrine. They do not alter the spiritual truth of the Bible in the slightest.

CONTRADICTIONS REGARDING EVENTS

John W. Haley, in "Alleged Discrepancies Of The Bible" [3], lists 116 apparent inconsistencies between separate accounts of the same incident, in terms of the details of the event itself. These inconsistencies are of a more serious nature than simple discrepancies regarding names or numbers. In most cases, however, the divergent accounts can be reconciled with rational analysis.

EXAMPLE 1

- *Matt 27:5. "So Judas threw the money into the temple and left. Then he went away and hanged himself."*

- *Acts 1:18. "With the payment he received for his wickedness, Judas bought a field; there he fell headlong, his body burst open and all his intestines spilled out."*

These passages are easily reconciled. Most scholars concur that Judas initially *"threw the money into the temple and left"*, but must have subsequently retrieved the money. He then bought a field with this blood money. He subsequently hanged himself there, and his rotting corpse was apparently left hanging there until it eventually fell to the ground where it burst open.

EXAMPLE 2

- Matthew 26:57, Mark 14:53 and Luke 22:54 indicate that, after his arrest, Jesus was taken to Caiphas, the high priest

- John 18:13-24 states that Jesus was taken first to Annas, the son-in-law of Caiphas, then to Caiphas.

Explanation: In this instance, John has added an additional detail – an initial interview with Annas. This does not represent an inconsistency; it merely reflects the ability of eyewitnesses to focus on different details of an event.

EXAMPLE 3

- Matthew 27:12-14 states that, at his trial, *"Jesus made no reply, not even to a single charge"*

- John 18:33-37 records that Jesus replied three times to Pilate's questions

Explanation: Jesus' silence in Matthew 27:12-14 was when he was being *"accused by the chief priests and elders"* (v.12), whereas Jesus' willingness to provide verbal answers (in John's Gospel) was in response to Pilate's less aggressive questions. There is no inconsistency at all.

The vast majority of apparent inconsistencies can be easily reconciled with this kind of rational analysis. A small number of inconsistencies, however, require a little more thought, but can also be reconciled if one considers the different perspectives and emphases of each writer.

EXAMPLE 4

There are varying descriptions of the exact wording of the inscription on the cross of Jesus:

- *Matt 27:37 "This is Jesus the King of the Jews."*

- *Mk 15:26 "The King of the Jews."*

- *Lk 23:38 "This is the King of the Jews."*

- *Jn 19:19 "Jesus of Nazareth, the King of the Jews."*

The difference in wording is very minor. One possible reconstruction is that the sign read, *"This is Jesus of Nazareth, the King of the Jews"*. In this case, each of the Gospel writers has quoted a portion of the whole sign, choosing the portion which best suits the purpose of their Gospel.

EXAMPLE 5

- In Matthew 27:44 and Mark 15:32, both criminals who were crucified with Jesus are recorded as taunting him.

- Luk 23:39-42, only one criminal taunts Jesus, and he is rebuked by the other for doing so.

It is possible that, initially, both criminals taunted Jesus, but as the day progressed one criminal sensed the divinity of Jesus and repented.

EXAMPLE 6

- Matthew 27:28 states that the soldiers gave Jesus a *scarlet* robe to wear on the cross

- Mar 15:17and John 19:2 record that the soldiers gave Jesus a *purple* robe to wear on the cross

The similarity between scarlet and purple is not sufficient explanation for this apparent discrepancy, because first century readers would have known that scarlet was the colour of sin and infamy, whereas purple was the colour of royalty. Leon Morris, in his commentary on Matthew's Gospel, provides a helpful explanation:

> "Since this kind of cloak was used by military officers, there would have been no great difficulty in getting one, perhaps an old one, discarded by an officer. The point of it was apparently that the color was somewhere near purple, the colour of royalty. By getting a cloak of a color not quite that of royalty the soldiers were mocking Jesus' claim to be a king." [4]

In other words, Matthew records the *actual* colour of the robe (scarlet) whereas Mark and John describe the implied colour, thereby highlighting the veiled reference to royalty.

EXAMPLE 7

Without doubt, the most problematic instance of internal inconsistencies is the divergent accounts in Mark and John regarding the time of the crucifixion:

- *Mark 15:25 "It was the third hour (9am) when they crucified him".*

- *John 19:14-15 "It was the day of Preparation of the Passover; it was about the sixth hour (12 noon). "Here is your king," Pilate said to the Jews. (15) But they shouted, "Take him away! Take him away! Crucify him!" "Shall I crucify your king?" Pilate asked. "We have no king but Caesar," the chief priests answered".*

There are 3 possible explanations for this apparent divergence:

1. The 3rd hour (in Mark) is referring to the beginning of the process of crucifixion, not the exact time when Christ was nailed to the cross. Approximately 5% of Bible scholars agree with this theory.

2. John was using the Roman time system, which commenced at midnight, and Mark used the Jewish time system, which commenced at 6am. Thus, Jesus appeared before Pilate at 6am (John) and was crucified at 9am (Mark). Approximately 55% of scholars subscribe to this theory.

3. A transcription error has taken place in one of the Gospels. Approximately 40% of scholars propose this explanation.

Once again, it must be stated that none of these apparent biblical inconsistencies affects a single Christian doctrine. The inconsistencies are all matters of small detail and have logical explanations.

THE NATURE OF GOD'S INSPIRATION OF THE BIBLE

These apparent inconsistencies within the biblical narratives require us to consider the nature of divine revelation. In what sense is the Bible inspired by God? To what extent do the words of the writers represent the voice of God? These are crucial questions that every thinking Christian needs to consider. Clearly, God did not directly dictate his message, word for word, otherwise these kinds of inconsistencies would not have eventuated.

At some point, every Christian needs to move beyond the simplistic view of the Bible that may have been sufficient in the early days of their faith, and develop a more intellectually robust, mature understanding of the nature of the Bible's inspiration; one that takes into account the hundreds of instances of apparent, and at times, actual, inconsistencies.

Many evangelical scholars use the term "verbal plenary inspiration" to describe the process of biblical inspiration. *"Verbal"* means that every word in the Bible is exactly the word God wanted written. This does not mean that God directly dictated the words but that his Spirit moved the writers internally to convey his truth. This view still allows the individual styles and personalities of each writer to be seen in their writing. A.C Meyers explains;

"individual backgrounds, personal traits, and literary styles were authentically theirs, but had been providentially prepared by God for use as his instrument in producing Scripture."[5]

The word *"plenary"* means that this process applied to the whole of Scripture, and not just to parts of it.

The **apparent** internal inconsistencies of the Bible pose no problem to this view of inspiration. These apparent inconsistencies are not the result of an error in the text, or a mistake by the writer, but of a lack of insight in the reader. Once a reader moves beyond a superficial skimming of the text and considers the logical possible explanations, these apparent inconsistencies disappear. Often these explanations involve understanding the complementary emphases and perspectives that different writers bring to the same account.

The **actual** internal inconsistencies, involving discrepancies in names and numbers between parallel narratives, require us to consider the **extent** of verbal, plenary inspiration. In October 1978, the world's leading Bible scholars met in Chicago, USA, to decide this very issue. As I explained in the previous chapter, the conference in Chicago concluded with a clear, final statement. The Chicago Statement on Biblical Inerrancy (October 1978) states:

> *"We affirm that inspiration and inerrancy, strictly speaking, apply only to the autographic text of Scripture."*

In other words, in the autographs (original manuscripts) of the Bible, there were no internal contradictions regarding names or numbers. These inconsistencies are simply the product of transcription errors during the copying process. The fact that God has not deemed these errors worthy of his protective intervention, tells us that they are of no spiritual consequence. Therefore, if they are not of great concern to God, they should not be of concern to us!

This may not be a completely satisfactory explanation for those of us who wish to maintain a view of the Bible that almost portrays it as having arrived on earth via courier directly from heaven! The reality is not as simple and neat as that. In many ways, the occasionally flawed process of the Bible's transmission through the ages is a reflection of the normal way in which God interacts with humanity. He continues to work in and through flawed human beings, not over-riding their imperfections, but choosing to display his truth and power in the midst of those imperfections. As God said to the apostle Paul, *"My power is made perfect in your weakness" (2 Corinthians 12:9).*

However, one thing we can be certain of is that God, in his sovereignty, has ensured that no doctrine of the Bible has had any doubt cast upon it by any variant or transcription error. Not a single word of spiritual truth is uncertain, altered or compromised.

DOCTRINAL AND ETHICAL CONTRADICTIONS

Throughout history, sceptics have sought to undermine the Bible's veracity by claiming that it is full of doctrinal and ethical contradictions. Many hostile, atheistic websites delight in making long lists of these supposed contradictions. They cite apparent contradictions such as the Old Testament's *"eye for an eye"* and Jesus' teaching of forgiving those who persecute you and turning the other cheek. Let me say, unequivocally, that there are *no* real doctrinal or ethical contradictions in the Bible. None! The supposed contradictions often claimed by sceptics are the result of a lack of understanding in two major areas:

1. Lack of understanding of the basic principles of interpretation

2. Lack of understanding of the nature of progressive revelation

Investigating these two areas will take up much of our enquiry in the next few chapters.

Chapter Footnotes

1. John W. Haley, *Alleged Discrepancies Of The Bible*, 1992, Whitaker House

2. IBID

3. IBID

4. Leon Morris, *"The Gospel According To St. Matthew"*, IVP, 1992, p.711

5. A.C. Meyers, "The Eerdmans Bible Dictionary", 1987, Grand Rapids, entry on Inspiration

Reflection Questions 3

1. How has this chapter challenged your preconceptions of the Bible?

2. What, if anything, surprised you as you read this chapter?

3. Has your view of the inspiration and inerrancy of the Bible changed?

4. What has encouraged you as you read this chapter?

5. Read 2 Peter:1:19-21. This is a reference to written Scripture, where the inspired insights of God's prophets have been recorded. How does this help us to have confidence in the Bible as God's inspired word? In what sense is it "completely reliable"? (Verse 19).

6. Read Romans 15:4. How does this give us confidence in the reliability of the Bible?

7. Read Luke 24:1-27. Note, particularly, verse 27. How does Jesus' reference to the authority of the Scriptures give us confidence in their reliability?

CHAPTER 4

BIBLE TRANSLATIONS

The work of textual critics is to examine all the available manuscripts of the Bible and publish a Greek text that is as close to the original as possible. This published Greek text is a work in progress: New manuscripts are regularly being discovered, and textual criticism is continually improving, resulting in regular revisions of the accepted Greek text.

Bible translators start their work where textual critics finish off. The task of Bible translators is to translate the Bible from the accepted autographic text, published by the textual critics, into the living receptor languages.

Textual Critics

Bible Translators

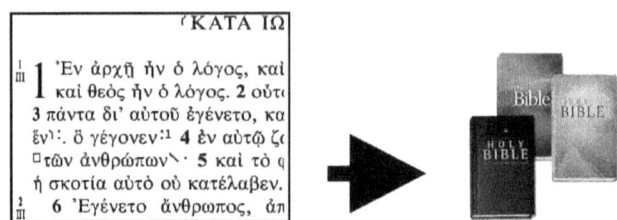

THE AUTOGRAPHIC LANGUAGES

The Bible was written in three languages. Jesus would have spoken and read these three languages:

Hebrew

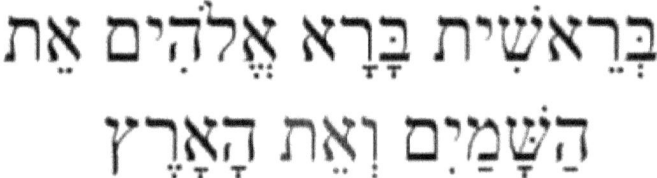

Hebrew was the ancient, formal language of the Jews. The temple and synagogue services were conducted in Hebrew, and the Old Testament was originally written in Hebrew.

Aramaic

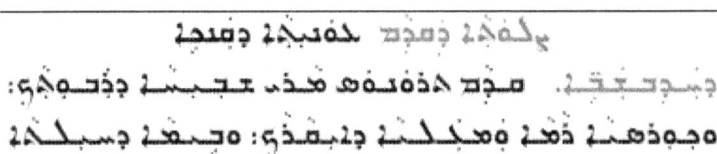

Aramaic was the common language of the Jews living in Palestine. This was the language that Jesus and his contemporaries spoke every day. Occasionally the Gospel writers, when quoting significant words spoken by Jesus, quote him in the actual Aramaic that he would have spoken aloud. A well-known instance of this is Matthew's quotation of Jesus' cry of anguish on the cross, "*Eli, Eli, lema sabachthani*", ("*My God, my God, why have you forsaken me*" - Matt 27:46). Almost all the words of Jesus and every other character in the New Testament were spoken in Aramaic, but only a few key statements are retained in that language by the New Testament writers.

Greek

βούλεσθε μᾶλλον ἐπιόντας, καὶ ἐς τύχας πρὸς πολλῷ δυνατωτέρους ἀγωνιζόμενοι καταστῆναι, ἐπιστάμενοι καὶ τὸν βάρβαρον αὐτὸν περὶ

Koine Greek was the language that was common throughout the Roman empire, and which had become the standard language in which everything was written. The New Testament was written in Greek, so that it could easily be disseminated around the world. By the middle of the second century B.C., the whole of the Old Testament had also been translated into Greek. This translation is known as the Septuagint (LXX), derived from the Latin word meaning "70", which is a reference to the fact that it was translated by approximately 70 translators. It is clear from the wording of Old Testament quotes in the New Testament that this is the translation that Jesus and the New Testament writers used.

CHALLENGES FACED BY BIBLE TRANSLATORS

There are 6 significant challenges facing Bible translators as they seek to produce an accurate and meaningful translation of these ancient Scriptures:

1. The autographic languages are dead languages

In other words, these languages have not been written or spoken for nearly 2,000 years. Ancient Hebrew and Koine Greek are very different from the modern Greek and Hebrew languages, and Aramaic has no modern equivalent at all (it is only *very* remotely related to modern day Arabic).

An Ancient Greek Scroll:

This leads to the second challenge facing translators:

2. We don't know how words were pronounced

For example, the Greek word, "agape" (unconditional love), has at least nine possible pronunciations - agapay, agapear, agapee, agarpay, agarpear, agarpee, argapay, argapear, argapee). We simply don't know how ancient people pronounced their vowels, consonants and combinations of the two. Of course, this isn't a major problem for most of us, because very few of us want to read aloud from the Greek text!

3. Lexical Uncertainty (uncertainty regarding the precise meaning of ancient words)

This is a more serious challenge. Sometimes, scholars are unsure of the meaning of a Greek or Hebrew word. The only way they can discover the meaning of these ancient words is from the context of other writings. There are no ancient speakers of these dead languages of whom we can ask, *"What does this word mean?"* There is no Koine Greek dictionary for English speakers that has been conveniently excavated by archaeologists! Translators are constantly having to grapple with obscure words and concepts.

For example: John 1:5 says, *"The light shines in the darkness, but the darkness has not καταλαμβάνω (katalambano) it"*. Translators are unsure as to the exact meaning of this word. Here are some of the different renderings of this word in various Bible translations:

- *"extinguished"* - Contemporary English Version (CEV).

- *"comprehended"* - King James version (KJV).

- *"understood"* - New International Version (NIV). (footnoted: "overcome")

- *"overcome"* - Today's New International version (TNIV). (This is the latest scholarship on this word).

In good Bible translations, alternate possible meanings of words are footnoted at the bottom of the page. For this reason, it is always helpful to read the footnotes in case there are possible alternate meanings for words.

4. Lexical Incompatibility

Even when translators know the meaning of the original word, sometimes there is no equivalent in the receptor language. For example:

λόγος (logos) is translated "word" in our English Bibles. But it means so much more; a thought or idea, the reason behind something, the cause of something, the logic behind something, the authoritative explanation of something, the communication or announcement of something. All this meaning is packed into one little word - and we don't have any single word that is close to its equivalent!

A second intriguing example highlights the difficulties in finding equivalent words in the receptor language. When Bible translators started translating the New Testament for tribes in Papua New Guinea, the indigenous people had never seen a sheep, and they had no word for "sheep" or "shepherd" in their language. The nearest they had was "pig" and "pig herder". So, when translators translated the Bible into the various tribal languages, Jesus had to become the good pig herder!

5. Grammatical Incompatibility

Many of the Greek and Hebrew tenses and genders have no English equivalent. For example, Ephesians 5:18 exhorts Christians to "πληρόω (pleroo) with the Spirit". In English it is translated as, "be filled", but in the Greek language, it is a verb in the present imperative tense, which means "continually go on being filled", indicating that this is not a single event, but an ongoing one. Furthermore, the word itself means much more than filling. It is a complex word that means to cram full, to complete, to satisfy, to level off, to influence. No single word in English can adequately convey either the meaning or the tense of this word.

6. Word Plays and Euphemisms are not easily translated

For example, Genesis 2:25-3:1. Most English versions read something like this:

> "And the man and wife were both naked (arome - ערום) and were not ashamed. Now the serpent was more crafty (arume - ערום) than any beast of the field which the LORD God had made..."

What is not apparent in our English translations is that the Hebrew words which are translated as 'naked' (arome) and 'crafty' (arume) are almost identical in spelling in Hebrew, and sound very similar. This is a deliberate play on words that links the two chapters together and also contrasts Adam and Eve's innocence with their impending loss of innocence. The best attempt I have seen to convey this aspect in an English translation is to make the words rhyme: *"And the man and his wife were nude... Now the serpent was more shrewd..."*.

As this example shows, the translator often has to choose between translating the literal original text, word for word, at the risk of being unclear, or translating the actual meaning of the passage, while being a little more relaxed about the specific words.

RE-AFFIRMING INERRANCY

This is why the Chicago Statement on biblical Inerrancy (October 1978) says, "*We affirm that inspiration and inerrancy, strictly speaking, applies only to the autographic text of Scripture*". This is because:

- We are very close to knowing the exact wording of the autographic text, but we are still uncertain of about 2.7% of the text.

- There is a small percentage of Greek and Hebrew words, whose meanings are still unclear.

- There is a small percentage of words which cannot be easily translated into modern receptor languages.

- There are some biblical inconsistencies regarding names and numbers which cannot be resolved until earlier, more complete manuscripts are discovered.

Improvements In Lexical Understanding

As each year passes, more manuscripts are uncovered, more lexical research is undertaken, and our knowledge of the original languages increases. Our understanding of the meaning of Greek and Hebrew words today is vastly superior to the 1600's when the King James Version was originally translated.

TYPES OF TRANSLATIONS

Transliterations

Transliterations (also called Interlinear Bibles) are a literal word for word rendering from the original language to the receptor language, retaining the form of the original sentence structure, without imposing the grammatical rules of the receptor language. These are particularly helpful when used in conjunction with a Greek / English lexicon, to gain an understanding of the meaning of the original words. A transliteration will often have the Greek and English text printed side by side or one above the other. For example:

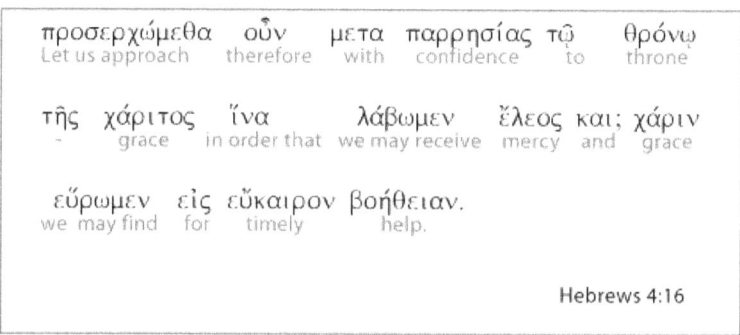

προσερχώμεθα οὖν μετα παρρησίας τῷ θρόνῳ
Let us approach   therefore   with   confidence   to   throne

τῆς χάριτος ἵνα λάβωμεν ἔλεος και; χάριν
grace   in order that   we may receive   mercy   and   grace

εὕρωμεν εἰς εὔκαιρον βοήθειαν.
we may find   for   timely   help.

Hebrews 4:16

The interlinear example above renders Hebrews 4:16 as *"Let us approach with confidence to throne grace in order we may receive mercy and grace we may find for timely help."*

Transliterations are "clunky" to read, because the receptor language's idioms and grammatical structures have not yet been applied to the text. For this reason, transliterations are more of a study tool than a Bible for personal, devotional reading.

Translations

Translations take the next step, by incorporating the grammar and idioms of the receptor language, to make the text more readable and understandable. Within this category of Bibles, however, there is a significant divergence in terms of how closely the translators have attempted to align the wording of the receptor language to the original language. Translations that stick very closely to a "word for word" translation are referred to as "literal", whereas those that adopt a "thought for thought" approach are called "dynamic".

Paraphrases

Paraphrases attempt to translate the ideas rather than the words themselves, using modern language, often without reference to the original manuscripts. They are not fresh translations from the original languages, but simply re-wordings from, say, English to English. These are occasionally helpful to provide a fresh perspective on a verse or passage, but they should not be relied upon if you want to accurately understand the Bible.

The continuum between word-for-word and thought-for-thought translations is illustrated below, demonstrating the relative position along the continuum of many of today's common translations.

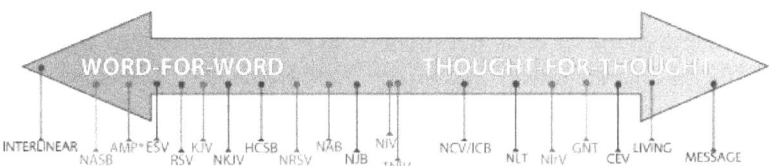

The following chart further indicates where many of today's translations and paraphrases lie in the continuum between literal, word for word and thought for thought rendering of the original text:

COMPARISON OF TRANSLATIONS

TRANSLITERATION	TRANSLATION		PARAPHRASE
	LITERAL	DYNAMIC	
	Formal Equivalence	Functional Equivalence	
Hebrew / English	KJV	NIV	GNB
Greek / English	NKJV	TNIV	LB
	NASB	NAB	NLT
	RSV	NJB	NIRV
	NRSV		MESSAGE
	ESV		

COMPARISONS OF LITERAL AND DYNAMIC TRANSLATIONS

There is always going to be a divergence of opinion concerning the best way of translating an ancient language into a modern, readable text. Within the continuum that we call "translations" there is a constant tension between a literal approach (word for word) and a dynamic approach (thought for thought). At first glance, it might seem that the literal approach is going to produce the most accurate translation, but that is not always the case. There are many occasions when a word for word translation will not capture the original meaning of the text as well as a thought for thought approach. Consider the following example, from Amos 8:1-2.

The KJV and RSV Bibles translate this verse as,

> "God said, "Amos, what do you see?" And I said, "A basket of **summer** fruit". Then the LORD said to me, "The **end** has come upon my people Israel"."

This is a word for word translation. Unfortunately, this does not capture the play on words between "*summer*" and "*end*" in Hebrew. "*Summer*" and "*end*" were almost the same words in Hebrew, ("*qys*" and "*qs*"), which were pronounced virtually identically. The KJV and RSV literal translation of "*summer*" and "*end*" completely misses this wordplay, and so God's statement "*The end has come*" seems to have no relevance to the preceding statement.

By contrast, the NIV and TNIV translate this verse,

> "What do you see, Amos?" God asked. "A basket of **ripe** fruit," I answered. Then the LORD said to me, "The time is **ripe** for my people Israel"."

These translations have attempted to capture the wordplay which links the two statements. Although the KJV and RSV are more literal interpretations at this point, the NIV and TNIV translations capture the true meaning of the passage. This demonstrates the difference between literal and dynamic translations, and why, on some occasions, a dynamic translation is preferable to a literal one.

A second example will help to further illustrate the functional difference between literal and dynamic translations. The KJV translates 2 Kings 9:8 as,

> *"For the whole house of Ahab shall perish: and I will cut off from Ahab him that pisseth against the wall".*

This is a word for word translation. But who are these people who are urinating against walls? Are they to be punished for unseemly public urination? No. The reference to those who *"pisseth against the wall"* was an ancient colloquial expression for *"all males"*. Accordingly, the NIV and TNIV translate this verse as,

> *"The whole house of Ahab will perish. I will cut off from Ahab <u>every last male</u> in Israel."*

Although this is not a word for word rendering of the original text, it is a much more helpful translation, as it more accurately conveys the original meaning.

It is important to note that translations like the NIV and TNIV are literal translations 95% of the time. On the rare occasions when they translate dynamically, it is because a literal translation would not accurately convey the original meaning.

COMMENTS ON SOME TRANSLATIONS

KING JAMES VERSION (KJV)

The King James Version (1611) was a good translation at the time, but is now outdated, not just because of its archaic language, but mainly because of its reliance on inaccurate Greek texts. The King James translators only had access to a total of six major Greek manuscripts upon which to base their translation. Today's translators have over 5,600 Greek manuscripts at their disposal.

The Greek manuscripts available to the King James translators came from the Byzantine family of manuscripts (referred to as the Textus Recepticus), dating from the 5th century and later. The Byzantine text was the dominant Greek text from the 8th century until 1889. By the 1800's, however, thousands more Greek manuscripts had been discovered, including many that were dated much earlier and were more reliable than the Byzantine text. These earlier manuscripts include the much more reliable Vaticanus. Although this had been discovered in 1475, it remained locked away in the Vatican vaults and the KJV translators were refused access to it. This was because of the Catholic church's opposition, at that time, to translations of the Bible into anything other than their own Latin version. The Vaticanus was only released and made available to Bible translators in 1889.

Other, more reliable, Greek manuscripts which weren't available to the KJV translators include the Alexandrinus (discovered in 1621, just 10 years after the KJV was published), and the Sinaiticus, the earliest, and most reliable, complete Greek New Testament in existence, discovered in a monastery in Sinai in 1875, and dated at 330 A.D. By 1889 these, and many other Greek manuscripts had begun to circulate. When compared to these, the Byzantine text, upon which the King James Version had been based, was vastly inferior – containing many transcription errors and interpolations. The Byzantine text is no longer relied upon by modern translators.

Because of its reliance upon flawed Greek texts, the KJV published many interpolations which we now know were not in the original text. For example, the KJV renders 1 Corinthians 6:20 as, *"Therefore, glorify God in your body and in your spirit, which are God's"*. The underlined words, *"and in your spirit, which are God's"* are an interpolation, found in the Masoretic and other later texts, but not in any earlier texts. In other words, these words are *not* in the original text of 1 Corinthians 6:20. This interpolation was introduced by monastic copyists in the 8th century, at a time when Greek philosophy, which emphasised the spirit and de-emphasised the body, had influenced Christian theology. Modern translations do not publish this interpolation in their text.

This is just one of hundreds of problematic interpolations published in the KJV, as a result of its reliance on later, less reliable manuscripts. These flawed Greek manuscripts were combined into a published Greek text called the Textus Receptus, and it was this published text that was used for the KJV translation. The accepted Greek text that is used by today's Bible translators differs from the flawed Textus Receptus in over 2,000 textual locations!

As previously explained, one outcome of the KJV's use of the Textus Receptus is that there are a number of verses that were published in the KJV (and, therefore, given verse numbers), which are not published in modern Bibles, because they are now known to be interpolations. These verses include *Matthew 17:21, Matthew 18:11, Matthew 23:14, Mark 7:16, Mark 9:44, Mark 9:46, Mark 11:26, Mark 15:28, Luke 17:36, Luke 23:17, John 5:4, Acts 8:37, Acts 15:34, Acts 24:7, Acts 28:29 and Romans 16:24.* None of these verses appear in modern translations, but in order to retain a consistent verse numbering system, modern Bibles simply skip that verse number. For example, in most modern Bibles, Matthew 17:20 is immediately followed by Matthew 17:22. Verse 21 is either footnoted or does not appear at all.

Apart from textual inaccuracy, the KJV also suffers from obtuse language and cumbersome sentence structure, often making it difficult for modern readers to understand. John 18:34 is a case in point. The KJV renders it, *"Jesus answered him, "Sayest thou this thing of thyself, or did others tell it thee of me?"."* The NIV and TNIV offer a more readily understandable version; *"Is that your own idea?" Jesus asked. "Or did others talk to you about me?"*

The "King James Only" Movement

Despite the overwhelming evidence of modern biblical scholarship, there remains a small minority of people who are adamant in their support of the King James Version. These fall into two main categories:

1. Those who prefer the KJV to other translations, because they like the ornate language or because it is the translation they grew up with.

2. Those who maintain that the KJV is the *only inspired translation* of the Bible. Some of these people tend to be fanatical in their allegiance to the KJV. Some have concocted all kinds of conspiracy theories about how all other translations have been corrupted because of the influence of anti-Christian elements who have secretly infiltrated the ranks of translators and publishers in order to undermine Christianity. All kinds of bizarre theories abound, linking different translations to the New Age movement, the Illuminati, secularism, and humanism. As worldwide biblical scholarship continues to shed light on some of the inadequacies of the KJV, these fanatics have reacted by becoming more extreme and ridiculous in their claims.

NEW INTERNATIONAL VERSION

The NIV, first published in 1978, was the most accurate translation at that time. In the 360 years since the KJV was published, the science of Bible translation has improved enormously. Not only are there thousands more Greek manuscripts available today, but our knowledge of the ancient Greek language has also vastly improved. In 1978, the NIV represented the most accurate translation of the Bible to that point. The NIV Preface states:

> *"The Greek text used in translating the New Testament was an eclectic one. No other piece of ancient literature has such an abundance of manuscript witnesses as does the New Testament. Where existing manuscripts differ, the translators made their choice of readings according to accepted principles of New Testaments textual criticism. Footnotes call attention to places where there was uncertainty about what the original text was. The best current printed texts of the Greek New Testaments were used."*

During the years following the initial publication of the NIV, textual criticism continued to improve, and new manuscripts were discovered, and so a minor revision of the NIV was published in 1984.

TODAY'S NEW INTERNATIONAL VERSION

Textual criticism continued to improve and so, in 2002, a major revision was undertaken and the TNIV was published. The New Testament TNIV was published in 2002 and the complete Bible TNIV was published in 2005. The TNIV is the most up to date and accurate English translation currently available. It corrects a number of translation inaccuracies that had surfaced during the last 20 years. It also incorporates gender-neutral language, which has caused some "push back" from conservative Christians. About 7% of the text was updated from the old NIV.

COMPARING TRANSLATIONS

Things to look for:

- How recent is the translation? The most recent translations will be the product of the latest scholarship and the latest manuscript discoveries. In the table below, the first publication date is the most important. The revision date is generally an update of English words and does not indicate a fresh translation of the original text.

- Who were the translators / publishers? This may sometimes be an indication of theological bias.

- How many translators worked on the project? The most scholarly translations use a large number of translators from a variety of denominations and countries.

The table below lists some of the most common modern translations and compares some of these key characteristics regarding how they were translated and by whom.

BIBLE TRANSLATIONS

COMPARISON OF TRANSLATIONS:

	DATE	Revised	Read Age	TRANSLATORS / PUBUSHERS	COMMENT
NAB New American Bible	1970	1991	13	Catholic Biblical Scholars and U.S. Conference Of Catholic Bishops	Very literal but not very readable.
NASB New American Standard Bible	NT: 1963 OT: 1971	1995	17	32 translators, Lockman Foundation, (U.S evangelical publishing company)	The NASB is a revision of the 1901 American Standard Version. Very literal translation, but not very readable.
NJB New Jerusalem Bible	1985		11	Less than 50 Catholic translators	Uses less reliable 9th C. Masoretic text for O.T. rather than 2nd C, Septuagint
KJV King James	1611		18	50 translators	Based on less reliable Greek ms
NKJV New King James	1982		14	100+ translators. Thomas Nelson Publishers	Uses some additional texts from the KJV, but rejects many of the accepted more reliable texts.
RSV Revised Standard Version	NT: 1946 OT: 1952		16	National Council Of Churches Of Christ, USA.	Not a fresh translation from original ms; a revision of the ASV (1901). Fairly accurate but not very readable
GNT	1966	1992	11	American Bible Society	Formerly GNB and TEV. Loose translation, inaccurate. Originally for speakers of English as a 2nd language
ESV English Standard Version	2001		15	100+ translators, led by Dr; J I Packer Standard Bible Society.	Very liter-al translation, but also very readable. The best of the literal translations.
NIV New International Version	NT: 1973 OT: 1978	1984	13	100+ international Translators. International Bible Society	Best balance between formal and functional equivalence.
TNIV Todays' New International	NT: 200 OT: 2005		14	100+ international Translators. International Bible Society and Zondervan	Incorporates gender neutral language and latest scholarship.
CEV Contemporary English Version	NT 199 OT: 1995		11	100 international, inter-denominational Translators. American Bible Society.	Very loose translation but very readable
NIRV New International Readers version	1996		8	International Bible Society and Zondervan	Paraphrase of NIV. Vocabulary aimed at 3rd class level. Not very accurate for adult study.
NLT New Living-Translation	1996	2006	12	90 translators. Tyndale.	Not a paraphrase, like the LB. A fresh translation from the original ms. Very readable but. not: as accurate- as TNIV.

Reflection Questions 4

1. What new insights have you gained from this chapter?

2. What translation of the Bible do you currently read and why?

3. Is there anything in this chapter that has challenged your thinking?

4. Read Psalm 119. This is a wonderful affirmation of the inspiration and authority of God's Word. Discuss each verse separately. What does each statement teach us about the Bible and about our response to it?

5. Read 2 Thessalonians 2:15-17. What are we encouraged to do? What do you think this means in practice?

PART II

GETTING THE BIG PICTURE

CHAPTER 5

CHALLENGES IN INTERPRETING THE BIBLE

THE NEED FOR INTERPRETATION

People often talk about the *"simple meaning of Scripture"*, as if all you have to do is read a Bible passage and the meaning is obvious. While this concept sounds very appealing, and even spiritual, the truth is that there is rarely anything simple about the process of reading and interpreting the Bible. Give two people the same passage to read and very often they will reach two very different conclusions about its meaning and its application to their lives.

For example, some Christians claim that the Bible *"plainly teaches"* that your salvation is eternally secure (*"once saved always saved"*), while others maintain that the Bible *"plainly teaches"* that it is possible to fall away and lose your salvation. Both groups are reading the same Bible, and both groups are sincerely trying to be faithful to what the Bible *"plainly says"*.

The fact that so many Christians disagree about so many things that the Bible *"plainly says"* should tell us that interpreting the Bible is anything *but* simple. Part of the difficulty lies in our own fallible human nature, and part of the difficulty is the nature of the Bible itself. In terms of our own human nature, we inevitably bring our own bias to the text we are reading. No one is immune to this. As we read a text, we filter it through the lens of our preconceptions, our experiences and our already established, often preciously guarded, doctrinal beliefs.

For example, people who have been taught that *not* all Christians can speak in tongues will read the book of Acts and they will discover that it supports their premise. On the other hand, people who have been taught that all Christians *can* speak in tongues will read Acts and they will discover that the book of Acts supports *their* premise. Both groups are reading the same book but are filtering it through the lens of their own preconceptions. It is extremely difficult to avoid doing this, as it usually occurs at the level of our subconscious mind. But one of the skills of *"correctly handling the Word of Truth" (2 Tim 2:15)* is learning to consciously put aside our preconceptions in order to read God's Word with an unfiltered mind.

The other part of the difficulty in interpreting the Bible, is the nature of the Bible itself. Even before we bring our own preconceptions to our reading, the Bible is already an incredibly complex and difficult book. It is an ancient book, originally written by and for an ancient people, penned in 3 ancient languages which are not completely transferrable into English, and set in a cultural and historical framework that is light-years away from our own understanding of the world. We are attempting to interpret a book that is between 2,000 and 4,500 years old, which we read from a point of extreme dislocation – historically, linguistically and culturally. Apart from the Bible, when was the last time you read a book that was 4,000 years old?

THE DIFFICULTY OF INTERPRETING THE OLD TESTAMENT

The Old Testament is the most difficult part of the Bible to interpret and apply, because it involves the added complication of containing components which belong to the obsolete old covenant. If we are to interpret the Old Testament accurately, there are some key questions that need to be answered:

- In what sense is the Old Testament authoritative for Christians?

- How do we interpret the Old Testament in the light of the New Testament?

- How should we treat old covenantal ethics, promises and practices?

Inadequate understanding of these kinds of issues has led many well-intentioned Christians down false trails of theology and ethics.

The question of how to interpret the Bible, particularly the Old Testament, is one that many Christians have not fully resolved. Having listened to many sermons over the years, I have concluded that even many pastors struggle with these issues. What relevance do the Old Testament stories have for today? In what sense can we take the words of a prophet, originally addressed to specific issues within the nation of Israel thousands of years ago, and apply them to Christians today? Are they applicable *at all*? It is at this point that many preachers and teachers resort to allegorism.

DAVID AND GOLIATH

A classic example is the well-known story of David and Goliath, in 1 Samuel 17. Let us "visit" 3 different churches, to see how they apply this story to Christians today:

- A Baptist Sunday School teacher is telling the story of David and Goliath, and has two helpers dressed as David and Goliath. She explains that Goliath represents the temptations we face as Christians which can, potentially, lead us away from God. She sticks a series of labels on the chest of Goliath – lust, pride, greed, dishonesty. She then explains that David's stones represent the weapons we use to overcome these obstacles. The stones are labelled Faith, Prayer, Bible Reading, Fellowship.

- In the Presbyterian church down the road, a different Sunday School teacher is teaching the same story to an adult Sunday School class. He explains that Goliath represents the secular forces in the world which oppose God's Kingdom. He sticks labels on Goliath's chest – materialism, secularism, atheism, humanism. He explains that David's stones represent the rationalist tools with which Christians must engage these secular forces. He holds up rocks labelled Apologetics, Philosophy, Theistic Rationalism and Creationism.

- Across the road, the pastor of the Pentecostal Church is preaching on the same passage. He says that Goliath represents the negative forces that will stop you reaching your full potential in God: negative words of non-Christians, negative words of Christians, past negative experiences, self-doubt, the accusations of the devil. The stones represent your need to surround yourself with positive people, saturate your mind with promises of God, speak positively about yourself and your future, ask and believe for great things in your life, and overcome obstacles through the power of prayer.

Which one of these teachers is right? Are they all right? Are any of them right? Is it appropriate to allegorise the Old Testament in this way, particularly when the applications seem quite arbitrary? They are not drawn from the passage itself; they are concocted by the Bible teacher.

What is wrong with allegorisation? More will be said about this shortly, but at this point let us affirm two important principles:

1. The Bible cannot mean what it never meant.

We must not place meanings upon the text which were not there originally. Every passage has an original meaning, and it is our job to discover what that original meaning is. In other words, we cannot use the Bible as a convenient springboard to launch into whatever topic we want to discuss.

2. We must derive the meaning from the text itself, not read our own meaning into it.

This is the difference between *exegesis* and *eisegesis*. Exegesis refers to the process of extracting meaning *out of* a passage; in other words, getting the meaning from the passage itself. Eisegesis refers to the dangerous practice of reading our own meaning *into* a passage. If we are to become people who *"correctly handle the Word of Truth" (2 Tim 2:15)*, we must learn the skill of laying aside our own preconceptions, and learn to see what a passage is *actually* saying, rather than what we *want* it to say.

These must be our two guiding principles as we read the Old Testament. We must not use the Bible as a convenient coat hanger to support whatever we want to say. We must work hard at uncovering the *actual* meaning of a text, rather than giving it an allegorical one. Otherwise we are no better than the secular motivational speaker who might use the story of David and Goliath to talk about self-assertiveness, or the sports coach who might use it to talk about underdogs who win.

So, what is the *actual* meaning of the story of David and Goliath?

There is one important fact that almost all allegorical interpretations of the story of David and Goliath overlook; and that is the fact that the oppression by the Philistines (including Goliath) was <u>God's punishment</u>

for the disobedience of the Israelites. It was their ongoing punishment for disobeying God by not driving out the inhabitants of the land of Canaan when they first arrived (Judges 1). It was also a more immediate punishment for choosing a King for themselves (Saul).

This is an important point. The oppression the Israelites were experiencing wasn't simply some inconvenient obstacle to be overcome in order to receive the blessing that God had in store for them; it was the punishment of **God himself** for their rebellion. All of the allegorical interpretations that we've looked at so far have completely missed the point of the story, because they overlooked this one key fact.

Here, then, is the meaning of the story of David and Goliath:

- Israel had disobeyed God and were under his judgment (in this case, oppression by the Philistines).

- They were, consequently, oppressed by an enemy too powerful for them to overcome; they were unable to save themselves.

- God had mercy upon them and decided to send them a saviour. God decided to save his people from his own judgment.

- The Israelites did not recognise David as their saviour because he did not meet their expectations of what a warrior saviour would look like.

- David stepped forward to represent the entire nation; one person doing battle on behalf of everyone.

- David, the unassuming shepherd boy, saved the entire nation by his one heroic act.

Can you begin to see the meaning of this story now? It's all about Jesus! The Saviour who comes to a people who are under the judgment of God; who steps forward to represent everyone – to take our place; a Saviour who is not recognised because he doesn't meet most people's expectations; a Saviour who takes our place and stands in the gap between us and our "enemy" (in this case, God the Judge, himself); a Saviour who, by his one heroic act, saves all mankind (at least, all who will follow him as Lord).

If there is any allegorical meaning in the story of David and Goliath, any hidden meaning at all, apart from the simple historical facts themselves, it is this one! It's not about me and my fulfilment, or overcoming the obstacles in my life; it's all about Jesus! Of course, it is entirely appropriate to make some applications to our own lives from the story of David and Goliath. We can consider David's courage and his trust in God, and seek to emulate those qualities ourselves. We can note the fact that God can use anyone for his purposes, even those whom the world dismisses as unimpressive. There are certainly appropriate applications for us in the story, without the need to allegorise. But if we have failed to see the foreshadowing of Christ our Saviour in this incident, we have missed the main point!

Now, you may be thinking, *"What makes your interpretation the correct one? Why is this interpretation right, and the others wrong?"* The answer is simple; it's not **my** interpretation, it's the **Bible's**, because this is the meaning that the New Testament attaches to the story of David and Goliath. On 17 occasions the New Testament refers to Jesus as the *"Son of David"*, and on 59 occasions the Bible points out the parallels between Jesus and David. For example:

> **Acts 13:23** *"From David's descendants God has brought to Israel the Saviour Jesus, as he promised"*

This is in response to the many prophecies in Isaiah, Jeremiah and Ezekiel that God would one day raise up another David, who would save God's people forever:

> *Ezekiel 37:25* *"They and their children and their children's children will live there forever, and David my servant will be their prince forever".*

> *Isaiah 9:7* *"Of the increase of his government and peace, there will be no end. He will reign on David's throne and over his kingdom, establishing and upholding it with justice and righteousness from that time on and forever".*

This is why, at the start of Jesus' ministry, the people asked, *"Could this be the Son of David?" (Matt 12:23)*. Jesus also made a point of identifying himself as the long awaited Davidic Saviour: *"I, Jesus, give you this testimony for the churches. I am the Root and the Offspring of David, and the bright Morning Star." (Rev 22:16)*.

David is the strongest "type" of Jesus in the Old Testament. We will look at typology in detail later, but, for now, it is enough for us to understand that the life of David is a prophetic foreshadowing of all that Jesus would be and do. By interpreting the story of David and Goliath as an allegory of the saving work of Jesus, we aren't forcing some arbitrary meaning upon the text (one that is not intended in the story), but rather, we are identifying the underlying theme that runs throughout the entire Old Testament; that the Old Testament is, ultimately, all about Jesus.

We know this, because Jesus and the New Testament writers identify this underlying theme for us. Chapter 11, *"Reading The Old Testament Christologically"*, will develop this theme in detail. For the moment however, it is sufficient for us to realise that Jesus, himself, proposed that the Old Testament is really all about him:

> *"He explained to his disciples what was said about him in **all** the Scriptures, beginning with **Moses** and the prophets" (Luke 24:27).*

This reference to "Moses" is a reference by Jesus to the Pentateuch, the first five books of the Old Testament, that were written by Moses. Jesus was saying that even these books of historical narrative within the Old Testament were all about him.

In a separate post-resurrection appearance Jesus made a similar appeal to the Old Testament: He said to his disciples,

> *"This is what I told you while I was still with you: Everything must be fulfilled that is written about me in the Law of Moses, the Prophets and the Psalms." (45) Then he opened their minds so they could understand the Scriptures". (Luke 24:44-45)*

This does not conflict with the first principle of interpretation that we looked at previously; that the Bible cannot mean what it never meant. According to Jesus and the New Testament writers, this allegory about Jesus was always there in the Old Testament, as a hidden sub-text. It only became apparent, however, after it was fulfilled in the life of Jesus and revealed by the inspired writings of the New Testament.

This brings us to a third important principle for reading the Old Testament:

3. The only time we can safely allegorise the Old Testament is when the New Testament reveals that allegory for us.

There is a danger in allegorising the Bible arbitrarily, because you can end up teaching and believing things that the Bible doesn't teach. In fact, you can read into a passage anything you want if you try hard enough! Arbitrary allegorisation turns the Bible into a convenient ideological coat hanger to support whatever you want to say.

Of course, just because someone has allegorised a Bible passage doesn't *necessarily* mean that the content of their message is wrong. In the case of David and Goliath, there are many good points made by the allegorical interpretations we have previously mentioned. Bible reading, prayer and fellowship *are* good ways of resisting and fighting temptation. But it would be far better to find a passage that *actually teaches* those ideas, rather than arbitrarily imposing them upon a passage that has *nothing to do with those concepts.*

SOLOMON'S TEMPLE

Consider the example of Solomon's Temple. In 1 Kings 6, we are given a detailed description of the layout of Solomon's Temple. It consists of layers of courts, from outer to inner: Court of Gentiles, Court of Women, Court of Israel (Men), Court of Priests (the Holy Place), and finally, the Holy of Holies.

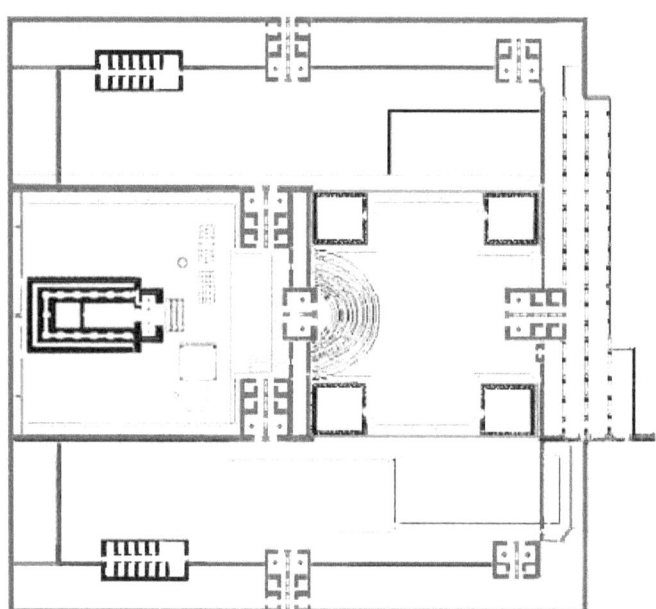

I once heard a creative sermon suggesting that the different courts of the Temple are an allegory for the different compartments of our lives, which must all be brought under the Lordship of Christ.

- Court Of Gentiles = our body and its physical needs & desires

- Court Of Women = our emotions

- Court Of Israel (Men) = our mind

- Court Of Priests = our soul

- Holy Of Holies = our spirit

The preacher's allegorical interpretation was quite creative, and, in one sense, what he was saying was quite true; we do need to allow the Lordship of Christ to permeate all aspects of our lives. But there was also a sense in which the message was quite misleading, because comparing the areas of our lives to the courts of the temple could cause us to develop a compartmentalised view of life; it might lead us to believe that each of these areas are quite separate and independent from each other. This is a false teaching called pluralism. Nowhere in the Bible are we encouraged to view ourselves as compartmentalised beings, with our physical life quite separate from our spiritual life, or our church life separate from our private life. In fact, this false teaching is strongly denounced in several passages in the New Testament, because it leads to hypocrisy.

Admittedly, 1 Corinthians 6:19 does say that our bodies are temples of the Holy Spirit, meaning that he now lives in us and speaks through us. As Christians, we are walking temples; we take God's message into the world and represent him to those around us. Therefore, we should ensure that the way we live honours him and does not grieve his Spirit within us. If we are to allegorise the temple to refer to ourselves, *that* is how we should allegorise it - not as an inward looking, compartmentalised dissection of myself, but as an allegory of my role now in taking God to the world around me. The New Testament also reveals a second allegorical interpretation of the Temple. In the Gospels, Jesus spoke of the Temple as allegorically referring to his body (Jn 2:19-21). The book of Hebrews picks up the same allegory, by describing the Temple's sacrificial system as an allegory of the final sacrifice of Christ.

In the case of the previously mentioned Temple sermon, it sounded convincing, it sounded very clever, but the preacher was actually contradicting the New Testament. This example illustrates why allegorisation is potentially dangerous, and why the only time we should contemplate it, is when the New Testament identifies the allegory for us.

Allegorising the Old Testament, except when it is revealed in the New Testament, is dangerous for three reasons:

1. The interpretations are extremely arbitrary.

2. It involves *eisegesis* (inserting our meaning *into* the text) rather than *exegesis* (extracting the true meaning *out of* the text).

3. It gives the *appearance* of being based on the Bible, whereas it can actually be *contradicting* the Bible. A lot of false teaching is perpetrated this way - under the guise of *biblical* teaching.

One way of ensuring that you are not misinterpreting a passage is to refer to a reliable Bible commentary or a Study Bible. The explanatory notes in a Study Bible, for example, provide a basic, reliable, verse-by-verse exposition of the major themes of the text, and also point out where that passage or topic has been mentioned elsewhere in Scripture.

SUMMARY

So far, we have examined three important principles for interpreting the Bible:

1. A passage cannot mean what it did not originally mean.

2. We must derive the meaning from the text itself, not read our own meaning into it.

3. The only time we can safely allegorise the Bible is when the Bible reveals that allegory for us.

We have only just begun our journey into the process of interpreting the Bible. It is a complicated process. There is much that needs to be understood if we are to avoid misinterpreting its message. There are new skills to be learnt and old habits to be discarded. But it is a journey worth taking. As the Apostle Paul writes to Timothy, the young pastor of the church at Ephesus:

"Do your best to present yourself to God as one approved, a worker who does not need to be ashamed and who <u>correctly handles the word of truth</u>." (2 Tim 2:15)

Reflection Questions 5

1. What new insight have you gained from this chapter?

2. Has this chapter highlighted any challenges for you?

3. Have you heard any examples of arbitrary allegorisation of Bible stories? Do you think there are times when it is valid?

4. Consider 2 Timothy 2:15, "Do your best to present yourself to God as one approved, a worker who does not need to be ashamed and who correctly handles the word of truth." What are some ways you can "correctly handle the word of truth"?

5. Read the story of David and Goliath in 1 Samuel 17. What elements of the story provide us with a prophetic foreshadowing of the work of Christ? What elements of the story are appropriate for us to apply to ourselves, as people seeking to live a life of faith?

CHAPTER 6

THE TWO COVENANTS

There is no single issue more vital for correctly interpreting the Bible than the necessity to understand the fundamental differences between the old and new covenants. Failure to appreciate these differences, together with a lack of understanding regarding the nature of progressive revelation throughout the Old and New Testaments, are the most common causes of biblical misinterpretation and theological error within the Christian church today. Even many pastors have an inadequate understanding of these foundational issues. The promotion of the prosperity doctrine by many prominent television evangelists and preachers, as well as their advocacy of old covenantal blessings, curses and promises, displays what can only be described as a serious deficiency in their understanding of these concepts.

What is the relationship between the Old and New Testaments and the old and new covenants? Are there parts of the Old Testament which are no longer relevant for us today? Are there any parts of the old covenant which can be directly applied to Christians? How do we decide which parts of the Old Testament still apply and which parts do not? The answers to these questions will have a significant impact upon the way we apply the teaching of the Bible to our lives today.

THE CONCEPT OF COVENANT

The concept of covenant is vital to our understanding of the relationship between the Old and New Testaments. In biblical times, covenants were very common. They were written agreements between two parties outlining the responsibilities and rights of each party. Covenants were the equivalent of our modern-day contracts. For example, a person leasing land to graze sheep would have a covenant specifying the terms of the lease. The covenant would detail the length of the lease, the rights and responsibilities of both parties, as well as clearly defined reimbursements, fines, rewards and punishments, which formed part of the legally binding conditions of the covenant. Under the terms of such a covenant, the lessee may be required to pay an annual percentage of the new-born lambs or a percentage of the wool, with penalties for late payment. At the end of the lease period a completely new covenant would need to be negotiated, and the old covenant would be destroyed. If it was written on a clay tablet (as was common in the early Old Testament period) it would be smashed. If it was written on parchment or papyrus it would be torn up or burned.

Once a new covenant was negotiated and signed, the old covenant was completely obsolete. The fact that the new covenant might have elements that were identical or similar to the old covenant did not mean that parts of the old covenant were still current. Whatever had been written in the old covenant was irrelevant; only what was written in the new covenant was binding. The new covenant *totally replaced* the previous one even though it may have some similar or identical elements. This understanding of covenants is *essential* to our reading of the Bible.

THE NEW COVENANT

Just before his death, Jesus announced that he was instituting a *new* covenant: *"After supper he took the cup, saying "This cup is the new covenant in my blood, which is poured out for you.""* *(Luke 22:20).* In biblical times, important covenants were sealed with the shedding of blood; the more important the covenant, the more costly the animal that was slaughtered. In this case, Jesus himself was the sacrifice that would seal the new covenant between God and mankind;

"This cup is the new covenant in my blood" (Luke 22:20)

How does the new covenant that was instituted by Jesus relate to the old one? The book of Hebrews answers that question unequivocally:

"By calling this covenant "new" he has made the first one obsolete" (Heb 8:13).

The writer to the Hebrews is appealing to the first century common understanding of covenantal obsolescence. If a "new" covenant exists, in any sphere of life, the old is automatically obsolete.

This is crucial for our understanding of the biblical old covenant. It is completely obsolete: All of it! All the rituals, all the ceremonies, all the blessings, all the curses, all the laws. They are no longer in operation for those who follow Christ. Every commandment in the Old Testament, including the Ten Commandments, are part of the old covenant which is now *"obsolete"*. The fact that the new covenant contains some laws that were in the old covenant, (for example, nine of the ten commandments are in the new covenant), does not mean that parts of the old covenant are still current. The old covenant is obsolete, and the new covenant *totally replaces* the previous one.

There is a common misconception among many Christians that Christ only fulfilled the ceremonial laws of the old covenant and that the moral laws are still current. I held this view, myself, in my early years as a

Christian, because this is what I had been taught. According to this view, part of the old covenant is still current, and part is not. Not only is this confusing (how do we distinguish which laws are ceremonial and which are moral?), but it fails to appreciate the ancient concept of covenantal obsolescence. The first covenant has been torn up, burned, smashed, destroyed. It is *"obsolete"*. There are no parts of it that remain current. Only what is written in the new covenant is binding. The early Christians, living in a world where covenants were common, would have understood this implicitly.

This does not mean that the Old *Testament* is obsolete. It is the old *covenant* that is obsolete, not the Old *Testament*. The Old Testament *contains* the old covenant, including the written record of the terms and conditions of that covenant; promises, blessings, curses, laws etc. But the Old Testament contains much more than this. It also contains timeless theological truths, important historical narratives and profound words of prophecy. It reveals God's character and the history of his dealings with mankind. It lays important theological foundations for our understanding of the gospel, by describing the fall of mankind, our inability to save ourselves, and our dependence upon God's redemptive intervention. It lays the groundwork for the coming of the Messiah. The Old Testament is an important part of God's inspired Word for Christians because it provides us with a deeper understanding of the nature of mankind and the character of God, and gives us a richer appreciation of the work of Christ.

Furthermore, although the old covenant's obsolescence means that it no longer applies to us, this does not infer that we should skip over those elements as we read the Old Testament. There is much value to be had in reading and understanding the old covenant, for, in so doing, we will gain a richer appreciation of the grace that is made available in the new covenant through the saving work of Christ.

Old Covenant Laws Are Applicable Only When Renewed in the New Covenant

Christians cannot apply the laws and promises of the Old Testament to themselves. They are part of a covenant that is now obsolete. Only when a law or promise is repeated in the New Testament is it applicable to us under the new covenant. The terms and conditions of the new covenant are recorded in explicit detail in the New Testament. It contains some laws that are the same as the old covenant, some that have been modified from the old covenant, and some that are completely new.

Laws That Are Carried Over into The New Covenant

Some old covenantal laws have been carried over into the new covenant. The wording may not be identical, but the concept is the same:

LAWS THAT ARE CARRIED OVER	
OLD COVENANT	NEW COVENANT
"You shall have no other Gods before me" (Exod 20:3)	"Worship the Lord your God an serve him only" (Matt 4:10)
"You shall not make any idols... or worship them" (Exod 20:4)	"Dear children, keep yourself from idols" (1 Jn 5:21)
"Honour your father and mother" (Exod 20:12)	"Honour your father and mother" (Eph. 6:2)
"You shall not covet your neighbour's house ... wife... servant ... ox... donkey" (Exod 20:17)	"Watch out! Be on your guard against all kinds of greed; a man's life does not consist in the abundance of his possessions" (Luke 12:15)
"Do not steal" Exod (20:15)	"Do not steal" (Matt 19:18)

Laws That Are Modified in The New Covenant

Some of the old covenantal laws have been given a facelift in the new covenant. But, rather than watering them down, they have been raised to an even higher level. Because the followers of Christ now have the indwelling Holy Spirit to empower and transform them, God's expectation of people living under the new covenant is greater than his expectation of those under the previous covenant. The following are examples of old covenantal laws that have been modified in the new covenant:

LAWS THAT ARE MODIFIED	
OLD COVENANT	NEW COVENANT
"You shall not make any idols... or worship them" (Exod 20:4)	"No immoral, impure or greedy person – such a person is an idolator – has any inheritance in the kingdom of Christ and of God" (Eph 5:5)
"You shall not misuse the name of the Lord" (Exod 20:7)	"Above all, brothers and sisters, do not swear, not by heaven or earth of anything else" (Jas 5:12)
"You shall not murder" (Exod 20:13)	"You have heard it said, 'Do not murder'... but I tell you, whoever is angry with his brother will be subject to judgement" (Mt 5:21-22)
"You shall not commit adultery" (Exod 20:14)	"You have heard it said, 'Do not commit adultery'... but I tell you that anyone who looks at a woman lustfully has already committed adultery in his heart" (Mt 5:27-28)
"You shall not give false testimony" Exod (20:16)	"Do not lie to each other" (Col 3:9)
"Love your neighbour as yourself" Lev (19:18)	"A new command I give you: Love one another. As I have loved you, so you must love one another" (Jn 13:34)

Laws That Are Not Renewed In The New Covenant

There are many laws in the old covenant that are not carried over into the new covenant. This includes not only the large number of ceremonial laws, but also a variety of other moral, ethical and judicial laws. Here are a few examples:

Reciprocal Justice

Under the old covenant, God instituted a system of proportional reciprocal justice:

> "If there is serious injury, you are to take life for life, eye for eye, tooth for tooth, hand for hand, foot for foot, burn for burn, wound for wound, bruise for bruise." (Exod 21:23-25)

> "Anyone who injures a neighbour is to be injured in the same manner: fracture for fracture, eye for eye, tooth for tooth. The one who has inflicted the injury must suffer the same injury." (Lev 24:19-20)

These laws of reciprocal justice have not been renewed in the new covenant. In fact, they have been completely overturned:

> "You have heard it said, "Eye for eye, and tooth for tooth", but I tell you, do not resist an evil person. If anyone slaps you on the right cheek, turn to them the other cheek also." (Matt 5:38-44)

> "Love your enemies, do good to those who hate you, bless those who curse you, pray for those who mistreat you." (Luke 6:27-29)

The reason for this repudiation of the principle of reciprocal justice will be explained in the next chapter, but at this point it is enough simply to understand that it has been made obsolete.

Keeping the Sabbath

> *"Remember the Sabbath day by keeping it holy. Six days you shall labour ... but the seventh day is a Sabbath to the Lord your God. On it you shall not do any work ..." (Exod 20:8-10)*

The commandment to keep the Sabbath is the only one of the famous Ten Commandments that is not repeated in the New Testament. In fact, Jesus angered the religious leaders of his day by breaking the Sabbath command on several occasions. He *"worked"* on the Sabbath. On at least seven occasions he healed people on the Sabbath:

- The demon possessed man (Luke 4:35)
- The woman with bleeding (Luke 13:14)
- The man with the withered hand (Matt 12:13)
- The crippled woman (Luke 13:12)
- The leper (Luke 14:4)
- The paralysed man (John 5:9)
- The blind man (John 9:14).

On another occasion Jesus and his disciples deliberately broke the Sabbath by walking on a long journey and by harvesting and eating grain as they did so (Mark 23-28).

When asked about these violations of the Sabbath law, Jesus replied, *"The Sabbath was made for man, not man for the Sabbath" (Mark 2:27)*. By this he meant that the concept of the Sabbath was meant as a blessing to people, not to be a burden that made life more difficult.

Not only is the Sabbath command not renewed in the new covenant, the New Testament specifically overturns it, stating that no longer is any single day more special than another. Every day is now to be lived in service to and worship of God. Anyone who wishes to maintain Sabbath observance may still do so, but they must not look down on those who choose not to, because it is no longer a mandatory law of the new covenant:

> *"One man considers one day more sacred than another; another man considers every day alike. Each one should be fully convinced in his own mind. He who regards one day as special, does so to the Lord. He who eats meat, eats to the Lord, for he gives thanks to God; and he who abstains, does so to the Lord and gives thanks to God".* (Rom 14:5-6)

> *"Therefore, do not let anyone judge you by what you eat or drink, or with regard to a religious festival, a New Moon celebration or a Sabbath day"* (Col 2:16).

The New Testament teaches that the old commandment of the Sabbath was a foreshadowing of the Sabbath rest that God's people would one day enter into, through the redeeming work of the Messiah. The physical Sabbath was a foreshadowing of the spiritual rest that was to come. The book of Hebrews states that we have now entered that Sabbath rest through Christ:

> *"... the promise of entering his rest still stands, for we have had the gospel preached to us, ... Now we who have believed have entered that rest ... For somewhere he has spoken about the seventh day in these words: "And on the seventh day God rested from all his work." (Heb 4:1-4).*

Tithing

The command to tithe was clearly stated in the Old Testament (Mal 3:10), but it is not renewed in the New Testament. Instead, Christians are exhorted to give *"generously"* (Rom 12:8; 2 Cor 9:6). It is left up to individual Christians to determine what this means for them (2 Cor 9:7). There is no evidence anywhere in the New Testament to suggest that tithing was practised by the early church or that it was a requirement for Christians. The old legalistic requirement of tithing is gone, replaced with the *higher* ideal of giving that is prompted by the Holy Spirit, motivated by compassion and characterised by generosity.

Any attempt by today's preachers, pastors or churches to portray tithing as obligatory upon Christians represents a basic failure to understand the nature of covenants generally, and, in particular, the central truth that *"we are no longer under the law"* (Rom 6:14; Gal 3:25).

Eating Blood

> *"Be sure you do not eat the blood, because the blood is the life, and you must not eat the life with the meat"* (Deut 12:23).

This old covenant command is not repeated in the New Testament, except for a temporary injunction in Acts 15 to keep the peace between Gentile and Jewish Christians. (A full treatise on this issue is given in Chapter 9, *"Progressive Revelation in The New Testament"*). Instead, we are told that all food is now acceptable in the new covenant, and that we should not pass judgment on one another based on what we eat or drink (Rom 14; 1 Cor 8). Jesus taught that the food laws no longer apply in the new covenant:

> *"Are you so dull?" he asked. "Don't you see that nothing that enters a man from the outside can make him 'unclean'? For it doesn't go into his heart but into his stomach, and then out of his body." (Mk 7:18-19)*

This theme was later taken up by Paul as he sought to combat the false teaching of some Jewish Christians who insisted that Gentile Christians should obey the Mosaic food laws:

> *"Since you died with Christ to the basic principles of this world, why, as though you still belonged to it, do you submit to its rules: "Do not handle! Do not taste! Do not touch!"? (Col 2:20-21)*

> *"They forbid people to marry and order them to abstain from certain foods, which God created to be received with thanksgiving by those who believe and who know the truth". (1Ti 4:3)*

Sadly, there are Christians today who are still bound up by the food laws, and many of the other ritual laws of the old covenant. There exist some extreme Christian fundamentalists who view the Old Testament commands as the neglected laws of God that only the faithful few still follow. These fundamentalist groups argue that all but the sacrificial laws are to be obeyed.

For instance, they read in Deuteronomy 22:5, *"A woman must not wear men's clothing"*, and argue that, on that basis, a woman should not wear slacks or shorts, because these are deemed to be men's clothing. But those same people choose to disregard the other instructions in that same passage, in which the Israelites were commanded to build parapets around the roofs of their houses (v.8) and sew tassels onto the hems of their coats (v.12). I am yet to meet a tassel-wearing, parapet-housed Christian fundamentalist! So even those who attempt to obey the old covenant laws fail to do it consistently.

Fundamentalists who insist that Christians should follow the laws of the old covenant have not grasped the concept of the new covenant completely replacing the old. Sadly, this misunderstanding often results in elitist cultic behaviour, as they view themselves as God's faithful remnant. They have also not fully grasped the concept of salvation by grace through faith:

> *"A man is not justified by observing the law, but by faith in Jesus Christ. So we, too, have put our faith in Christ Jesus that we may be justified by faith in Christ and not by observing the law, because by observing the law no one will be justified". (Gal 2:16)*

Curses

In the same way that many of the old covenant laws were not renewed in the new covenant, the accompanying punishments and curses were also not renewed. The topic of rewards and punishments in the Old Testament will be examined in detail in the next chapter, but for the moment it is worth pointing out that Christians should beware of applying old covenant punishments and curses to themselves or others today.

The concept of multi-generational curses that need to be *"broken"* through some form of specifically targeted prayer is an unfortunate, yet common, misapplication of old covenantal theology, based upon verses like Exodus 20:5 and Numbers 14:18:

> *"You shall not bow down to idols or worship them; for I, the LORD your God, am a jealous God, punishing the children for the sin of the fathers to the third and fourth generation of those who hate me." (Exo 20:5)*

> *"The LORD is slow to anger, abounding in love and forgiving sin and rebellion. Yet he does not leave the guilty unpunished; he punishes the children for the sin of the fathers to the third and fourth generation." (Num 14:18)*

Firstly, it is important to note that it is God who does the cursing here, not the devil or demons.

Secondly, towards the end of the old covenant, the promise was given that a new covenant was coming in which no one would be punished for someone else's sin:

> *"In those days people will no longer say, 'The fathers have eaten sour grapes, and the children's teeth are set on edge.' Instead, everyone will die for his own sin; whoever eats sour grapes—his own teeth will be set on edge". (Jer 31:29-30)*

These kinds of curses are not renewed in the new covenant, and should have no part in our thinking. The New Testament specifically states that Christ broke all the curses of the law when he died on the cross in our place:

> *"Christ redeemed us from the curse of the law by becoming a curse for us, for it is written: 'Cursed is everyone who is hung on a tree.'" (Gal 3:13)*

As the next chapter will explain, these old covenant curses were for a pre-regenerate people who needed severe consequences in order to keep them from straying into sin. Any kind of superstitious teaching that proposes that these kinds of curses are applicable to Christians today represents a complete misunderstanding of the fundamental differences between the two covenants, and contradicts the clear teaching of the New Testament.

COMPARISON OF THE TWO COVENANTS	
OLD COVENANT	**NEW COVENANT**
Lower Standards: No Adultery, No Murder, Reciprocal Justice,	**Higher Standards:** No Lust, No Hate, Love Enemies,
Laws Written On Stone Tablets	Laws Written On Heart By Holy Spirit
Need For Continual Animal Sacrifices	Christ's Perfect Sacrifice: Once For All
Immediate Tangible Rewards	Future Spiritual Rewards
Justification = Obedience To The Law	Justification = By Grace Through Faith
Condemned By The Law	Set Free From The Law: No Condemnation
Obedience To The Law: In Order To Be Justified	Obedience To The Law Because We Are Justified
Brings Death	Brings Life
Obsolete	Eternal

THE VALUE OF THE OLD TESTAMENT

What, then, is the value of the Old Testament for Christians? If it contains a covenant that is now obsolete, is there any point in reading it at all? Of course there is! The Old Testament is still God's Word for Christians because it reveals *more* than just the old covenant:

- It reveals the character of God. Even those laws which no longer apply to us today, reveal much about God's character; his holiness, justice and compassion for the lowly.

- It describes the history of God's dealing with mankind, including narratives describing many extraordinary divine interventions in human history. From these, we learn a great deal about the character of God and the undeserving, fickle nature of mankind.

- It illustrates, in literary technicolour, the great redemptive themes of sin, separation, sacrifice and salvation that will be fully developed in the New Testament, and lays the theological foundations for our understanding of the gospel. Even reading the old covenantal laws, blessings and curses, assists us in reaching a deeper understanding of the new covenant.

- It prefigures the redemptive work of Christ and gives us a richer appreciation of his atoning sacrifice.

There is great value in reading the Old Testament, but in doing so, we must avoid the mistake of assuming that its covenantal laws still apply to us.

"We are no longer under the law"

(Rom 6:14; Gal 3:25)

Reflection Questions 6

1. How has this chapter changed your view of the relationship between the old and new covenants?

2. Are there laws or promises from the old covenant that, until now, you have assumed still apply to us today?

3. Are there issues you are still uncertain of, regarding laws and promises from the Old Testament?

4. Read Hebrews 8:8-13. (This passage includes a quote from Jeremiah 31:31-34).

- Verse 9. In what ways is the new covenant "not like" the old covenant?

- Verse10. What major difference does this verse indicate?

- Verse 11. What major difference does this verse indicate?

- Verse 12. What major difference does this verse indicate?

- Verse 13. What does it mean that the old covenant will "soon disappear"?

5. Read Luke 22:20. Why was the shedding of Christ's blood necessary?

6. Read Galatians 2:16. How does this verse relate to both old and new covenants?

CHAPTER 7

INTERPRETING THE OLD TESTAMENT

The Old and New Testaments are equally inspired, but they are not equally applicable. As we saw in the previous chapter, the Old Testament contains the terms and conditions of an ancient covenant between God and the Israelites; a covenant which was made obsolete by the new covenant instituted by Christ. This has significant repercussions for how we read and apply the Old Testament. Christians cannot read the Old Testament as if it is the New Testament. While we affirm that the Old Testament is inspired Scripture, we cannot apply its many laws, blessings and punishments to ourselves as if they are part of God's covenant with us today.

If we are to read and apply the Old Testament appropriately, we must learn to distinguish between timeless truths and obsolete covenantal conditions.

TIMELESS TRUTHS

The Old Testament is full of eternal theological truths which form an important part of our Christian understanding of God, the world and ourselves:

> "The heavens declare the glory of God; the skies proclaim the work of his hands". (Psa 19:1)

> "God said, 'You cannot see my face, for no one may see me and live.'" (Exo 33:20)

> "The LORD is slow to anger, abounding in love and forgiving sin and rebellion." (Num 14:18)

> "In the beginning God created the heavens and the earth". (Gen 1:1)

> "So God created human beings in his own image, in the image of God he created them; male and female he created them". (Gen 1:27)

> "The LORD is my shepherd, I lack nothing". (Psa 23:1)

> "So do not fear, for I am with you; do not be dismayed, for I am your God. I will strengthen you and help you; I will uphold you with my righteous right hand". (Isa 41:10)

Propositional statements such as these are timeless theological truths that describe the character of God and indicate what it means to live in relationship with him. These truths did not cease to exist with the obsolescence of the old covenant. The glory of God is still seen in the stars. God is still slow to anger and abounding in love. He is still a shepherd to his people. These are not laws with associated blessings or curses; they are eternal theological truths.

LAWS, BLESSINGS AND PUNISHMENTS

The parts of the Old Testament that no longer apply to us are the old covenantal laws, blessings and punishments. As was explained in the previous chapter, ancient covenants specified conditions or laws which the covenantal parties had to abide by, as well as clearly defined reimbursements, fines, rewards and punishments which formed part of the legally binding conditions of the covenant. So it is with God's covenant with Israel. It contained the laws which defined Israel's obligations towards God (613 laws to be precise!), as well as specific rewards for compliance to those laws, and punishments for disobedience. Christians cannot apply *any* of these to themselves.

Not all Christians completely understand this. There is a common tendency to take a covenantal promise given to the Israelites in the Old Testament and treat it as if it was part of the new covenant. For instance:

> ***Mal 3:10*** *"Bring the whole tithe into the storehouse, that there may be food in my house. Test me in this," says the LORD Almighty, "and see if I will not throw open the floodgates of heaven and pour out so much blessing that there will not be room enough to store it".*

This is a popular verse among some Christians who believe that God will bring financial blessing to those who tithe. This promise of God's abundant blessing, however, is linked to the old covenant law of tithing, which is not repeated in the new covenant, and is therefore obsolete. In particular, it is linked to one of the *punishment* clauses of the old covenant. God's promise to *"throw open the floodgates of heaven"* is a promise to end the drought that he had sent as a *punishment* for the nation having turned away from him to worship other gods. The whole book of Malachi is a plea from God towards his adulterous people, who were now offering their tithes to pagan gods; *"Return to me, and I will return to you, says the Lord Almighty"*. (Mal 3:7). They were under a covenantal *curse* and Malachi 3:10 is God's promise to lift that curse if they repented.

A more complete examination of the so-called "prosperity doctrine" will be made later, but at this point it essential to understand that we cannot lift either the old covenant laws, or their associated blessings and curses, out of the Old Testament and treat them as if they are part of God's covenant with us today. They are not. They are part of a covenant that was superseded over 2,000 years ago.

Interestingly, Christians are not so eager to claim the old covenant curses for themselves today:

- Put to death everyone who has sex outside of marriage (Deut 22:13-30).

- Stone your son to death if he will not obey you (Deut 21: 21).

- Break your son's arm if he accidently breaks someone else's arm (Lev 24:20).

- Cut off the hand of a woman who touches a man's genitals while trying to break up a fight **(Deut 25:11-12).**

- Knock out your son's tooth if he knocks out someone else's tooth (Exod 21:24).

- If you develop a rash, you must leave your community and live in the wilderness until you get better (Lev 13:46).

Most Christians would agree that these, and many other old covenant punishments and curses, are no longer applicable - otherwise there would be a lot more one-handed, toothless, bush-dwelling Christians! We must learn to be consistent in our interpretation of God's Word. We cannot take the blessings and leave the punishments. They are irrevocably linked. They are *all* integral components of a covenant that is now obsolete.

DIFFERENTIATING BETWEEN OLD COVENANT AND OLD TESTAMENT

It is important to differentiate between the old covenant and the Old Testament, because they are not identical. While the word "testament" is another word for covenant, the Old Testament in the Bible contains *more* than just the old covenant laws and their associated blessings and punishments. It also contains:

- **Historical Narrative:** The description of the creation of the world, the fall of mankind, the flood, the calling of God's people, the lives of the patriarchs, God's numerous redemptive interventions, the fickleness of mankind, the faithfulness of God, etc. This is our history as human beings; the history of our planet! From these historical accounts we learn a great deal about God and ourselves.

- **Poetry:** Songs and psalms of praise and rejoicing, hymns full of theological truths, poems celebrating the joy of love, and heart-wrenching cries expressing sorrow, sadness, grief and loss. These are all still beautiful expressions of faith and hope and love, even, at times in the midst of great heartache, and they can continue to inspire and comfort us as we go through similar experiences.

- **Prophecy:** Promises of a coming Messiah, visions of a new age when God's people would have his Spirit within them, glimpses of things yet to come, and assurances of the sovereignty of God over all the world and over all of history.

These elements of the Old Testament remain an essential and relevant component of our Christian Scriptures, for they form the theological foundation upon which the New Testament is built. Old Testament scholar, Graeme Goldsworthy, comments;

"The Old Testament is not completely superseded by the gospel, for that would make it irrelevant to us. It helps us understand the

gospel by showing us the origins and meanings of the various ideas in the New Testament" (According to Plan, Graeme Goldsworthy, p.107).

In this sense, the Old Testament is an important part of God's inspired Word for Christians. Although the old covenant has been made obsolete, the Old Testament has not. We must, therefore, learn to read the Old Testament discerningly; sifting out the covenantal laws, blessings and punishments that no longer apply to us, while retaining those parts that are foundational and timeless.

THE OLD COVENANT FULFILLED

The reason why the laws and conditions of the old covenant have been made obsolete is not because they have been *cancelled*, but because they have been *fulfilled*. This is an important distinction. Jesus made this very clear:

> *"Do not think that I have come to abolish the Law or the Prophets; I have not come to abolish them but to **fulfil** them. (18) Truly I tell you, until heaven and earth disappear, not the smallest letter, not the least stroke of a pen, will by any means disappear from the Law until everything is accomplished". (Matt 5:17-18)*

According to Jesus, the old covenant has not been cancelled, it has been fulfilled. The reason the old covenant was made obsolete and a new covenant instituted was not because God somehow changed his mind or decided that the old covenant was not working. The old covenant was set in place *until it was completely fulfilled*. This was always God's intention. The old covenant was meant to lead mankind to Christ, who is the only one who could perfectly fulfil all its requirements:

> *"So the law was put in place to lead us to Christ that we might be justified by faith". (Gal 3:24)*

> *"Christ is the end of the law so that there may be righteousness for everyone who believes". (Rom 10:4)*

The purpose of the old covenant was not to help us achieve righteousness by obedience to the Law, but to show us that we are incapable of meeting its requirements, and unable to achieve righteousness before God. It was designed to reveal our need of a Saviour:

> *"Clearly no one is justified before God by the law, because the righteous will live by faith." (Gal 3:11)*

> *"For what the law was powerless to do in that it was weakened by the sinful nature, God did by sending his own Son in the likeness of sinful man to be a sin offering. And so he condemned sin in sinful man" (Rom 8:3)*

HOW DID JESUS FULFIL THE OLD COVENANT?

Moral Laws

Jesus lived the perfect life. He was *"without sin" (Heb 4:15)*. He completely met every moral condition of the old covenant. He lived the obedient life that we were incapable of. The moral conditions of the old covenant were finally fulfilled in his sinless life.

Ritual Laws

The old covenant contained a multitude of laws pertaining to food, hygiene and procedural correctness. These were intended to teach God's people the necessity to be separate from the world, and to impress upon them the need to be pure. Jesus' sinless life and pure dedication to the Father fulfilled the spirit of these laws as well.

Sacrificial Laws

At the heart of the old covenant was the principal that blood needed to be shed in order to secure forgiveness for sins:

> "The law requires that everything be cleansed with blood, and without the shedding of blood there is no forgiveness." (Heb 9:22)

The old covenant required that sacrifices be constantly made for sin. This served to illustrate both the universality and seriousness of sin. The animals that were sacrificed, however, did not actually provide atonement for sins; they were merely a constant reminder of the need for such an atonement. It would require a perfect sacrifice to truly atone for sin; the death of God's Son:

> "The blood of goats and bulls and the ashes of a heifer sprinkled on those who are ceremonially unclean sanctify them so that they are **outwardl**y clean. (14) How much more, then, will the blood of Christ, who through the eternal Spirit offered himself unblemished to God." (Heb 9:13-14)

Christ's sinless life was essential for him to be an acceptable and final sacrifice for the sins of the world:

> "Such a high priest truly meets our need—one who is holy, blameless, pure, set apart from sinners, exalted above the heavens. (27) Unlike the other high priests, he does not need to offer sacrifices day after day, first for his own sins, and then for the sins of the people. He sacrificed for their sins once for all when he offered himself." (Heb 7:26-27)

Because of this, only one single sacrifice was needed to fulfil all the sacrificial laws and satisfy God's justice for all time:

> "For Christ died for sins, once for all, the righteous for the unrighteous, to bring you to God." (1 Pet 3:18)

Now that he has done this, the old covenant has been completely fulfilled, setting us free from its requirements;

> *"For this reason Christ is the mediator of a new covenant, that those who are called may receive the promised eternal inheritance—now that he has died as a ransom to set them free from the sins committed under the first covenant." (Heb 9: 15)*

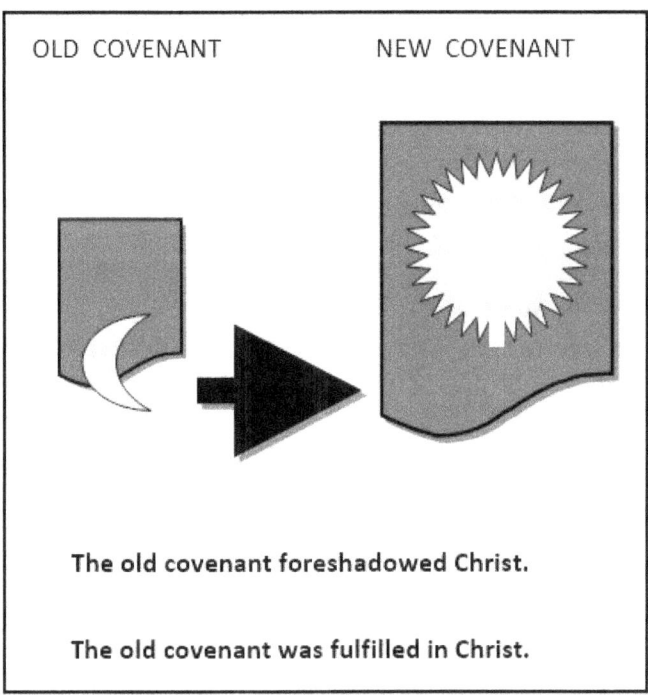

A *NEW* COVENANT, NOT A MODIFIED ONE

In Matthew 5:17-18, after stating that he had not come to *abolish* the law but to *fulfil* it, Jesus then made an emphatic statement:

> *"Truly I tell you, until heaven and earth disappear, not the smallest letter, not the least stroke of a pen, will by any means disappear from the Law until everything is accomplished"* (Matt 5:18)

In what sense are we to understand this? Clearly Jesus does not mean that we are to continue to sacrifice animals or observe the other laws of the old covenant, for we *"are no longer under the law" (Gal 5:18)* because *"Christ Jesus has set us free from the law" (Rom 8:2)*. Jesus had previously stated that he had come to establish a *"new covenant" (Luke 22:20)*.

In fact, this is precisely the point. Jesus is stressing that he is not changing the laws of Moses to suit his purposes (which appears to have been a criticism levelled at him by the Pharisees). He is not "fiddling" with the old covenant; he is introducing a *totally new covenant* which fulfils the purpose of the old. This is not just a fine-tuning of the old covenant; changing a few words or letters here and there. In fact, Jesus declares that the old covenant had been perfect for its intended purpose. It didn't need a re-write; *"not the smallest letter, not the least stroke of a pen"*. But it has now been *"fulfilled"*, and the new covenant has arrived. The writer to the Hebrews captures this meaning beautifully:

> *"By calling this covenant "new," he has made the first one <u>obsolete</u>; and what is obsolete and aging will <u>soon disappear</u>." (Heb 8:13)*

This is a crucial concept for us to understand if we are to read the Old Testament *Christianly*.

THE HIGHER LAWS OF THE NEW COVENANT

Being set free from the law does not mean, however, that we are free from moral and ethical restraint. In fact, in many ways, the laws of the new covenant are more demanding than the laws of the old covenant. According to the New Testament, God's standards for his people have been raised to even higher levels in the new covenant. For example:

THE HIGHER LAWS OF THE NEW COVENANT

OLD COVENANT	NEW COVENANT
Justice	Grace and Mercy
Reciprocal retaliation	Forgiveness and Love
Treat multiple wives fairly	Love one wife for life, as Christ loved the church

In a significant discourse, recorded in Matthew's Gospel, Jesus spoke of raising the Old Testament laws to a new level:

> "You have heard that it was said, 'Eye for eye, and tooth for tooth.' (39) But I tell you, do not resist an evil person. If anyone slaps you on the right cheek, turn to them the other cheek also. (40) And if anyone wants to sue you and take your shirt, hand over your coat as well. (41) If anyone forces you to go one mile, go with them two miles. (42) Give to the one who asks you, and do not turn away from the one who wants to borrow from you. (43) "You have heard that it was said, 'Love your neighbour and hate your enemy.' (44) But I tell you, love your enemies and pray for those who persecute you, (45) that you may be children of your Father in heaven. He causes his sun to rise on the evil and the good, and sends rain on the righteous and the unrighteous. (46) If you love those who love you, what reward will you get? Are not even the tax collectors doing that? (47) And if you greet only your own people, what are you doing more than others? Do not even pagans do that? (48) Be perfect, therefore, as your heavenly Father is perfect". (Matt 5:38-48)

In this passage, Jesus explains that the old covenant laws were the stepping stones to the higher new covenant laws; they were the intermediate precursors to a new way of life that is more in tune with the heart of God and closer to his perfect standards. The old covenant laws have not been cancelled; they have been raised to a higher level. Jesus summed up the essence of these higher laws in a single, pithy statement:

> "A new command I give you: Love one another. As I have loved you, so you must love one another". (John 13:34)

That we are called to love one another is not new. The Old Testament had already made this clear; *"love your neighbour as yourself"* (Lev 19:18). In fact, Christ quoted this command in Matthew 22:39 as a good summary of the old covenant laws of social responsibility. What is **new** about Jesus' command is that, under the new covenant, we are to love **as Christ loved us**. How did Christ love us? He loved us unconditionally and sacrificially, ultimately dying for us, and even showing love and forgiveness towards those who were crucifying him. This is the highest love of all; agape love, God's love. This is more than merely loving your neighbour **as** yourself; it is loving your neighbour **more** than yourself. This represents a significant lifting of the bar, from the old covenant to the new.

Of course, this begs the question: *"Why didn't God introduce these higher laws from the beginning?"*

That is the topic of the next chapter.

Reflection Questions 7

1. What have you learnt or been challenged by in this chapter?

2. What has been your view of Malachi 3:10 up to this point?

3. Can you think of any other Old Testament promises that Christians often claim?

4. Read Matthew 5:17-18. Firstly, how did Jesus "fulfil" the requirements of the old covenant? Secondly, what does verse 18 mean?

5. Read Hebrews 9:11-27. What major differences between the two covenants do these verses indicate?

6. Read Hebrews 7:26-27. What major difference between the covenants do these verses indicate?

CHAPTER 8

THE OLD TESTAMENT AS PRE-CHRISTIAN

Why did there need to be two covenants? Why couldn't God simply introduce the higher, new covenant laws and principles from the very beginning? The answer revolves around the two most important concepts for our understanding of the Bible and its application to our lives:

- The Old Testament as Pre-Christian
- The Concept Of Progressive Revelation

The pre-Christian nature of the Old Testament will be dealt with in this chapter; the concept of progressive revelation will be explored in the next.

THE OLD TESTAMENT AS PRE-CHRISTIAN

The Old Testament was not addressed to Christians. Let me say that again: The Old Testament was not addressed to Christians! It was addressed to **pre-Christians**. This is the consensus view of respected evangelical Bible scholars:

> *"The Old Testament is pre-Christian. The people of Israel were not Christians and cannot be said to live Christian lives." (Graeme Goldsworthy, "According to Plan", p.26).*

> *"The basic problem with the Old Testament is that, in all its texts, it occupies a perspective that is not, and cannot be, our own. It stands on the other side of Christ" (John Bright, "The Authority of The Old Testament, p.183)*

> *"The Old Testament is not, of and by itself, a Christian message" (John Bright, "The Authority of The Old Testament", p.183),*

This is one of the most important concepts for Christians to grasp if we are to properly understand and interpret the Old Testament. The people of Israel were *unregenerate*. They were not born again. They did not have the indwelling Holy Spirit to illuminate, guide and empower them. Nor did they have anything but the most basic understanding of God and how to relate to him.

In terms of their beliefs and their behaviour, the Israelites were far from Christian. When God called Abraham, he and his family were most likely idol-worshipping polytheists, who demonstrated a mixture of pagan superstitions and questionable morals. The Old Testament is the unfolding story of God patiently and graciously attempting to lead these people out of the darkness of paganism, superstition, idolatry and immorality, into the light of his Truth.

I say "attempting to", because the Old Testament is not really a success story. It is a story of little progress with many set-backs. By the end of the

Old Testament era, the nation of Israel was still rife with pagan beliefs and practices, prompting God's decisive act of punishment by allowing the surrounding nations to overwhelm them and take them into captivity. In fact, the Old Testament ends with a whimper rather than a bang, with 10 of the 12 tribes disappearing into oblivion, never to be heard from again, while only a straggling remnant of the other 2 tribes return to Canaan to attempt to rebuild Jerusalem and the temple.

The diagram, entitled *"Outline Of Biblical History"*, at the end of this chapter, provides a concise overview of the flow of Old Testament history. Such an overview is helpful for understanding how each individual event in the Old Testament fits into the big picture of the gradually developing Kingdom of God on earth.

The pre-Christian Israelites were powerless to obey God; they were slaves to sin, ignorant of spiritual truth, and their hearts were unresponsive because they did not have the indwelling Holy Spirit. This is what prompted Ezekiel's famous prophecy:

> *"I will give you a new heart and put a new spirit in you; I will remove from you your heart of stone and give you a heart of flesh. And I will put my Spirit in you and move you to follow my decrees and be careful to keep my laws"* **(Ezek 36:26-27)**

This prophecy looked ahead to the New Testament era when Christians would be set free from the power of sin through the death and resurrection of Jesus and by the regenerative work of the indwelling Holy Spirit (Rom 6:1-7).

This concept of the Israelites being **pre-Christian** is crucial for interpreting the Old Testament, because God's way of dealing with them was very different from the way he deals with Christians today. In many ways the Israelites were like little children in terms of their understanding and behaviour, and this is precisely how God dealt with them. In fact, this is why they were so often referred to as the "children of Israel", because they were mere infants spiritually, and had to be treated as such. We see this most clearly in the Old Testament system of discipline and rewards. Because they were spiritual infants, God had to motivate and discipline the Israelites using methods similar to the way we deal with little children: the carrot and the stick (although, hopefully, not a literal stick!).

THE CARROT AND THE STICK

When my own children were little, it was a challenge to get them to eat their vegetables. I would sometimes promise them a jellybean, or something similar, if they ate all their peas (an appalling dietary contradiction, I now realise!). If, on the other hand, a spoonful of the dreaded peas was thrown onto the floor, a light smack on the hand was soon to follow (please don't report me for child abuse!). These rewards and punishments were immediate and tangible, and were appropriate strategies for pre-school aged children. They would have been laughably ineffective and inappropriate, however, for older teenage children. As my children matured, different means of motivation and discipline were employed. Rewards didn't have to be immediate and tangible. The promise of a future trip to a favourite place or activity proved highly effective in motivating them in all sorts of situations.

The same is true of the way God dealt with the ancient Israelites, compared with the way he deals with Christians today.

THE CARROT

Just like little children, the Israelites needed rewards that were immediate and tangible. Promises of future blessings in eternity were not really on the agenda because, as we shall see later, the concept of eternal life was not fully developed until the New Testament. God's primary means of motivating the Israelites to obedience and faithfulness was the ancient equivalent of jellybeans; milk, honey, grapes, figs and crops in abundance. Consider the following examples of God's promises to the Israelites:

> **Lev 20:24** *"I will give you this land as an inheritance; a land flowing with milk and honey"*
>
> **Deut 28:2-6** *"If you obey the Lord your God you will be blessed in the city and blessed in the country. The fruit of your womb will be blessed, and the crops of your land and the young of your livestock – the calves of your herds and the lambs of your flocks. Your basket and your kneading trough will be blessed. You will be blessed when you come in and blessed when you go out."*
>
> **Deuteronomy 28:11** *"The LORD will grant you abundant prosperity—in the fruit of your womb, the young of your livestock and the crops of your ground—in the land he swore to your forefathers to give you."*
>
> **Deuteronomy 30:9** *"Then the LORD your God will make you most prosperous in all the work of your hands and in the fruit of your womb, the young of your livestock and the crops of your land. The LORD will again delight in you and make you prosperous, just as he delighted in your fathers."*

Israel's rewards for obedience were immediate and tangible; an abundance of crops, livestock and offspring. Occasionally this prosperity also included silver and gold, as God allowed them to take possession of the plunder from nations and cities that they had overcome:

> **Exo 12:35-36** *"The Israelites did as Moses instructed and asked the Egyptians for articles of silver and gold and for clothing. (36) The LORD had made the Egyptians favourably disposed toward the people, and they gave them what they asked for; so they plundered the Egyptians."*

> **Jos 22:8** *"Return to your homes with your great wealth—with large herds of livestock, with silver, gold, bronze and iron, and a great quantity of clothing—and divide with your brothers the plunder from your enemies."*

These material rewards were the carrots, or jellybeans, that God used to motivate a spiritually infantile people under the old covenant. At the same time, however, the Old Testament also contained many warnings against the seductiveness and danger of wealth:

> **Deut 8:13-14** *"For when your herds and flocks grow large and your silver and gold increase and all you have is multiplied, (14) then your heart will become proud and you will forget the LORD your God, who brought you out of Egypt, out of the land of slavery."*

> **Deut 17:17** *"He must not take many wives, or his heart will be led astray. He must not accumulate large amounts of silver and gold."*

> **Job 31:25-28** *"If I have rejoiced over my great wealth, the fortune my hands have gained ... so that my heart was secretly enticed ... then these also would be sins to be judged, for I would have been unfaithful to God on high."*

> **Ezek 28:5** *"By your great skill in trading you have increased your wealth, and because of your wealth your heart has grown proud."*

These promises of material blessings in the Old Testament belong to a covenant which is now obsolete. They were a temporary means of motivating a spiritually immature people, until the new covenant was put in place by Christ. At the end of the Old Testament era, Habakkuk looked ahead to a time when God's people would worship and obey God out of love rather than from a desire for physical reward:

> **Habakkuk 3:17-18** *"Though the fig tree does not blossom, and there are no grapes on the vines, though the olive crop fails, and the fields produce no food, though there are no sheep in the pen and no cattle in the stalls, yet I will rejoice in the Lord, I will be joyful in God my Saviour"*

This is the mark of the mature Christian. Now that we have the indwelling Holy Spirit to give us hearts of obedience, God no longer needs to bribe us like little children. Instead, Jesus spoke of a higher reward that those under the new covenant could look forward to:

> **Matt 6:19-20** *"Do not store up for yourselves treasures on earth, where moth and rust destroy, and where thieves break in and steal. Instead, store up for yourselves treasures in heaven ..."*

The physical promised land in the old covenant was a foreshadowing of the heavenly promised land in the new covenant. The material blessings promised to the pre-Christian Israelites have now been superseded by the infinitely greater spiritual blessings now promised to all who are in Christ:

> **Heb 8:6** *"But the ministry Jesus has received is as superior to theirs as the covenant of which he is mediator is superior to the old one, and it is founded on <u>better promises</u>."*

Charles Spurgeon, the great revival preacher of the 19th century, once said;

> *"The old covenant was a covenant of prosperity. The new covenant is a covenant of adversity whereby we are being weaned from this present world and made fit for the world to come."*

Christians who "hanker" after the physical rewards of the old covenant reveal that they are mere infants; ensnared by the same worldliness as the idolatrous Israelites. If this worldliness and greed is left unchecked, it has the potential to corrupt the heart and derail one's salvation:

> **Mat 6:24** *"No one can serve two masters. Either he will hate the one and love the other, or he will be devoted to the one and despise the other. You cannot serve both God and Money.*
>
> **1 Tim 6:9-10** *"People who want to get rich fall into temptation and a trap and into many foolish and harmful desires that plunge them into ruin and destruction. For the love of money is a root of all kinds of evil. Some people, eager for money, have wandered away from the faith."*

The New Testament is very clear that we who are under the new covenant should not expect wealth and prosperity. Instead we are warned against it:

> **Matt 6:19** *"Do not store up for yourselves treasures on earth …"*
>
> **Matt 19:21** *"If you want to be perfect, sell your possessions and give to the poor, and you will have treasure in heaven"*
>
> **Luke 6:24** *"Woe to you who are rich, for you have already received your comfort"*

Mark 10:25 *"It is easier for a camel to go through the eye of a needle than for a rich man to enter the kingdom of heaven"*

You may sometimes hear a preacher refer to the "fact" that there was a gate in Jerusalem known as the "Needle's Eye", through which camels could squeeze only by having their loads unpacked. The point of this "interpretation" is that camels **can** go through the eye of the needle, but only with great difficulty. The trouble with this exegesis is that it is simply not true. There never was a gate like this in Jerusalem. In fact, the idea originated in the speculations of an 11th century Greek commentator, named Theophylact, who struggled with the apparent harshness of this text. It was speculation only, with no historical evidence, but the idea has taken root with some commentators and preachers who have not bothered to check the historical facts. No Jerusalem gate called *"The Eye of The Needle"* has ever been discovered by archaeology, nor was one ever mentioned in ancient literature. This is the Christian equivalent of an urban myth.

Instead of material wealth, the people of the new covenant are promised a much greater reward for obedience and service to God: treasure in heaven. Precisely what form this treasure will take, we are not told, but clearly it is of much greater worth than any worldly treasure:

> **Matt 6:20** *"Store up for yourselves treasures in heaven, where moth and rust do not destroy, and where thieves do not break in and steal"*

> **1 Cor 2:9** *"No eye has seen, no ear has heard, no mind has conceived what God has prepared for those who love him"*

These undefined and intangible rewards would not have motivated the immature Israelites. We who are in Christ, however, are considered by God to be mature enough to *"not set our hearts on wealth" (1 Tim 6:17)*, but to *"seek first his kingdom and his righteousness" (Matt 6:33)*. Such esoteric ideals were beyond the ability of the pre-Christian Israelites to grasp, however, so God dealt with them as little children.

THE STICK

Unfortunately, positive motivation was rarely enough to keep the Israelites on the straight and narrow. They were easily seduced by idolatry and immorality. As a nation they demonstrated a remarkable ability to perform spiritual back flips; completely turning away from God in a very short space of time.

Just how quickly the Israelites could forsake God and revert to their old ways is illustrated in the events at Mount Sinai, in Exodus 32. Not long after being delivered from Egypt and witnessing a series of extraordinary miracles, the Israelites made camp at Mount Sinai and Moses ascended the mountain to receive instructions from God. While he was away, however, the people made an idol and began worshipping it, engaging in debauchery and pagan sexual rituals. Amazingly, this occurred while the visible presence of the true God was right in front of their eyes, in the form of a pillar of cloud by day and a pillar of fire by night! Yet even this was not enough to stop them from worshipping idols.

This chameleon-like ability to revert to paganism and idolatry remained a constant problem throughout Israel's history. From the call of Abraham, through the time of the patriarchs, the judges, the kings and, finally, the prophets, Israel remained spiritually bi-polar; renouncing their idolatry and immorality, promising to follow God wholeheartedly, only to quickly fall away again, needing to be brought back to repentance once more.

This constant cycle demonstrates how fragile their allegiance to God was and indicates the superficiality of their transformation into his people. Their allegiance to God was only ever a thin veneer, and it didn't take much to scratch through it to uncover their previous pagan ways.

We have already quoted Ezekiel's famous prophecy, but it is worth mentioning again because it demonstrates God's acknowledgment that the only permanent cure to Israel's habitual spiritual adultery was a heart transplant:

> *"I will give you a new heart and put a new spirit in you; I will remove from you your heart of stone and give you a heart of flesh. And I will put my Spirit in you and move you to follow my decrees and be careful to keep my laws"* (Ezek 36:26-27)

This prophecy looked ahead to the saving work of the Messiah and the regenerating power of the Holy Spirit whom he would subsequently send. During the time of the Old Testament, however, this solution was still a long way off.

In the meantime, God needed to ensure that the Israelites did not abandon him completely and permanently. There needed to be a remnant of faithful Jews left for the Messiah to save! The Old Testament disciplinary system was the answer. God set in place very clear, and very tough, consequences for those who broke his laws. These consequences had a threefold purpose:

1. To discourage people from sinning

2. To bring about repentance in those who did sin

3. To stop sin from spreading further

The table on the next page lists some of the extreme consequences that God set in place.

SIN	PUNISHMENT	REF
Murder	Death	Exod 21:12
Assault your parents	Death	Exod 21:15
Kidnap	Death	Exod 21:16
Curse mother or father	Death	Exod 21:17
Sorcery and witchcraft	Death	Exod 22:18
Idolatry	Death	Exod 22:20
Adultery & incest	Death	Lev 20:11-12
Homosexuality	Death	Lev 20:13
Marry your mother-in-law	Death	Lev 20:14
Blasphemy	Death	Lev 24:16
Inflict injury	Same injury	Lev 24:20
Pre-marital sex	Death	Deut 22:24

THE REASONS FOR GOD'S HARSH PUNISHMENTS

Some of God's old covenant punishments seem very harsh to us today. To help us understand why God acted so harshly, it is important to realise two important concepts; a cultural one and a theological one.

Cultural Reasons

The ancient world was a violent, brutal world. Life was cheap, and punishments were harsh, not just those of the Hebrew God. The justice systems of the surrounding nations exhibited extreme harshness and brutality in their punishments. In fact, the greater the King, the harsher his punishments, in order to show his strength and power. People were used to harsh penalties, and if God had dealt more softly with sin, he would have been perceived as a weak God and his laws would have been regarded as not worthy of obedience.

Theological Reasons

Theologically, there was an even more important reason for the harsh punishments. The consequence of not punishing sin would have been much worse than his punishments. If sin was allowed to go unchecked and unpunished, it would have spread like a cancer throughout the nation and all would eventually have been lost. The eternal salvation of the entire nation of Israel hung in the balance. If they rejected God and never repented, they would be lost forever. Compared to that, the death of a small number was inconsequential. In fact, the death sentence was God's way of cutting out a cancer before it could spread any further. It was the act of a loving God who was protecting his people from a fate worse than death itself. It was the act of a spiritual surgeon who was cutting out the diseased portion in order to save the whole.

Critics who decry the harshness of God's Old Testament punishments, particularly the death penalty, are failing to appreciate God's eternal perspective. Our brief mortal lives are the merest, fleeting shadow compared to the infinitude of eternity that awaits us. In the case of those whom God punished with death, he was merely bringing forward their eternal punishment by a few years or decades; cutting short their lives and taking them straight to judgment. In doing so, God, in his infinite, all-seeing wisdom, may well have determined that these people would never have repented and, furthermore, may have led many others astray if they had been left alive. In many ways, we sophisticated 21st century citizens place too much value upon this brief mortal existence, and not nearly enough value upon the eternal existence that lies on the other side of death.

GENERAL PUNISHMENTS

As well as punishments for specific sins, there was also a general set of punishments for the nation as a whole, if they wandered away from God. These punishments were, essentially, the opposite of God's promises of prosperity as a reward for obedience. Deuteronomy 28 is the clearest description of God's general, national rewards and punishments, and it is worth reading in full, in order to gain a clear understanding of God's "carrot and stick" methodology with the Israelites. A significant section (63 verses) is quoted below:

Deuteronomy 28 (TNIV)

"1 If you fully obey the LORD your God and carefully follow all his commands I give you today, the LORD your God will set you high above all the nations on earth. 2 All these blessings will come on you and accompany you if you obey the LORD your God:

3 You will be blessed in the city and blessed in the country.

4 The fruit of your womb will be blessed, and the crops of your land and the young of your livestock—the calves of your herds and the lambs of your flocks.

5 Your basket and your kneading trough will be blessed.

6 You will be blessed when you come in and blessed when you go out.

7 The LORD will grant that the enemies who rise up against you will be defeated before you. They will come at you from one direction but flee from you in seven.

8 The LORD will send a blessing on your barns and on everything you put your hand to. The LORD your God will bless you in the land he is giving you.

9 The LORD will establish you as his holy people, as he promised you on oath, if you keep the commands of the LORD your God and walk in obedience to him. 10 Then all the peoples on earth will see that you are called by the name of the LORD, and they will fear you. 11 The LORD will grant you abundant prosperity—in the fruit of your womb, the young of your livestock and the crops of your ground—in the land he swore to your ancestors to give you.

12 The LORD will open the heavens, the storehouse of his bounty, to send rain on your land in season and to bless all the work of your hands. You will lend to many nations but will borrow from none. 13 The LORD will make you the head, not the tail. If you pay attention to the commands of the LORD your God that I give you this day and carefully follow them, you will always be at the top, never at the bottom. 14 Do not turn aside from any of the commands I give you today, to the right or to the left, following other gods and serving them.

Curses for Disobedience

15 However, if you do not obey the LORD your God and do not carefully follow all his commands and decrees I am giving you today, all these curses will come on you and overtake you:

16 You will be cursed in the city and cursed in the country.

17 Your basket and your kneading trough will be cursed.

18 The fruit of your womb will be cursed, and the crops of your land, and the calves of your herds and the lambs of your flocks.

19 You will be cursed when you come in and cursed when you go out.

20 The LORD will send on you curses, confusion and rebuke in everything you put your hand to, until you are destroyed and come to sudden ruin because of the evil you have done in forsaking him. 21 The LORD will plague you with diseases until he has destroyed you from the land you are entering to possess. 22 The LORD will strike you with wasting disease, with fever and inflammation, with scorching heat and drought, with blight and mildew, which will plague you until you perish. 23 The sky over your head will be bronze, the ground beneath you iron. 24 The LORD will turn the rain of your country into dust and powder; it will come down from the skies until you are destroyed.

25 The LORD will cause you to be defeated before your enemies. You will come at them from one direction but flee from them in seven, and you will become a thing of horror to all the kingdoms on earth. 26 Your carcasses will be food for all the birds and the wild animals, and there will be no one to frighten them away. 27 The LORD will afflict you with the boils of Egypt and with tumours, festering sores and the itch, from which you cannot be cured. 28 The LORD will afflict you with madness, blindness and confusion of mind. 29 At midday you will grope about like a blind person in the dark. You will be unsuccessful in everything you do; day after day you will be oppressed and robbed, with no one to rescue you.

30 You will be pledged to be married to a woman, but another will take her and ravish her. You will build a house, but you will not live in it. You will plant a vineyard, but you will not even begin to enjoy its fruit. 31 Your ox will be slaughtered before your eyes, but you will eat none of it. Your donkey will be forcibly taken from you and will not be returned. Your sheep will be given to your enemies, and no one will rescue them. 32 Your sons and daughters will be given to another nation, and you will wear out your eyes watching for them day after day, powerless to lift a hand. 33 A people that you do not know will eat what your land and labour produce, and you will have nothing but cruel oppression all your days. 34 The sights you see will drive you mad. 35 The LORD will afflict your knees and legs with painful boils that cannot be cured, spreading from the soles of your feet to the top of your head ......

.... 53 Because of the suffering that your enemy will inflict on you during the siege, you will eat the fruit of the womb, the flesh of the sons and daughters the LORD your God has given you. 54 Even the most gentle and sensitive man among you will have no compassion on his own brother or

the wife he loves or his surviving children, 55 and he will not give to one of them any of the flesh of his children that he is eating ....

...... 58 If you do not carefully follow all the words of this law, which are written in this book, and do not revere this glorious and awesome name— the LORD your God— 59 the LORD will send fearful plagues on you and your descendants, harsh and prolonged disasters, and severe and lingering illnesses. 60 He will bring on you all the diseases of Egypt that you dreaded, and they will cling to you. 61 The LORD will also bring on you every kind of sickness and disaster not recorded in this Book of the Law, until you are destroyed. 62 You who were as numerous as the stars in the sky will be left but few in number, because you did not obey the LORD your God. 63 Just as it pleased the LORD to make you prosper and increase in number, so it will please him to ruin and destroy you. You will be uprooted from the land you are entering to possess."

Here is God's carrot and stick portrayed in the clearest possible manner! It is expressed in vivid imagery, designed to shock and deter a spiritually infant nation from departing from God's ways. God's threatened punishments involved a five-tiered litany of escalating devastation as the passage unfolds:

Verses 16-17. Loss of inner peace, mental depression, fear, paranoia, lack of success in business and agriculture, poverty, sickness, and defeat in battle.

Verses 18-20. Loss of national prestige and honour, the cessation of God's gracious provision for the nation and a great barrenness in the land.

Verses 21-22. Plagues, no control over natural enemies, a general inability to subdue the earth, the death of children, and the beginnings of great desolation among the people.

Verses 23-26. Increased attacks by enemies, invasions by foreign powers, extreme economic adversity, poor productivity, even in the production of necessities, resulting in famine. Some national sovereignty remains, but invaders have ever-widening influence in all areas of life. There are increases in plagues and disease.

Verses 27-68. Complete loss of personal and national sovereignty, the destruction of the family and the nation, slavery, descent into cannibalism as a result of severe famine, and the assimilation of its surviving citizens into other cultures.

Sadly, even these threats and promises did not stop a large part of the nation from ultimately turning their back on God and consequently fading into oblivion in captivity, thereby fulfilling the dire prophecies of this passage. The fact that the extravagant blessings and terrible curses of the old covenant could not deter the Israelites from ultimately rejecting God reveals how hard-hearted they were and how deeply ingrained their paganism was.

Yet God's "carrot and stick" methodology did not completely fail. In fact, it achieved its purpose. A small remnant of Jews, tiring of their banishment, and seeking once more the blessings of God, eventually returned from captivity. Under the guidance of Nehemiah and Ezra they rebuilt Jerusalem, rededicated their lives to serving God, and settled in the land to await the coming of God's promised Messiah.

This is how the curtain closed on the Old Testament era. A small remnant was all that was left of a once great nation. There were perhaps only several hundred people who came back with Ezra and Nehemiah; a mere drop in the bucket compared to the millions who had once comprised Israel. I said before that the Old Testament ends with a whimper, not a bang; but it is a whimper of hope! A remnant has survived! The stick and the carrot have done their job. A small number have, against all odds, decided that God is worth following after all. The prophecy of Deuteronomy 28:62 came true; *"You who were as numerous as the stars in the sky will be left but few in number"*. There aren't many who remain faithful, but there are still some. The blazing sun of Israel's past glory has set, but there is still a flicker, a candle burning in the dark, a small flame of faith that refuses to be extinguished.

It is to that small flame of faith that the Messiah will come, and fan into flame a fire that will sweep through the world and forever change mankind. It is stirring stuff! And God's stick and carrot, his blessings and curses, are the means by which he preserved that remnant.

GOD'S DISCIPLINE OF CHRISTIANS

The point of this chapter has been to show that God's methods of discipline in the Old Testament were:

- Tailored to the specific spiritual condition of the Israelites, who were unregenerate, spiritual infants, who needed very clear, firm, consequences to keep them in line.

- Designed for a specific purpose: To ensure the eventual existence of a remnant.

Neither of these two conditions relates to Christians, so it is not surprising that God's method of disciplining Christians is considerably different. The presence of the indwelling Holy Spirit means that we now have hearts that are responsive to God; hearts whose desire is to love and obey him. There is no longer any need for a big stick.

Of course, God still disciplines Christians: *"Those whom I love, I rebuke and discipline" (Rev 3:19)*. This discipline may, at times, take the form of sickness (1 Cor 11:32) or hardship (Heb 12:7), although these are more commonly the result of living in a fallen, imperfect world. The only other possible reference to God's discipline in the New Testament is in Acts 5 where Ananias and Sapphira deliberately try to deceive God and are struck dead. This sobering incident reveals that God is still to be feared and respected, but fortunately it appears to be an exceptional case.

Gone is the big stick of the Old Testament. In its place is the affirmation that *"there is now no condemnation for those who are in Christ Jesus, because through Christ Jesus the law of the Spirit who gives you life has set you free" (Rom 8:1).*

CONCLUSION

The blessings and punishments of God in the Old Testament do not directly apply to Christians today. They were given to a people who were pre-Christian, under a covenant that has now been fulfilled. The concept that the Old Testament is pre-Christian is vital for our interpretation of the Bible. It means that the Old Testament can't be applied directly to Christians because it wasn't addressed to us; it was addressed to pre-Christians. While the Old Testament remains a foundational part of the inspired word of God, serving to illustrate many key biblical doctrines, many parts cannot be applied directly to Christians, but need to be interpreted through the lens of the New Testament.

Christians cannot read the Old Testament in isolation, or use it as a manual for faith and practice. We cannot read it as if there is no New Testament, nor can we turn to it for proof texts to support doctrines we want to espouse. We cannot simply lift a verse or passage out of the Old Testament and apply it directly to ourselves, as if there is no difference between us and the people of Israel; no difference between the new covenant and the old. As we have seen already, the differences between the two covenants are significant, as are the differences in the way God deals with the recipients of those covenants.

The New Testament is the lens through which we must read and interpret the Old Testament. Rather than arbitrarily trying to interpret the Old Testament for ourselves, the New Testament is our definitive guide as to which commands or promises still apply, which have been modified, and which have not been carried over into the new era. The process of how to interpret the Old Testament through the lens of the New Testament will be fully discussed in a subsequent chapter, but, for the moment, it is enough that we understand the need for such an interpretive lens. A book that was written for, and about, pre-Christians, needs to be reinterpreted for Christians before any life-applications can be made.

At the beginning of this chapter, I mentioned that there were two important concepts for understanding the Old Testament. We have examined the first of those concepts; that the Old Testament is pre-Christian. The second of these concepts is the concept of progressive revelation. That is the subject of the next chapter.

THE OLD TESTAMENT AS PRE-CHRISTIAN

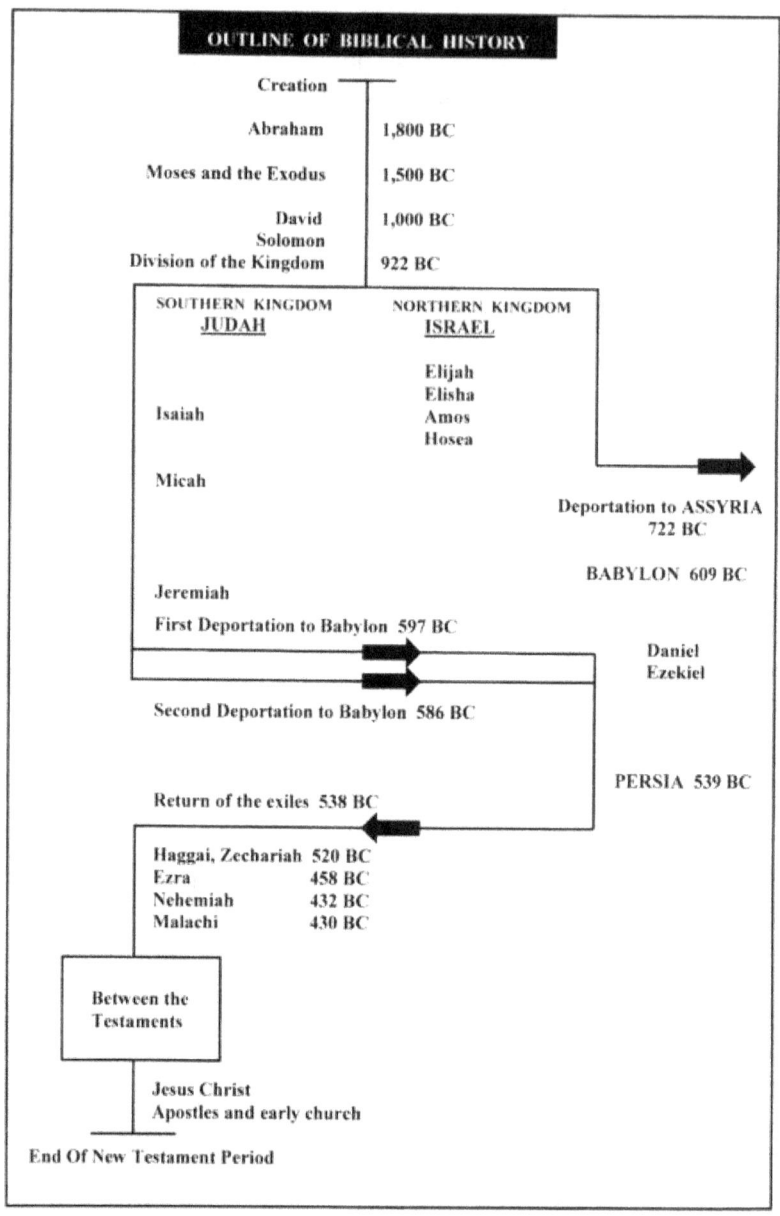

Reflection Questions 8

1. What have you learnt or been challenged by in this chapter?

2. Is there anything in this chapter that you are unsure of or struggling with?

3. How do you regard the harsh punishments of the old covenant?

4. Are there any old covenant promises that you have previously applied to yourself?

5. Read Ezekiel 36:26-27. What fundamental difference sets apart those living under the new covenant, compared to those living under the old? What practical impact do you think this has upon the way we live?

6. Read Matthew 6:19-20. What does this exhortation mean in practice; what application does this verse have for us? In what ways is it possible to do the opposite of this?

7. Read Habakkuk 3:16-19. The prophet is living during a time of national and personal hardship. How is his attitude an example to us? What applications can we draw from this?

CHAPTER 9

PROGRESSIVE REVELATION

IN THE BIBLE

In the previous chapter it was noted that there are two important concepts for understanding and interpreting the Old Testament. The first is that the Old Testament is *pre-Christian*. It was written about, and for, an immature, unregenerate people under a covenant that has now been fulfilled. While the Old Testament remains a foundational part of the inspired Word of God, establishing many key biblical doctrines, its directives cannot be directly applied to Christians, because they were designed for a pre-Christian people who were spiritual infants.

The second important concept for understanding and interpreting the Old Testament, is the concept of the Bible as *progressive revelation*.

THE CONCEPT OF PROGRESSIVE REVELATION

The difficulty of referring to the Old Testament as pre-Christian, is that some people will interpret this to mean anti-Christian, which, of course, is not true. The Old Testament doesn't contradict the New Testament; it is the precursor to the New Testament, and contains within it the seeds of the more complete revelation that Christ and the New Testament writers would eventually reveal. The Old Testament portrays the gradual unfolding of God's revelation to humanity. God did not just dump his whole moral code and doctrinal truth on mankind at the beginning, because they would not have understood it. Respected biblical scholars are unanimous on this point:

> *"Progressive revelation means that God's revelation was not given all at once in the beginning, but was revealed by stages until the full light of truth was revealed in Jesus Christ"* (Graeme Goldsworthy, According to Plan, p. 81)

> *"Since God's redemptive acts were progressive, preparing the way for Christ who should come in the fullness of time (Gal 4:4), the accompanying truths that were progressively revealed show in most cases a progressive development. That is, God graciously unfolded both his redemption and his revelation in ways corresponding to man's capacities to receive them."* (J. Barton Payne, Theology of the Old Testament, p. 18).

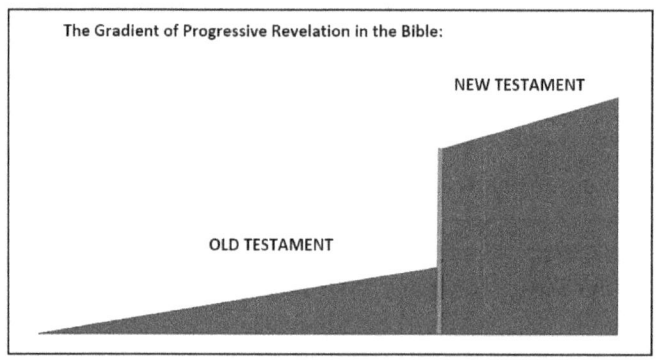

The above diagram provides a rough visual representation of the gradual process of spiritual revelation in the Old Testament, followed by the significant increase in revealed truth introduced by Christ and the New Testament writers.

Compared to the depth of theological insight evident in the New Testament, the Old Testament's teaching is partial and elementary. Evangelical scholar and theologian, Bernard Ramm, states:

> "This perspective of progressive revelation is very important to the interpreter. He will expect the full revelation of God in the New Testament, and will be aware of the **partial and elementary nature of Old Testament revelation**. Progressive revelation states simply that the fullness of revelation is in the New Testament." (Bernard Ramm, Protestant Biblical Interpretation, pp. 103-104)

The need for spiritual truth to be revealed gradually and progressively is most evident in regard to the process of salvation. God did not send the Saviour to mankind immediately after Adam and Eve sinned; it took thousands of years until people were ready for a saviour. In the initial stages, God was dealing with a primitive people who were at an extremely low level spiritually and morally, and who had little concept of God. Polytheism was endemic, as were pagan rituals, occult practices and immorality. There were many beliefs and behaviours that had to be unlearned, as well as many new lessons to be learned, and God needed to implement these changes gradually and incrementally:

> "In the Old Testament we see God taking people from a pagan culture and teaching them how to be the people they were created to be. He did not try to change them in a day, but instead took 2,500 years (from Abraham until Jesus came) to lead them to the point at which some could accept Jesus as the Messiah. God's revelation to us [in terms of inspired Scripture] ended when the last book of the New Testament was written." (http://www.evangelical.us/)

Progressive revelation does not mean that the Old Testament is somehow less true than the New Testament. It was not a progression from untruth to truth – it was a progression from less information to more complete information. We see progressive revelation at work in every area of God's revelation; doctrine, morals, ethics and social justice.

1. DOCTRINE

In terms of Christian doctrines, the Old Testament is not contradictory when compared with the New Testament; it is merely elementary and incomplete. Many of the doctrines that are fully developed in the New Testament are only vaguely hinted at in the Old Testament. This is because the pre-Christian Israelites were not ready to receive God's full revelation; in the same way that a small child is not ready to study calculus or quadratic equations.

> *"God graciously unfolded both his redemption and his revelation in ways corresponding to man's capacities to receive them." (J. Barton Payne, Theology of the Older Testament, p. 18)*

Paul makes reference to the partial and elementary revelation of God in the Old Testament:

> *"Now to the One who is able to strengthen you according to my gospel and the proclamation of Jesus Christ, according to the revelation of the mystery that was kept secret for long ages but is now disclosed ..." (Rom 16:25)*

In some ways, the relationship between the Old and New Testaments is similar to the relationship between a seed and a tree. Every element of the tree is present within the seed, but the final shape and form cannot yet be glimpsed. This is the sense in which Paul refers to Old Testament revelation as a *"mystery"* and a *"secret"*. It is often said that Genesis 1-11 contains the seed of every significant doctrine subsequently developed in the Bible. Many of these *"seeds"* were not obvious to the pre-Christian

Israelites, and can only be glimpsed retrospectively, through the lens of the New Testament.

Let us examine some examples of doctrinal progressive revelation in the Old Testament.

GOD

God's revelation of himself to a polytheistic, idolatrous people began with the simplest of concepts. In the first few chapters of Genesis, we find God revealing himself as **creator** (Gen 1:1), **sustainer** (Gen 2:16), the **law-giver** (Gen 2:17) and the **wrathful judge of sin** (Gen 3; Gen 6-9; Gen 11). The early concept of God as one who must be obeyed, and whose punishments are to be feared, was foundational to the development of a people who would follow him. The Old Testament is replete with detailed commands and consequences, dire warnings and punishments. The wrath of God is mentioned 169 times in the Old Testament and only 36 times in the New Testament. The Old Testament reveals a comparatively well-developed doctrine of God as the law-giving ruler who must be feared and obeyed.

Very early in Old Testament history, the concept of **God's unapproachability** was revealed. This was a very strong concept throughout the Old Testament. Because God was perfect in holiness, a vast gulf separated him from sinful, fallen mankind. He could not be approached directly, nor could a person survive even momentarily in his unfiltered presence. When God gave Moses the 10 Commandments at Mt Sinai, Moses was instructed to tell the people that they were not to approach the mountain or even set foot on its flower slopes or they would be struck down by God (Exod 19:12). Even Moses, himself, was told that he would not survive if he was to look upon God's face directly, because *"no one may see me and live" (Exod 33:20)*. Later in Israel's history, anyone who touched the ark of the covenant (the symbolic dwelling place of God within Israel) was struck down instantly (2 Sam 6:7). The New Testament still affirms that *"God lives in unapproachable* *light" (1 Tim 6:16)*, but also states that we can now *"approach God's throne of grace with confidence" (Heb 4:16)* because of the atoning sacrifice of Christ.

Other concepts of God that were less developed in the Old Testament were:

God is the God of intimate relationship.

In Genesis 3:8, God is described as walking in the Garden of Eden with Adam and Eve. In Isaiah 41:8 God and Abraham are described as "friends". This concept, however, was overshadowed by the overwhelming dogma of God's unapproachability. Friendship and intimacy with God would only widely become a possibility through the work of Christ, *"through whom we have now gained access to God" (Rom 5:2)*. In the Old Testament, such an intimate view of God was only dimly glimpsed.

The God of mercy and forgiveness.

Psalm 103 is a beautiful song celebrating God's merciful, forgiving nature:

> *"Praise the Lord ... who forgives all your sins ...who redeems your life from the pit ...The Lord is compassionate and gracious, slow to anger, abounding in love. He will not always accuse, nor will he harbor his anger forever; he does not treat us as our sins deserve ... for as high as the heavens are above the earth, so great is his love for those who fear him; as far as the east is from the west, so far has he removed our transgressions from us" (Psa 103:1-12).*

This passage, and several others like it in the Old Testament, was a musical prelude to the symphony that would be developed in the New Testament. Yet because such forgiveness was only ultimately possible through the work of Christ on the cross, this concept of God remained only an occasional, prophetic counter-melody in the Old Testament, overshadowed by the stronger melody of God's unapproachable holiness.

Finally, there were aspects of God's nature that were barely hinted at in the Old Testament:

The Trinity

The concept of the Trinity is, primarily, a New Testament doctrine. The Old Testament contains the tiniest of seeds of this doctrine, but these are only discernible retrospectively, through the lens of the Old Testament.

In Genesis 1:2 we are told that *"the Spirit of God was hovering over the waters"*. Although the term *"the Spirit of God"* appears twelve times in the Old Testament, and *"Holy Spirit"* appears twice, it was always understood as simply referring to God's presence in the world. The overwhelming concept of God was that of Deuteronomy 6:4; *"Hear O Israel: The Lord our God, the Lord is one"*. Only in the New Testament is the concept of tripartite monotheism (three persons in one) developed. In the New Testament, the Holy Spirit is identified as a separate divine member of the Godhead: He speaks (Acts 8:29), forbids (Acts 16:6), teaches (John 14:26), testifies (John 15:26), convinces (John 16:8), reveals (John 16:13), has a mind (Rom 8:27), can be grieved (Eph 4:30), can be despised (Heb 10:29), can be lied to (Acts 5:3) and can be resisted (Acts 7:51). Jesus referred to the Holy Spirit as "he" and "him" (John 14:17; 15:26; 16:7), and spoke of him as separate and distinct from himself and the Father *("the Holy Spirit, whom I will send you from the Father", John 15:26)*.

The divinity of the Holy Spirit is evidenced by the fact that lying to the Holy Spirit is lying to God (Acts 5:3-4), blasphemy against the Holy Spirit is forbidden (Matt 12:31), and the Spirit's indwelling makes our bodies temples of God (1 Cor 3:16; 6:19). The Holy Spirit also possesses the divine qualities of omnipresence (present everywhere; Psalm 139 and Heb 9:14), and omniscience (all-knowing; 1 Cor 2:10-11).

Similarly, the New Testament reveals that Jesus Christ is a member of the divine Godhead. John 1 reveals that Christ was simultaneously *with* God and *was* God himself at the beginning of creation (John 1:1), and was the one through whom all creation was made (John 1:3). Furthermore, the New Testament informs us that Christ is *"in very nature God" (Phil 2:6)*, and *"in him all the fullness of the Godhead dwells in bodily form" (Col 1:19)*. After his resurrection, Jesus commended Thomas for finally acknowledging him as *"my Lord and my God" (John 20:28)*.

These and many other New Testament verses proclaim the inescapable truth that there are three who are God, and yet there is still only one God (Mark 12:29). Such a mind-boggling paradox would have been too confusing for the Israelites.

Yet, even so, the Old Testament contains hints of this paradoxical truth; tiny seeds hidden and lying dormant in the garden of God's revelation. The most common Hebrew name for God, *"Elohim"*, used over two thousand times in the Old Testament, was always written in the plural tense. Similarly, in Genesis 1:26 we find God saying to himself, *"Let us make man in our image"*. In Genesis 18:1-22, God appeared to Abraham in the form of three people. In Psalm 110:1, we read *"The Lord says to my Lord, sit at my feet while I make your enemies your footstool"*, a conversation which Jesus would one day identify as having taken place between himself and the Father before the creation of the world (Matt 22:43-45).

To the Old Testament Israelites, these references were simply a poetic device reflecting the majesty and greatness of God. The fact that they had no concept of the Trinity is evident by the vehement opposition of the Jews to the doctrine of the trinity as it developed in the New Testament church.

REDEMPTION

Progressive revelation is also seen in the development of the doctrine of redemption. The New Testament letters of Romans and Galatians explain, in great detail, that the purpose of the Old Testament law was to convict people of their inability to save themselves; to convince them of their need for a saviour and, ultimately, to lead them to Christ (Rom 5:12-21; Gal 3:1-22). The seeds of this doctrine are evident in the sacrificial system commanded by God in the Old Testament. This system established and reinforced a number of crucial truths:

- No one could fully meet the requirements of the Law – sacrifice was continually needed.

- Sin was serious; blood must be shed for the forgiveness of sins (Exod 12:12; Heb 9:22).

- The life being sacrificed had to be pure and spotless; without blame. Only an innocent life could be sacrificed for the sins of the nation (Exod 12:5).

The sacrificial system was a continual reminder to Israel that they needed saving; that their sins needed atonement. This system of sacrifice was, of course, a prophetic preparation for the work of Christ on the cross, which would accomplish what the Old Testament sacrifices could not: complete redemption as a result of a single, perfect sacrifice.

The sacrificial system was not the only prophetic picture of redemption in the Old Testament. The great saving events of the Old Testament were all prophetic pictures of the future work of Christ the Saviour: the saving of Noah from the flood, the calling of Abraham out of a pagan culture, the exodus from Egypt, the saving of Israel from famine through the suffering servant Joseph, the salvation of Israel from her enemies under King David, the return of the remnant from Babylonian captivity. All of these events are interpreted by the New Testament writers as foreshadowing the work of Christ in purchasing our salvation.

These powerful pictures of redemption are only obvious to us from the perspective of the New Testament. To the Israelites, the concept of redemption was, at best, dimly understood. This was partly due to their unregenerate, unenlightened hearts, and partly due to the partial and elementary nature of this doctrine in the Old Testament.

THE MESSIAH

Nowhere is the concept of progressive revelation more apparent than in the development of the doctrine of the coming Messiah. From the perspective of the New Testament it is evident that the life, death and resurrection of Jesus was the fulfilment of many prophecies embedded within the Old Testament. These prophecies can be summarised into various topics:

- His Family Lineage - Genesis 3:15; 21:12; Numbers 24:17; Genesis 49:8-12; Isaiah 11:1; Jeremiah 23:5

- His Place of Birth - Micah 5:2

- That He will be King - Isaiah 9:6-7; Daniel 7:13-14; Zechariah 6:11-13; 9:9

- That He will be a Priest - Psalm 110:4; Zechariah 6:11-13

- That He will be a Prophet - Deuteronomy 18:15-19

- That He will be a Servant - Isaiah 49:6; 53:11

- That He will be Lord - Psalm 110:1

- That He will be The Son of God - Psalm 2:7,12; Proverbs 30:4

- That He will be God - Isaiah 9:6; Jeremiah 23:5-6

- The Name of The Messiah - Zechariah 6:11-13

- The Time of his Appearing - Daniel 9:23-26

- That He will Bring Salvation - Isaiah 49:6; Zechariah 9:9-10

- That He will Atone for Sins - Isaiah 53:5-6,8,10-12

- That He Will Heal the Sick - Isaiah 35:5-6

- That He Will Set the Captives Free - Isaiah 42:7

- That He Will Teach in Parables - Psalm 78:2(a)

- That He Will be a Light to the Gentiles - Isaiah 42:6; 49:6

- That He Will Claim to be The Messiah - Isaiah 49:5-6

- That He will be Rejected - Isaiah 53:1-3

- That He will Suffer - Isaiah 53:1-12

- That He will Die - Isaiah 53:8-9,12

- That He will be Raised from the Dead - Psalm 16:10; Isaiah 53:8-12

- That He will Eventually be Recognised - Zechariah 12:10-14

While these prophecies seem clear to those reading them through the lens of the New Testament, they would not have been clear to the Old Testament Israelites. Most of these prophecies were very obscure, and many were not recognisable as prophecies until after their fulfilment.

Consider the following examples:

> *Deuteronomy 18:15* *"The Lord your God will raise up for you a prophet from among you, from your own people ..."*

These words of Moses were initially fulfilled in the person of Joshua, whom God raised up to replace Moses and lead the people into the Promised Land. The Jews would have viewed this prophecy as fulfilled, and no longer awaiting any further fulfilment. Only from our New Testament perspective can we understand that there was a second, greater fulfilment in the person of Jesus.

> *Numbers 24:17 "A star will come out of Jacob; a sceptre will rise out of Israel"*

This prophecy was fulfilled by Joseph, in the first instance, and, more distantly, by King David. Once again, only from our New Testament perspective can we see that Jesus was the ultimate fulfilment of this prophecy.

> *Genesis 49:8-12 "The sceptre will not depart from Judah, nor the ruler's staff from between his feet, until he to whom it belongs shall come and the obedience of the nations be his ..."*

This prophecy was initially fulfilled by King David, yet the New Testament writers point to Jesus as the ultimate fulfilment of this promise. The Old Testament Israelites, however, would not have had any idea that there was a second, greater fulfilment to come.

> *Genesis 3:15 "I will put enmity between you [the serpent] and the woman, and between your offspring and hers; he will crush your head and you will strike his heel"*

This is the earliest messianic prophecy in the Bible. It is a dual-layered pronouncement; on the one hand describing the natural enmity between mankind and snakes, set in place as part of the curse after the fall, and on the other hand describing the death of Jesus (*"you will strike his heel"*) and his victory over Satan (*"he will crush your head"*). Once again, the immediate fulfilment would have been obvious to the Jews, while the deeper, spiritual fulfilment would have been completely obscure.

Many of the Old Testament's messianic prophecies are of this nature: having an initial fulfilment in the course of Old Testament history and giving no obvious indication that there was a further, deeper fulfilment yet to come.

Towards the end of the Old Testament era, the messianic prophecies did become clearer:

> *Isaiah 11:1-2 "A shoot will come up from the stump of Jesse; from his roots a branch will bear fruit. The spirit of the Lord will rest on him ..."*
>
> *Isaiah 42:1-7 "Here is my servant, whom I uphold, my chosen one in whom I delight. I will put my Spirit on him, and he will bring justice to the nations..."*
>
> *Malachi 4:5,6 "See, I will send you the prophet Elijah before that great and dreadful day of the LORD comes. He will turn the hearts of the fathers to their children, and the hearts of the children to their fathers; or else I will come and strike the land with a curse"*

Yet, even these seemingly obvious prophecies are only clear to us because we have the advantage of hindsight. To the Old Testament Jews, these were puzzling statement that evoked much debate as to their interpretation. Were these passages speaking about yet another prophet that God would raise up? Were they speaking of a final Great Prophet? Were they speaking of a Messiah? Was God going to physically resurrect Elijah, or was God going to implant Elijah's spirit into a new prophet?

So unclear was the interpretation of these and other prophecies, that many Jews at the time of Jesus had no concept of a coming Messiah. Some chose to interpret these prophecies as speaking metaphorically of the nation of Israel as a whole, while others viewed the Isaiah prophecies as having been fulfilled in the coming of the later prophets such as Jeremiah, Haggai, Zechariah, Joel and Amos.

The clearest of all Old Testament messianic prophecies, and the most famous, is Isaiah 53:

> <u>Isaiah 53:7-8</u> *"He was led like a sheep to the slaughter, and as a lamb before its shearer is silent, so he did not open his mouth ..."*

Yet even this seemingly clear prophecy was not transparent in its interpretation without a post-Calvary perspective. In fact, this is the very passage that the Ethiopian eunuch was reading when Phillip met him on the road to Gaza, in Acts 8:26-40. The Ethiopian, who was sincerely trying to understand the passage, had to ask Phillip, *"Tell me, please, who is the prophet talking about, himself or someone else?" (Acts 8:34)*. It took a post-Calvary, New Testament perspective to understand that this passage was even talking about a Messiah. This is why so many Jews failed to recognise Jesus as the Messiah. Some were not even expecting a Messiah, while others were confused by the vagueness of the prophecies and the conflicting possible interpretations.

Such is the nature of progressive revelation. Progressive revelation does not mean that everything had already been fully and clearly revealed in the Old Testament and was simply awaiting fulfilment. Progressive revelation means that the New Testament not only fulfils the Old Testament, but also brings with it a greater, clearer revelation.

> *"God, in fact, reserves his greatest revelation until the point of fulfilment. Jesus does not simply fulfil the promises. Rather, he is the final and fullest revelation of what the promises are really about" (Graeme Goldsworthy, "According to Plan", p.83).*

This is the point that the Apostle Paul makes when he writes,

> *"Now to him who is able to establish you in accordance with my gospel, the message I proclaim about Jesus Christ, in keeping with the revelation of the mystery hidden for long ages past, but now revealed and made known through the prophetic writings by the command of the eternal God ..." (Rom 16:25-26)*

ETERNAL LIFE

The concept of eternal life was far from clear in the Old Testament. In the first part of the Old Testament there is no concept at all of life beyond the grave. In the book of Job, the earliest Old Testament book (in terms of the date it was written), the question is posed, *"If a man dies, shall he live again?" (Job 14:14)*. The only answer given refers to a belief in a place called, Sheol, which appears to be the place of the dead. In early Old Testament literature Sheol seems to refer to a place where the dead go and are no more; *"As the cloud fades and vanishes, so he who goes down to Sheol does not come up" (Job 7:9)*. The souls of the dead in Sheol were believed to be in a state of unconsciousness; *"For in death there is no remembrance of you; in Sheol who will give you praise?" (Psalm 6:5)*.

About the time of the Psalms, however, there arises a glimmer of hope that there might be an alternate destiny to the soul sleep of Sheol:

> *Psalm 49:15* "But God will ransom my soul from the power of Sheol, for he will receive me"

> *Psalm 86:13* "For great is your steadfast love toward me; you have delivered my soul from the depths of Sheol"

> *Proverbs 23:14* "If you strike him with the rod you will save his soul from Sheol"

That Elijah was taken up into heaven in a whirlwind, amidst chariots and horses of fire (2 Kings 2:11), was not apparently considered the destiny of common man, but a special reward for God's holy prophet. Towards the end of the Old Testament period, however, stronger glimmers of belief in eternal life emerged:

> *Isaiah 26:19* "But your dead will live, Lord, their bodies will rise – let those who dwell in the dust wake up and shout for joy."

> *Daniel 12:2 "Multitudes who sleep in the dust of the earth will awake: some to everlasting life, others to shame and everlasting contempt"*

Despite these glimpses, however, belief in eternal life remained speculative within Israel. By the time of Christ, the Jews were divided over this issue; the Sadducees did not believe in life after death, whereas the Pharisees did. This ongoing debate between the two major Jewish sects prompted several questions directed at Jesus. It was also an issue that Paul was able to turn to his advantage after his arrest:

> *Acts 23:6 "Brothers, I am a Pharisee, a son of Pharisees. It is with respect to the resurrection of the dead that I am on trial." When he said this a dispute broke out between the Pharisees and the Sadducees, and the assembly was divided. (The Sadducees say there is no resurrection, and that there are neither angels nor spirits, but the Pharisees believe all these things)."*

Only in the teachings of Jesus and the writings of the New Testament do we finally see clear, unequivocal teaching concerning the resurrection of the dead and life beyond the grave. The New Testament removes the veil of uncertainty and reveals the promise of universal resurrection:

> *John 5:28-29 "The time is coming when all who are in the grave will hear my voice and come out – those who have done good will rise to live and those who have done evil will rise to be condemned."*

The eternal destiny of both groups of people is also clearly explained. Those who have rejected Christ *"will go away to eternal punishment"* (Matt 25:46) in a place called hell *"where there will be weeping and gnashing of teeth"* (Matt 13:42), where there is an *"eternal fire that never goes out"* (Mark 9:43) and where *"the smoke of their torment rises forever and ever"* (Rev 14:10-11). Those who are in Christ, on the other hand, will witness the universe being remade in perfection (Rev 21:1) and will live with God in a state of perfect joy, perfect health and perfect peace (Rev 21:2-26).

(A much more detailed discussion of the nature and duration of Hell can be found in my book, *"Finding God When He Seems To Be Hiding"*, available in print and as an ebook through my website, SmartFaith.net, and from all major book retailers).

In fact, after the comparative paucity of information in the Old Testament on this subject, the New Testament provides a veritable flood of revelation concerning life beyond the grave. There are nearly 1,000 references in the New Testament to the resurrection of the dead and what is to follow, with the certain hope of eternal life being revealed as the overarching motivation for persevering in the Christian life (Matt 6:20; 1 Cor 15:19).

Once again, we see progressive revelation at work in the scope and flow of the Bible; a gradual dawning of belief in immortality in the Old Testament, culminating in a quantum leap in detailed revelation concerning eternal life in the New Testament.

2. MORALS AND ETHICS

Progressive revelation in the Bible was not limited to doctrine. The same process can also be seen at work in regard to moral and ethical standards. In terms of behaviour, God expected far less of the Israelites than he does of Christians. As an unregenerate people, not yet freed from their sinful natures by Christ, the Israelites were incapable of the kind of Christian character that the New Testament exhorts us to display. Because of this, God did not demand from the Old Testament Israelites a level of holiness that was beyond their reach. In dealing with them as little children, God set them realistic behavioural benchmarks.

For example, practices such as polygamy, the beating of slaves, and the system of reciprocal justice for wrong-doing were allowed to continue throughout the Old Testament, and were not finally addressed until the

New Testament. (Although, in each of these cases God instituted specific instructions in the Old Testament to limit harm and ensure some measure of justice).

Sceptics and critics of Christianity highlight these different standards between the Old and New Testaments and accuse God of being inconsistent. They refer to verses like Malachi 3:6, *"I, the LORD do not change"*, and claim that this is contradicted by the flow of biblical revelation. It is important to understand, however, that God did not change any of his standards. His standards remained the same; it was his *expectations* that changed. His standards have always been perfection; perfect love, perfect grace, perfect holiness – the kind of perfection that we see exemplified in Jesus, who taught his disciples, *"Be perfect, as your heavenly Father is perfect"*, *(Matt 5:48)*.

This perfect, unchanging standard was made clear in the Old Testament as well;

> *"God's works are perfect, and all his ways are just. He is a faithful God who does no wrong, upright and just is he" (Deut 32:4).*

God has not changed, neither have his standards, but God knew that the pre-Christian Israelites were incapable of meeting those standards without the indwelling of the Holy Spirit, so he set his *expectations* of them at a lower, more realistic level.

This should not surprise us. As human parents, we adopt the same strategy in raising our own children. For example, my standards of table etiquette include chewing with your mouth closed and not spitting food out or dribbling it down your chin onto your shirt. This has always been my standard for the dinner table! When our kids were babies and infants, however, they were incapable of meeting that standard, so I didn't enforce it on them. I didn't expect them to chew with their mouth closed and not dribble food down their chin when they were 18 months old! I didn't insist upon those standards until they were older and mature enough to meet them. My standards never changed, but my expectations had to be modified to a level that was consistent with my children's capabilities.

This is precisely what we see God doing in the Old Testament. God was effectively saying:

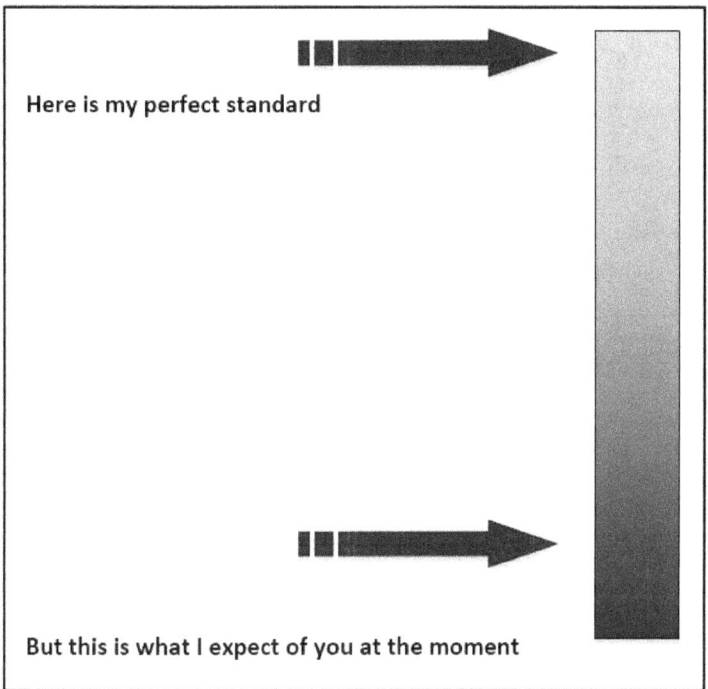

MARRIAGE

Polygamy was very common in the Old Testament world, partly out of necessity. It was a brutal world, and war was an almost constant fact of life. Men were often killed in battle, and sometimes whole armies were wiped out leaving towns and villages with few men left alive. The widows who were left would perish if they did not remarry, and the towns could not effectively repopulate unless every woman of childbearing age found a husband. Polygamy was the answer in a society with far more women than men. Polygamy enabled widows to remarry and be cared for, and also enabled towns to repopulate after wars or plagues. Polygamy was God's "social security plan" for widows.

God's ideal, of course, was always for one man to have one wife for life:

- *"... the wife of your marriage covenant. The Lord has made the two of you one." (Mal 2:15)*

- *"For this reason a man will leave his father and mother and be united with his wife, and they will become one flesh" (Gen 2:24)*

Jesus quoted this passage in Matthew 19:5 and expounded further upon it:

- *"For this reason a man will leave his father and mother and be united with his wife, and they will become one flesh. So they are no longer two, but one. Therefore what God has joined together, let no-one separate".*

The pastoral epistles of the New Testament clearly enunciate monogamy as God's standard;

- *1 Tim 3:12* "A deacon must be the husband of but one wife ..."

- *Titus 1:6* "An elder must be blameless, the husband of but one wife ..."

If God had outlawed polygamy in the Old Testament, however, he would have effectively condemned to death many widows, and perhaps even led to the nation of Israel fading into oblivion as their population dwindled. Polygamy was an important means of caring for widows and ensuring the viability of the nation.

On the other hand, polygamy, as it was practised in much of the ancient world, could be very unfair on some women, with a husband favouring one wife and treating his other wives harshly. God's answer to this situation was to allow polygamy, while also providing clear instructions for the fair treatment of all wives:

- <u>Deut 21:15</u> *"If a man has two wives …"* (followed by instructions for treating them and their children fairly).

- <u>Deut 25:5-10</u> Instructions indicating that if a man's brother dies, the surviving brother is to marry the widow in order to perpetuate his brother's line, even if he is already married.

In fact, God's instructions in the Old Testament about the fair treatment of multiple wives were revolutionary in a world where women had no rights and men could do what they liked. In this sense, God's instructions about polygamy in the Old Testament were an intermediate step towards the perfect ideal of monogamy, as revealed in the New Testament. This gradual and incremental reform is an example of God's progressive revelation regarding moral behaviour.

DIVORCE

Progressive moral revelation is also evident in the raising of standards regarding divorce from the Old to New Testaments. In the Old Testament a certificate of divorce could be written by a husband on almost any grounds:

> <u>Deut 24:1-4</u> *"When a man takes a wife and marries her, if then she <u>finds no favour in his eyes</u> because <u>he has found some indecency in her</u>, and he writes her a certificate of divorce and puts it in her hand and sends her out of his house, and she departs out of his house, and if she goes and becomes another man's wife, <u>and the latter man hates her</u> and writes her a certificate of divorce and puts it in her hand and sends her out of his house, or if the latter man dies, who took her to be his wife, then her former husband, who sent her away, must not take her again to be his*

wife, after she has been defiled, for that is an abomination before the LORD."

Jesus, however, significantly raised this standard in the New Testament:

> Matthew 5:31-32 *"It was said, "Whoever divorces his wife, let him give her a certificate of divorce". But I say to you that everyone who divorces his wife, except on the ground of sexual immorality, makes her commit adultery. And whoever marries a divorced woman commits adultery."*

Matthew 19 is a significant passage for our understanding of progressive revelation, not only in regard to the issue of divorce, but also in regard to progressive moral revelation generally. In this passage Jesus once again spoke about divorce, explaining God's perfect standard:

> *"From the beginning, the Creator made them male and female. For this reason a man will leave his father and mother and be united to his wife, and the two will become one flesh. So they are no longer two but one. Therefore what God has joined together, let no-one separate." (Matt 19:4-6)*

The Pharisees questioned Jesus about the obvious difference between his teaching and the teaching of Moses on this subject;

> *"They asked, 'Why then did Moses command that a man give his wife a certificate of divorce and send her away?'" (Matt 19:7).*

Jesus' reply explains the difference between Moses' standards and the standards of the new covenant;

> *"Jesus replied, 'Moses permitted you to divorce your wives because your hearts were hard. But it was not this way from the beginning. I tell you that anyone who divorces his wife, except for sexual immorality, and marries another woman commits adultery'." (Matt 19:8-9)*

In his answer, Jesus illustrates four important principles of progressive moral revelation:

1. The Old Testament was a temporary *intermediate* moral step. Jesus is very clear about this: God *"permitted"* divorce as a temporary measure.

2. This was necessary because their *"hearts were hard"*. In other words, the Israelites, in their pre-Christian, unregenerate condition, were incapable of meeting any higher standard, so God modified his expectations to a more moderate level.

3. This was never God's perfect, eternal standard *("But it was not this way from the beginning", Matt 19:8)*. God did not lower his standards; they have not changed.

4. It is now time for God's perfect standard to be introduced; the bar is about to be raised! (*"I tell you that anyone who divorces his wife, except for sexual immorality, and marries another woman commits adultery" Matt 19:9).*

The issue of divorce and remarriage is, of course, a very complex one, and there are other factors that need to be taken into account. Many Christians believe that, through Christ, there is forgiveness and the chance to start again when a previous marriage has failed. But the point here, is that the New Testament indicates a raising of the bar in terms of God's *ideal standard*.

SLAVERY

Slavery was an integral part of society in Old Testament times. It was an institution that we look back on as barbaric, but which, in the context of the times, also provided people with a valuable means of employment and survival. Poor families would sometimes sell a son or daughter to a wealthy land owner as a slave for a predetermined number of months or years, in return for a generous payment that would allow the family to survive and prosper. At the end of that set time, the son or daughter would be returned to the family. Sometimes a person would choose to become a bonded servant (a voluntary slave) to a kind and generous master, and would enjoy a lifestyle that would have been otherwise unattainable. Slavery was, in this sense, the ancient equivalent of full-time employment for many people.

Of course, the practice of slavery was open to all kinds of abuse. Many people were sold or forced into slavery against their will, and there were cruel masters who felt it was their right to mistreat slaves. In fact, in most cultures in the ancient world, a master could beat a slave to death for no reason, with complete impunity. This was the world in which the Israelites lived; a world without trade unions, workers' rights, or the protective legislation of enlightened governments.

In the Old Testament, slavery was allowed, and even, at times, encouraged by God. When the Israelites defeated their enemies, they were often instructed to take the women and children as slaves (Deut 20:14; Deut 21:10-14). In contrast to the other nations around them, however, God gave the Israelites specific instructions for the fair treatment of slaves; instructions that would have been revolutionary at that time.

- Exod 21:26. If a master caused the loss of a slave's eye or tooth, the slave should be freed.

- Exod 21:20. A master who beat his slave to death should be punished.

- Exod 21:1-4. A slave must be released after 6 years of service.

- Lev 25:46. A slave must not be *"ruled over ruthlessly"*.

- Exod 21:7-11. Slaves cannot be re-sold to foreigners.

These reforms represented a significant elevation of the stature of slaves in the ancient world. It has to be admitted, however, from our enlightened New Testament perspective, that they did not represent God's final, perfect standard. Many harsh activities were still allowed in relation to slaves:

- Exod 21:21. If a master beat his slave and the slave lived for 1 or 2 days and then died, the master could not be punished (because homicidal intent could not be proved).

- Exod 21:10-14. A man could capture a woman from another nation and make her his slave.

- Exod 21:1-4. Any children born from such a union belonged to the master as slaves.

As with the case of polygamy, God's instructions regarding slavery in the Old Testament represented an intermediate step towards God's higher ideals in the New Testament, where masters were told to treat their slaves with *respect* and to not even *threaten* them;

> "Masters, treat your slaves with respect. Do not threaten them ..." (Eph 6:9).

As Christianity spread, the question of what to do about slavery became an issue. Some Christians argued that slavery should be abolished; that if a master became a Christian, he should free all his slaves. Paul, however, recognised that this was too radical a move for the world of the first century. Instead he instructed:

- Each person is to remain as they were before they became a Christian – slave or free (1 Cor 7:17-23)

- Slaves are to respect their masters (Eph 6:5; Col 3:22; Tit 2:9)

- Slaves are to submit to their masters as to Christ (1 Pet 2:18)

While these injunctions do not go far enough for those of us living in the western, unionised world, the New Testament reveals the heart of God's higher principles of love, which were a significant step up from his expectations of pre-Christian Israel.

3. SOCIAL JUSTICE

The ancient world of the Old Testament was a harsh, brutal world. It was a world of independent city states, ruled over by kings who fulfilled the dual roles of government and judicial system; the law makers and the law enforcers. In order for a king to maintain control over his subjects, he had to be strong. If he was to maintain law and order, his punishments had to be tough enough to satisfy the wronged parties and dissuade them from engaging in an escalating cycle of vendettas and feuds. It was not unusual in the ancient world for two cities to go to war after a simple offense had escalated out of control in a series of increasingly violent retributions. Whole towns could be laid waste as a result of an initial simple offense. It was to remedy this problem that God instituted the famous "eye for eye" system of justice:

> *Evo 21:23-25* "*If there is serious injury, you are to take life for life, eye for eye, tooth for tooth, hand for hand, foot for foot, burn for burn, wound for wound, bruise.*"

> *Lev 24:19-20* "*Anyone who injures a neighbour is to be injured in the same manner: fracture for fracture, eye for eye, tooth for tooth. The one who has inflicted the injury must suffer the same injury.*"

This system of reciprocal justice was designed to limit the retribution to be *no more* than the original injury. In this way, justice was ensured, and society was protected from the dangers of escalating feuds. While such a system of proportional punishment might seem barbaric by today's standards, it was a necessary means of limiting the cruel and disproportionate punishments that were often administered in the ancient world.

The Old Testament system of reciprocal justice was an important intermediate step in reforming the practices of the pre-Christian Israelites. It represented a major improvement from the cruel, disproportionate punishments of the ancient world, and was a significant step towards God's perfect standard of love and forgiveness, eventually revealed in the New Testament:

> *Luke 6:27-29* "*Love your enemies, do good to those who hate you, bless those who curse you, pray for those who mistreat you.*"
>
> *Matt 5:38-44* "*You have heard it said, "Eye for eye, and tooth for tooth", but I tell you, do not resist an evil person. If anyone slaps you on the right cheek, turn to them the other cheek also.*"

In these passages Jesus once again demonstrates the principle of progressive revelation. God's perfect, eternal standards finally replaced the temporary, intermediate standards of the Old Testament.

SUMMARY

The fact that God did not condemn slavery, polygamy, divorce or the payback system in the Old Testament does not mean that he was condoning those practices. God was being a wise and loving parent, realising what standards the pre-Christian Israelites were capable of, and what they were not capable of. He was also demonstrating effective change management strategy; deciding which were the important moral reforms that needed immediate implementation, and which were the reforms that would have to wait until a later time. In acting in this way, God demonstrated 2 important principles:

1. It is not always possible to change everything at once. Many of these practices (like slavery, polygamy and the payback system) were endemic to the entire world at that time and, consequently, were deeply ingrained within Israel's system of social ethics. Change, if it was to be successful, needed to be gradual and incremental.

2. Do not expect more of people than they are capable of giving. Israel, in its unregenerate immaturity, was not capable of reaching God's higher standards - in the same way that an infant of 3 months isn't capable of toilet training and a child of 3 years isn't capable of reading Shakespeare. Trying to enforce behaviour that is beyond a child's developmental ability will only result in frustration, resentment and failure.

The Bible is the record of God's progressive revelation to mankind. It reveals a progression from simple to complex truth; from partial information to more complete information. The New Testament, and the person of Christ in particular, represents God's fullest and final revelation to mankind. The Old Testament represents the gradual and incremental revelation of truth to an initially pagan, ignorant people. We see this process at work in:

Doctrine: The revelation of doctrinal truth in the Old Testament was partial, elementary, often vague, and remained incomplete by the end of the Old Testament.

Prophecy: Many of the prophecies in the Old Testament, that Christ would eventually fulfil, were far from clear and unequivocal at the time they were given. Many of them can only be identified as prophecies retrospectively, when viewed through the lens of the New Testament. Even those that were initially regarded as prophecies were often vague and difficult to interpret.

Morals: God's moral code, revealed in the Old Testament, often represented an intermediary step towards the higher laws of the New Testament. This does not mean that God's standards changed; just that his expectations of us were gradually raised to meet his standards.

Walter A. Hendricksen, in his *"Layman's Guide to Interpreting the Bible"*, states:

"God does progressively reveal himself as history unfolds. But this does not mean that God's standards become progressively higher or that God changes along the way. Rather it is our understanding of God and his revelation that progresses. God never changes." (Layman's Guide to Interpreting the Bible, Henricksen, P. 77)

Progressive Revelation In The New Testament

Progressive revelation was not confined to the Old Testament. The same process continued throughout the New Testament as well, and this concept is important to understand if we are to read the New Testament with discernment and apply it with accuracy.

The concept of progressive revelation in the New Testament is the topic of the next chapter.

Reflection Questions 9

1. What new insights have you gained from this chapter?

2. Are there any aspects of the nature of progressive revelation that you find difficult to understand or accept?

3. Are there any moral or ethical practices that God allowed in the Old Testament that you find difficult to accept?

4. Read Romans 16:25-26. What is this mystery and why was it kept hidden for so long?

5. Read Matthew 19:1-9. How does Jesus' teaching about marriage and divorce differ from the old covenantal teaching? While this is the ideal, what role do you think grace and forgiveness also play? (See for example, 2 Cor 5:17).

6. Read Matthew 5:17-42. The statements, "You have heard it said" in verses 21, 27, 31 and 38 are references by Jesus to old covenantal teachings that he is now overturning. Yet Jesus precedes these comments by stating, in verses 17-20, that none of the old covenantal laws can be "set aside". Please explain!

7. In this same passage, Jesus articulates some new, higher laws regarding anger (vv.21-26) and lust (vv.27-30). Discuss the practical application of these as we seek to live lives that honour God.

CHAPTER 10

PROGRESSIVE REVELATION IN THE NEW TESTAMENT

Progressive revelation did not cease with the advent of the New Testament era. God's final revelation was not transmitted to us in a single "download" through the person of Christ. In fact, Jesus told his disciples that they would receive even deeper revelation from God after he left the world and the Holy Spirit came:

> *John 16:12-15* "*I have much more to say to you, more than you can now bear. But when he, the Spirit of truth, comes, he will guide you into all truth. He will not speak on his own; he will speak only what he hears, and he will tell you what is yet to come. He will glorify me by taking from what is mine and making it known to you. All that belongs to the Father is mine. That is why I said the Spirit will take from what is mine and make it known to you.*"

In the same way that revelation occurred progressively and incrementally throughout the Old Testament, it also continued progressively throughout the writing of the New Testament books. The New Testament documents reflect the development of increasingly detailed doctrines, inspired by the Holy Spirit and flowing from a deepening understanding of the person and work of Christ. The diagram below illustrates the concept of progressive revelation continuing throughout the New Testament period:

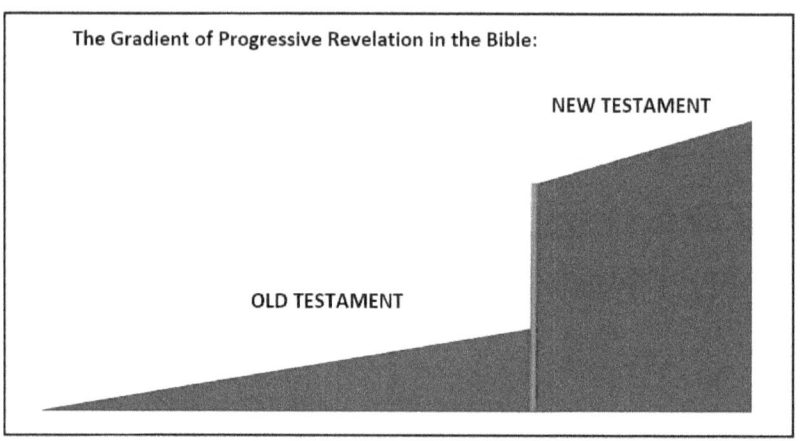

PROGRESSIVE REVELATION

Progressive revelation in the New Testament can be seen in the development of increasingly detailed and complex doctrines in the post-ascension New Testament epistles (letters). It should not surprise us, for example, that Paul's teaching in his letters is, in many instances, more theologically complex than the teaching of Jesus in the Gospels. Jesus was speaking to a pre-Christian audience, who would not be converted until the Day of Pentecost, whereas Paul's audience consisted of post-Pentecost Christians who were indwelt by the Holy Spirit. Even within the epistles, there is a marked increase in the complexity and depth of theological understanding when comparing the early New Testament letters such as James, 1 & 2 Thessalonians and Galatians with the later pastoral epistles (1 & 2 Timothy and Titus).

A timeline of the New Testament books is shown below:

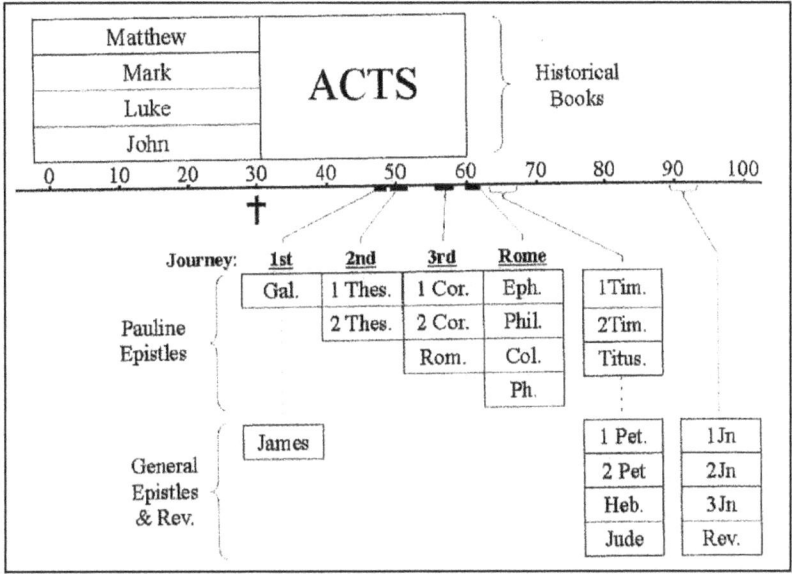

Tracing the development of doctrines from the early New Testament books to the later ones reveals a growing complexity and a deepening understanding of the Kingdom of God. This should affect the way we read the New Testament. If we want to study the New Testament's teaching on a certain subject, we should not limit our reading to the earlier books alone.

The progressive complexity of New Testament doctrines is seen in a number of areas. Two examples will suffice; the gospel and ecclesiology.

THE GOSPEL

The universal nature of the gospel was not immediately apparent to the early Jewish Christians. It took many decades for Christianity to fully embrace the concept that salvation through Jesus Christ was equally available to Gentiles as well as to Jews. This was despite the clear teaching of Jesus that *"You will be my witnesses in Jerusalem, and in all Judea and Samaria, and to the ends of the earth" (Acts 1:8).* The gradual dawning of this understanding of the universal nature of the gospel is outlined below:

Acts 1-8 (28-35 AD). Christianity is established in Jerusalem as a Jewish sect. Acts 6 records some tensions in the Jerusalem church between the "Hellenistic Jews" (Gentile converts to Judaism) and "Hebraic Jews" (Acts 6:1) At this point in time, there is no concept of the possibility of a Gentile accepting Christ without also converting to Judaism.

Acts 10 (36 AD). God reveals to Peter that the gospel is for Gentiles also (at the home of Cornelius). The conversion of a household of Gentiles is recorded, but it appears to have had little impact on the general mission of the fledgling church, who continued to see their role as attempting to convince Jews, rather than Gentiles, to accept Christ as their Messiah.

James (40-45AD). James, the Lord's brother and leader of the church in Jerusalem, writes to Christians who have been scattered abroad by persecution. Despite this persecution by traditional Jews, James still sees himself as a Jew, and he writes to the Christians as Jews; *"to the 12 tribes scattered among the nations" (Jms 1:1)*. He uses the Jewish term *"synagogue"* to refer to the meetings of Christians, and uses the Jewish title *"kyrios sabaoth"* (Lord Almighty) to refer to God. There is no indication in the letter that the gospel extends to any people beyond the Jews.

Acts 15 (50AD). Some Jewish Christians still insist that Gentile converts must be circumcised and become Jews. *"Some of the believers who belonged to the party of the Pharisees said, "The Gentiles must be circumcised and required to keep the law of Moses"" (Acts 15:5).* This verse is fascinating, because it reveals that 22 years after the death and resurrection of Christ, many Christians still saw themselves as Messianic Jews (and even Pharisees!) and believed that they were still obligated to obey all the commandments of the old covenant. Paul's disagreement with these Jewish Christians and his subsequent appeal to the Apostles in Jerusalem results in a decision that Gentile believers do not need to be circumcised, but that they need to *"abstain from food offered to idols, from blood, from the meat of strangled animals" (Acts 15:29)*. Adherence to these Old Testament food regulations was eventually overturned in Paul's letters to the Corinthians (55AD), when the full implications of the new covenant were realised. Here, then, is an example of a New Testament doctrine which would be misleading to read in isolation, without realising that it represented an incomplete, partially developed understanding of the gospel.

Galatians (51AD). Jewish Christians arrive in Galatia after Paul had preached there. These Jewish Christians convince the new Gentile believers that they must be circumcised as Jews and obey all the laws of Moses. The Apostle Peter, who was visiting there at the time, was even convinced by them and endorsed their teaching (Gal 2:11)! Galatians is Paul's scathing letter condemning this teaching and emphasising the freedom from the Law that the gospel brings. He insists that Christianity is no longer about fulfilling the old covenantal laws.

Corinthians (55AD). In 1 Corinthians 8, Paul overturns the necessity to obey the prohibitive Old Testament food laws, but advises Christians to abstain from eating certain things if, by so eating, they might offend the consciences of "weaker" (Jewish) Christians who have not yet fully grasped the nature of the new covenant.

Romans 14 (57AD). The church in Rome was divided between Jewish Christians who insisted that all the Old Testament laws still had to be obeyed, and the Gentile Christians who did not believe this. Paul again states that the Old Testament food laws no longer apply to Christians (Rom 14:20). More significantly, in response to this ongoing debate about obedience to the laws of Moses, Paul writes a more fully developed doctrine of justification by faith alone, independent from the laws of Moses.

Hebrews (69AD). Jewish Christians were being pressured to revert to Judaism and to a strict observance of the laws of Moses. The writer (possibly Paul) argues that Christ has fulfilled all the sacrificial laws of the Old Testament. This book provides the deepest exploration in the New Testament of how Christianity represents a completely new covenant, for which the old laws no longer apply.

Without a proper appreciation of the progressive nature of revelation in the New Testament, one might not realise that some of the early New Testament propositions were transitional in nature. For instance, one might read the Apostolic mandate, in Acts 15, that Gentile Christians are to obey Jewish food laws, and believe that this is a binding injunction upon all Christians for all time.

ECCLESIOLOGY

Ecclesiology refers to the doctrines concerning the formal structures and practices of the church. It is derived from the Greek word, *"ἐκκλησία"* (*"ecclesia"*), which means "congregation" or "gathering". Ecclesiology deals with such things as leadership structures, the purpose of the church and the roles of various functional offices (such as elders, deacons, pastors etc). The New Testament reveals a growing ecclesiological complexity. Consider, for example, the issue of church leadership:

The Gospels (25-27AD). Jesus' teaching, recorded in the Gospels, centres on the concept of the Kingdom of God on earth, rather than on the concept of "church". Jesus focuses on the ethics and values of the Kingdom of God, rather than the structures of the church as an organization.

Acts 1-5 (28-34AD). The church in Jerusalem is presided over by the Apostles.

Acts 6 (35AD). The increasing number of Christians, together with the growing demands of ministry, result in the Apostles deputising "deacons" to oversee practical aspects of ministry, such as the distribution of food to widows.

Acts 11 (43AD). The leaders of the church in Jerusalem are now referred to as "elders", inferring a widening of the leadership group to include others working alongside the Apostles. This may be due to the martyrdom of some of the Apostles. From Acts 15 onwards, this group is referred to as *"the Apostles and elders"*.

Acts 14 (47AD). Paul and Barnabus appoint elders in each church during their first missionary journey. They are *appointed*, not elected by the church (Acts 14:23). Formal qualifications for eldership have not yet evolved, nor has a clear job description.

Acts 15 (49AD). The Jerusalem council reveals that the elders of the churches in the outlying provinces are subject to the authority of the Apostles in Jerusalem.

1 Thessalonians (51AD). Paul mentions that, as an Apostle, he could have insisted on financial support from the Thessalonicans. This is the first mention of paid itinerant ministry, but it applies only to the Apostles. There were, as yet, no paid ministries *in situ*.

Acts 20 (56AD). Paul's final farewell to the Ephesian elders infers a complete handing over of responsibility for the Ephesian church into their hands (Acts 20:26-38). It also marks the first definitive statement in the New Testament of the role of elders, to *"be shepherds of God's church" (v.28)*, and to teach and protect the church from false doctrine. From this point on, the Jerusalem church ceased to exercise oversight over churches in other cities. This was due to three probable factors:

1. The Apostles had died out or moved on from Jerusalem;

2. There were too many churches and the distances were too great for any kind of central oversight;

3. The Christians in outlying churches had developed leaders who were mature enough to lead autonomously.

Romans (57AD). Paul's final greetings in Romans 16 indicate a decentralised house church network, meeting under the pastoral oversight of the owner of each house. In Romans 12, Paul lists leadership and teaching as important gifts to be exercised, but there is no mention of any leaders in full-time or paid positions.

Ephesians (60AD). In Ephesians 4:11 Paul lists the leadership gifts, given by God for the strengthening of his church, as Apostles, prophets, evangelists, pastors and teachers.

Philippians (61AD). In writing to the church in Philippi, Paul addresses the letter to the church as a whole, but with a special salutation to the "overseers and deacons" (Phil 1:1). Here is the first recognition of two separate formal offices within the church hierarchy. The weight of current scholarship understands these to be the roles of spiritual oversight (overseer) and practical assistance (deacon).

Timothy (64AD). 1 Timothy 5:17 is the first mention in the New Testament of teacher-elders who are paid to exercise their ministry in a full-time capacity in the church at Ephesus. Here is the first example of "professional ministry". 1 Timothy 3 also contains the first fully developed list of qualifications for elders and deacons.

Without a proper appreciation of the progressive nature of revelation in the New Testament, one might note, in Acts 15, the authority of the Apostles in Jerusalem over the elders of churches in the outlying provinces, and see this as a biblical mandate for denominational hierarchy, where individual congregations are subject to central denominational bodies. This view, however, fails to recognise that the ecclesiology evident in Acts 15 was transitional; that as churches and elders became more mature, and the Apostles died out, individual churches became completely autonomous. This is not to say that centralised denominational hierarchies are wrong; what is wrong is claiming an eternal biblical mandate for them based upon Acts 15, which was a unique, transitional situation.

New Testament ecclesiology demonstrates a progression over time from simple to complex, from unstructured to structured, from centralised to decentralised church leadership. The New Testament record, however, also displays a variety of concurrent leadership structures that frustrate any attempt to construct a single, prescriptive New Testament model of church leadership. Ranging from informal house churches in Rome (Rom 16) to the highly structured paid teaching-elders, general elders and deacons in Ephesus (1 Timothy), there appears to be a sense in which local churches evolved leadership and ministry structures that were appropriate to their own situations and circumstances. Such is the adaptable, organic nature of Christianity.

Reflection Questions 10

1. What new insights have you gained from this chapter?

2. How has this changed your view of the teaching of the New Testament?

3. Read John 16:12-15. How does this verse indicate the nature of progressive revelation within the New Testament? Is what sense does the Holy Spirit still do this for the followers of Christ today?

4. Read Acts 1:8. The early church was very slow in putting this mission statement into practice (as explained in the above chapter). How is your church doing in this regard? What are you doing well? How can you improve your commitment to wider, global mission?

5. Read Acts 14:23 and 20:26-38. These passages relate to the appointment and function of elders. How do the leadership structures of your church and denomination compare to those of the New Testament? Do you view the New Testament teaching regarding elders as prescriptive for the modern church?

6. Read Hebrews 13:17. Discus the practical application of this verse for your church, in regard to both the role of leaders / elders, and the response of the congregation to those leaders.

7. Spend some time praying for your church, for your leaders and for your missional endeavours.

CHAPTER 11

READING THE OLD TESTAMENT CHRISTOLOGICALLY

Christ is the key that unlocks the meaning of the Old Testament. In fact, according to Jesus, the Old Testament is all about him. After his resurrection, when he encountered two confused and disheartened disciples on the road to Emmaus (who had not yet heard of his resurrection), we are told:

> *"Beginning with Moses and all the Prophets, he explained to them what was said in all the Scriptures concerning Himself." (Luke 24:27).*

The "Scriptures" that Jesus explained to these disciples was the Old Testament, for the New Testament had not yet been written. He began with *"Moses"* (the Pentateuch – the first five books of the Bible) and the prophets, and went on to explain *"what was said in **all the Scriptures** [the whole Old Testament] concerning himself"*. What a wonderful Bible study this would have been! Jesus opened the eyes of these disciples to see that the whole of the Old Testament is really all about him – laying the ground work for his appearance and prophesying all that he would do to save mankind.

CHRIST IS THE FULFILMENT OF OLD TESTAMENT PROPHECIES

The New Testament describes Jesus as the final fulfilment of many Old Testament prophecies:

> *Act 13:32-33 "We tell you the good news: What God promised our fathers, he has fulfilled for us, their children, by raising up Jesus."*

There are hundreds of predictive prophecies in the Old Testament concerning the coming Messiah. They predicted the precise nature of Christ's birth, ministry, death and resurrection. Chapter 9 of this book contains a fuller discussion of Jesus' fulfilment of these messianic prophecies, but it is worth mentioning again that many of the prophecies were not clear until their fulfilment in Christ. In fact, some of them were not obvious as prophecies at all until Jesus and the New Testament writers interpreted them as such. This is in keeping with the nature of progressive revelation. The relationship of prophecy to fulfilment is often like that of seed to plant; the latter bearing little resemblance to the former.

There are over 300 Old Testament prophecies that were fulfilled by Christ. The *"Jews For Jesus"* organisation lists 365 on their website (http://Bibleprobe.com/300great.htm). As significant as these are, however, we are still only scratching the surface of the importance of Christ for understanding the Old Testament. Jesus did more than simply fulfil some prophecies: The *whole* of the old covenant finds its fulfilment in him.

CHRIST IS THE FULFILMENT OF THE OLD COVENANT

In Matthew 5: 17 Jesus declared that he had come to *"fulfil the Law and the Prophets"*. By this he was referring to the *whole* of the old covenant, including the Old Testament narrative itself. The Jews used the term *"the Law and the Prophets"* to refer to their Tanakh; their complete Scriptures (our Old Testament). By describing Himself as the fulfilment of *"the Law and the Prophets"*, Jesus reveals that he is the fulfilment of the whole of the Old Testament. The New Testament is unequivocal in affirming this:

> <u>Heb 1:1-2</u> *"In the past God spoke to our forefathers through the prophets at many times and in various ways, (2) but in these last days he has spoken to us by his Son, whom he appointed heir of all things, and through whom he made the universe".*

> <u>2 Cor 1:20</u> *"For no matter how many promises God has made, they are "Yes" in Christ. And so, through him the "Amen" is spoken by us to the glory of God".*

It is important that we understand what Jesus and the New Testament writers are inferring. Jesus did not simply fulfil some Old Testament prophecies. They are claiming that the Old Testament, when understood correctly, is *all about Christ.* This is what Jesus meant when, in his Emmaus Road post-resurrection appearance, *"he explained to his disciples what was said about him in all the Scriptures, beginning with Moses and the prophets" (Luke 24:27).* Moses wrote the Pentateuch, the first 5 books of the Bible, so Jesus was saying that even these books of historical narrative were all about him. In a separate post-resurrection appearance Jesus made a similar appeal to the Old Testament: He said to his disciples:

> *"This is what I told you while I was still with you: Everything must be fulfilled that is written about me in the Law of Moses, the Prophets and the Psalms." Then he opened their minds so they could understand the Scriptures. (Luke 24:44-45)*

At the macro (big picture) level, the vast sweep of the Old Testament narrative from Genesis to Malachi is a story of redemption that finds its ultimate fulfilment in Christ. In saying this, however, Christ is not simply the concluding chapter of the story: He is the beginning and middle as well. We must understand that the Old Testament is *all* about Christ, from beginning to end; it is the story of God's preparation of mankind for his coming.

At the micro level, the Old Testament is replete with redemptive moments that foreshadow the work of Christ:

- God's curse of the serpent and his promise to Eve in the Garden of Eden, that her descendent would crush the head of the serpent (the devil).

- The provision of animal skin clothing for Adam and Eve in the Garden of Eden. The death of these animals as a means of providing a covering for Adam and Eve in their fallen state, foreshadowed the ultimate sacrifice of Christ to provide a final covering and restitution for the sins of mankind.

- The story of God's redemption of Noah and his family through the flood.

- The story of Joseph, who was rejected and mistreated, but ultimately provided salvation from famine for his people.

- The Exodus story: Moses was God's appointed deliverer of the nation of Israel, who rescued the nation from slavery and oppression.

- Moses lifting up the bronze snake in the desert, so that those who were bitten by poisonous snakes and looked up to the bronze replica were healed (Numbers 21:9). Jesus specifically cites this as a foreshadowing of his redemptive work on the cross; *"And as Moses lifted up the serpent in the wilderness, so must the Son of Man be lifted up." (John 3:14)*

- Rahab hanging the scarlet cord out of her window, which caused the invading Israelite soldiers to spare her. This is a subtle foreshadowing of the blood of Christ as the means of salvation, and also pre-empts the scarlet robe that Jesus was given to wear by his mocking executioners.

- The story of David and Goliath. David was the maligned, under-rated shepherd boy who, by his one heroic act, saved the entire nation.

- David's benevolent rule as King of Israel is regularly referred to in the New Testament as a prophetic foreshadowing of the saving kingship of Christ.

These events, and many more throughout the Old Testament, are a "type" (an allegoric, prophetic foreshadowing) of the redemption that Christ would one day bring. On the surface, they are historical narratives describing the lives of key Jewish figures. But there is a deeper meaning. We are meant to see Christ in these stories, for they are ultimately about *him*.

When we read the story of Joseph, a man who was unjustly treated and left for dead, but through whom salvation was eventually procured for the whole nation, we are meant to understand it as a foreshadowing of the salvation that Christ, God's suffering servant, would one day bring.

When we read the story of David, a youth who was overlooked by his family but whom God chose to defeat a seemingly undefeatable warrior and single-handedly win a vicarious victory for the entire nation, we are meant to understand this as a foreshadowing of Christ's vicarious victory over sin and death on behalf of mankind. It is not just an inspiring story with a moral about trusting God, or overcoming obstacles, or defeating giants in our lives. It is all about Christ, and if we miss this, we have missed the main point.

It is easy to fall into the trap of thinking that the gospel is only a New Testament revelation. While it is true that the gospel is only fully and finally revealed with the coming of Christ in the New Testament, the gospel was also present, in embryonic form, throughout the Old Testament. Paul speaks of this embryonic, Old Testament gospel in his opening remarks in his letter to the Romans:

> *Rom 1:1-4* "…. *the gospel of God - the gospel he promised beforehand through his prophets in the Holy Scriptures regarding his Son, who as to his human nature was a descendant of David, and who through the Spirit of holiness was declared with power to be the Son of God by his resurrection from the dead: Jesus Christ our Lord".*

Paul is not inferring that we can turn to a chapter of the Old Testament and find the gospel laid out for us in full. The gospel that was *"promised beforehand through his prophets in the Holy Scriptures"* was not clearly, explicitly stated anywhere in the Old Testament. But there are glimpses of it throughout the Old Testament for those with eyes to see.

CHRIST IS THE INTERPRETIVE KEY TO THE OLD TESTAMENT

The key to interpreting the Old Testament, therefore, is Jesus Christ himself. He is the one who makes sense of it all, because it was written *about* him and in preparation *for* him. Without a proper understanding of Christ, the true meaning of the Old Testament will remain a mystery. Paul describes this beautifully in his second letter to the Corinthians:

> *2 Cor 3:14-16 "But their[the Jews] minds were made dull, for to this day the same veil remains when the old covenant is read. It has not been removed, because only in Christ is it taken away. Even to this day when Moses is read, a veil covers their hearts. But whenever anyone turns to the Lord, the veil is taken away".*

The inference is clear; the Old Testament does not interpret itself. On the surface it presents a story that is easy to follow; the story of God's dealing with the people of Israel. Underneath this, however, is a deeper meaning, a metanarrative ("big story") that only becomes apparent when the story is read through the interpretive lens of Christ. It is a story within a story; a hidden message that can only be discovered through the application of the correct key; Jesus Christ. The concept of God *hiding* a deeper message within the Old Testament is stated in Paul's concluding comments to the Romans:

> *Rom 16:25-26 "Now to him who is able to establish you by my gospel and the proclamation of Jesus Christ, according to the revelation of the mystery hidden for long ages past, (26) but now revealed and made known ..."*

The hidden meaning of the Old Testament, as Paul states above, is the gospel of Jesus Christ; the message of redemption though him. Elsewhere, Paul refers to it as the *"mystery of the gospel"* (Eph 6:19) and the *"mystery of Christ" (Eph 3:4).* In fact, the New Testament uses the word *"mystery"* nineteen times to refer to the hidden nature of the gospel within the Old Testament.

That God should "hide" it within the Old Testament might seem perplexing, but the reason for this is simple; the Old Testament Jews were not ready to receive the gospel because they were not yet capable of understanding it. For this reason, it was kept hidden for a later generation; for those who would follow Christ and receive his Spirit. The gospel is a spiritual message and it can only be understood through the illumination of the indwelling Holy Spirit:

> *Eph 3:3-5 "This mystery was made known to me …. the mystery of Christ, which was not made known to men in other generations as it has now been revealed by the Spirit"*
>
> *Col 1:26-27 "This mystery has been kept hidden for ages and generations, but is now disclosed to the saints. To them God has chosen to make known among the Gentiles the glorious riches of this mystery, which is Christ in you, the hope of glory".*

Only with the coming of Jesus Christ was this mystery finally unveiled. This unveiling, however, was met with an underwhelming response. The Jews of Jesus' day should have recognised him as the living fulfilment of the Old Testament and finally understood the message that had been hidden for so long. Their failure to do so prompted Jesus to rebuke the Pharisees, scribes and priests, for their blindness:

> *John 5:39-40 "You diligently study the Scriptures because you think that by them you possess eternal life. These are the Scriptures that testify about me, yet you refuse to come to me to have life".*

It was this inability to perceive the Christological metanarrative, the deeper meaning of the Old Testament, that prompted Paul to write;

> *"Even to this day when Moses is read, a veil covers their hearts" (2 Cor 3:15).*

If we are to understand the Old Testament properly, we must understand that it as a book about Christ. Only when we read it from this perspective will it make sense and its true meaning become apparent, because *"whenever anyone turns to the Lord, the veil is taken away" (2 Cor 3:16).*

READING THE OLD TESTAMENT CHRISTOLOGICALLY

Reading the Old Testament Christologically means reading it through the lens of our understanding of the person and work of Christ. Because the gospel begins and ends with Christ, our reading of the Old Testament must do the same. We do not simply read our way through the Old Testament until we discover where it is all leading at the end. Rather, we *start* with an understanding of Christ, and, as we read each passage, we ask ourselves, *"How does this passage speak to me about Christ? How does it fit into the big picture of God's redemptive plan?"*

Of course, not every passage in the Old Testament is full of typology or obvious gospel application. Whole sections can seem quite pedestrian to the casual reader, but reading even these passages Christologically will help us to see how they fit into the grand scheme of God's redemptive plan concerning Christ. For example, the tedious and seemingly irrelevant laws of Leviticus take on new meaning because we know that *"the Law was put in charge to lead us to Christ that we might be justified by faith" (Gal 3:24).* By reading these Mosaic laws Christologically, we can see the role they played in God's redemptive purposes. They prepared the way for Christ by emphasising:

- God's perfect standards

- Mankind's inability to meet those perfect standards

- The serious consequences of sin

- Our need of a Saviour

While the laws, themselves, no longer apply to us, they provide a valuable reminder of these aspects of the gospel, and should impress upon us the incredible privilege that is ours to be able to *"approach the throne of grace with confidence"* through Christ *(Heb 4:16)*.

If we read the Old Testament Christologically, there is no part that is irrelevant. Although there are many parts that are no longer *applicable*, they are all *relevant* because of their helpfulness in illustrating some part of the gospel of Christ. Our ability to see the Christological metanarrative in even the most mundane passages transforms our reading of the Old Testament so that it all has value. This Christological metanarrative is always present, although, because it is a *hidden* message, it is often not obvious or explicitly stated.

Consider, for example, the story of Abraham. Speaking about him, Jesus commented, *"Your father Abraham rejoiced at the thought of seeing my day; he saw it and was glad" (John 8:56)*. Yet when we read the story of Abraham, in Genesis 12 – 25, there are no messianic promises, no explicit statements about a coming redeemer. The promises that were given to Abraham were about being given a land of his own and about his descendants becoming a great nation through whom *"all nations on earth will be blessed" (Gen 18:18)*. Yet Jesus tells us that we are to understand that these promises were really speaking about him and the establishment of his kingdom on earth. Exactly how much of all this Abraham understood is not clear; perhaps very little. He glimpsed these things from afar. But you and I know the end from the beginning. Our understanding of the gospel of Christ allows us to imbue Abraham's story with a Christological meaning that Abraham could only dimly perceive.

How do we learn to do this consistently? How do we learn to accurately uncover the "Christ-story", the hidden metanarrative, in our reading of the Old Testament? We start by letting the New Testament be our guide.

THE NEW TESTAMENT: OUR GUIDE TO CHRISTOLOGICAL INTERPRETATION

Fortunately, in seeking to uncover the metanarrative seam of gold that underlies the bedrock of the Old Testament, Jesus and the New Testament writers have done a lot of the digging for us. They have not uncovered it all, for that would make the New Testament many times bigger than the Old, but they have uncovered enough so that we can see where the seam lies and can follow it further.

In the previous example of Abraham, the reason we can be sure of the Christological metanarrative in Abraham's story is because Jesus himself pointed it out; *"Your father Abraham rejoiced at the thought of seeing my day; he saw it and was glad" (John 8:56)*. There are many examples like this where the New Testament refers to an Old Testament event or person, and uncovers previously hidden Christological meaning.

Consider, for example, the story of how God miraculously provided Moses and the Israelites with water from the rock in the desert (Num 20:1-13). Speaking of this incident, in 1 Corinthians 10:4, Paul says, *"they drank from the spiritual rock that accompanied them, and that rock was Christ"*. In the original story there is no hint that either the rock or the water held any symbolism at all, yet Paul, under the inspiration of the Holy Spirit, has uncovered for us another glimpse of the Christological metanarrative. Christ is both the rock and the water; he is the rock upon whom we can build our life (Lk 6:48), and he is the spring of life-giving water that wells up to eternal life (Jn 4:14).

TYPOLOGY

At this point, typology becomes an important concept for us to understand. A "type", in the theological sense, is an Old Testament person, place or event that foreshadows some aspect of New Testament truth regarding Christ. It is a prophetic prefiguring of the person and work of Christ. For example, Jesus identified Jonah as a type of himself:

Mat 12:40 "*For as Jonah was three days and three nights in the belly of a huge fish, so the Son of Man will be three days and three nights in the heart of the earth*".

In identifying Jonah's three days in the belly of a fish as a "type" of his death and resurrection, Jesus has uncovered for us a part of the metanarrative seam that runs beneath the Old Testament. Typology is the study of these types in the Old Testament.

There are two extremes to be avoided in looking for types in the Old Testament.

The **first extreme** is stretching the type too far. In the previously mentioned case of Jonah, his three days in the belly of the fish is a type of Christ's burial in the tomb, but his initial refusal to obey God and his attempt to flee from God are clearly not typical of Christ (although he did express fear and reluctance as he approached his death). Just because some parts of a story or event are typical does not mean that all parts are; we must not stretch the type too broadly. Similarly, we must not stretch the type too deeply. The Tabernacle, as we shall see shortly, is a type of certain New Testament truths, but some teachers have gone to the extreme of investing even the cords and tent pegs of the Tabernacle with typological meaning. This sort of extreme typology can easily result in allegorical interpretations that are misleading and possibly dangerous. Usually the breadth and depth of a type will be fairly obvious and should not be stretched further than is reasonable or rational.

The **second extreme** is the belief that the only valid types are those that are identified in the New Testament. While this is not a potentially harmful position to hold (as is the first extreme), as this view will not lead you into error, it is somewhat limiting. This is similar to saying that the only valid Old Testament prophecies are those that are explicitly repeated in the New Testament. The Old Testament types identified by the New Testament are extremely helpful in showing us the kind of types to look for, but we should not think that there are no other types to be found. In considering possible types, however, the type should have an obvious correlation with a New Testament truth that does not require mental origami to perceive.

Examples of Old Testament Types Identified by The New Testament

The following are examples of Old Testament types and their New Testament fulfilments ("antitypes") that are identified by the New Testament writers:

OLD TESTAMENT TYPE		NEW TESTAMENT ANTI-TYPE	
Gen 28:12	Jacob's ladder	John 1:51	Christ, God's anointed one
Num 21:8	The brazen serpent	John 3:14	The cross of Christ
Gen 1:3	Creation of light	2 Cor 4	The light of the Gospel
Gen 6 – 8	Noah's flood	Mtt 24	The second coming of Christ
Gen 6 – 8	Noah kept safe	1 Pet 3	Salvation & baptism
Exod 17:6	Water from the rock	John 4:14	Christ's living water
Exod 16:14f	Manna from heaven	John 6:32	Christ, the bread of life
Exod 12	The Passover lamb	John 1:29	Christ, the lamb of God (1 Cor 5:7)
Lev 16:9-10	The sin offering goat	Heb 9	Christ's sacrificial death
Lev 16:21f	The scapegoat	John 1:29	The removal of sins
Lev 23:10	The festival of firstfruits	1 Cor 15:20f	Christ's resurrection
Jonah 1 – 2	Jonah in the fish	Mtt 12:40	Christ's death and resurrection
Gen 22	Abraham and Isaac	Rom 8:32	Death of God's Son
Exod 25-26	The Tabernacle	Heb 9	Christ the way to God
Gen 14:18	Melchizedek (& Psa 110:4)	Heb 5:6-10	Christ our priest and King

Examples of Additional Types Not Identified in The New Testament

Here are some examples of other possible types that are commonly suggested. Although the New Testament does not identify these as types, their typological similarities with Christ are too obvious to ignore.

Boaz (Ruth 1-4)

Boaz is a type of Christ, the redeemer, in the way he graciously redeemed Ruth, a Moabite, and married her, thus incorporating her into the people of God.

Moses (Exod 2 – 40)

There are several parallels between Moses and Christ:

MOSES	JESUS CHRIST
Baby Moses had to be hidden from Pharaoh	Baby Jesus had to be hidden from Herod
Moses turned water into blood	Jesus turned water into wine
Moses received the Law on Mt Sinai	Jesus took the punishment of the Law on Calvary
Moses: manna in the desert for the hungry people	Jesus: fed the people in the wilderness
Moses: water from the rock for thirsty people	Jesus: living water
Intercedes with arms held out by two men	Crucified with a criminal on each side

Moses can also be seen as a type of Christian: saved from certain death and adopted into the Pharaoh's family, foreshadowing our own salvation from certain death and our adoption as sons and daughters of the King of Kings.

Joseph (Gen 37-50)

The life of Joseph is overflowing with typology. Although Joseph is not identified anywhere in the New Testament as a type, it is hard to deny the obvious similarities with Christ:

JOSEPH	JESUS CHRIST
Beloved son	Beloved Son
Joseph was a shepherd	Jesus is the Good Shepherd
Coat of many colours: sign of nobility	Jesus, proclaimed King at his birth
Despised by his brothers	Rejected & scorned by his brothers
Sent by his Father on a mission	Sent by his Father on a mission
Brothers conspired against him	Jews conspired against him
Brothers did not accept his prophetic words	Jews did not accept his teaching and his claims
Stripped of his garments	Stripped of his garments
Cast into a pit	Placed in a tomb
Removed from the pit	Rose from the tomb
Sold into slavery – 20 pieces of silver	Sold for 30 pieces of silver
Resisted sin (Potiphar's wife)	Lived a sinless life
Unjustly condemned and imprisoned	Unjustly condemned and crucified
Rose to the highest authority under Pharaoh	Rose to the right hand of the Father
Saved his people from famine and death	Saved us from sin and hell

Principles For Reading The Old Testament Christologically

1. Become more familiar with the New Testament.

The more we read the New Testament, the better we will understand the Old Testament. The deeper our understanding of the gospel of Christ in the New Testament, the clearer will be our perception of it as the underlying metanarrative in the Old Testament.

2. When reading the Old Testament, ask questions of the passage.

"What reflections of Christ are there in this passage? What part of the gospel of Christ does this passage illustrate?" Don't be too concerned with whether something is officially a "type" or not. The important thing is that you see Christ in the passage.

3. Use a Bible with cross referencing and study notes.

The cross references will often link the Old Testament passage you are reading to relevant New Testament passages. Similarly, the study notes will point out obvious Christological meanings in the passage. Remember, most of the hard work has already been done by biblical scholars, so let them guide you.

4. Learn to see the big picture.

Have a simple outline of Bible history handy (such as the timeline at the end of Chapter 8 of this book). Know where a particular passage fits into the grand flow of Christ's redemptive story.

5. Read large portions.

When reading the Old Testament, it is often helpful to read large sections at a time, rather than becoming bogged down in minute detail. The "big picture" metanarrative often becomes clearer when we step back and read the Old Testament as a story, rather than as a prescriptive, verse by verse instruction manual. This is particularly true of the historical narrative sections. For instance, it is best to read the story of Ruth in a single sitting, in order to see the story of redemption within it. Similarly, it is better to read the other individual stories of the Old Testament (Noah, Abraham, Joseph, Moses, Joshua, the Judges, Samuel, Elijah, Elisha, David, Solomon, Ezra, Nehemiah, Daniel, Job) in large sections rather than spending weeks or months pouring laboriously over individual verses. The more we read these sections as stories, the clearer the metanarrative will become.

6. Read historical narrative sections in large instalments.

Following on from the previous point, make it a goal to read from Genesis to Job in a relatively short time, as this represents the major historical narrative section of the Old Testament. It is surprising how quickly you can read this important section of the Old Testament by setting aside a minimal period each day. This section of the Old Testament contains 436 chapters. Here are some examples of reading timetables:

- 1 month   =   15 chapters each day   =   30-45 minutes each day
- 6 weeks   =   10 chapters each day   =   20-30 minutes each day
- 2 months =   7 chapters each day   =   15 – 20 minutes each day
- 3 months =   5 chapters each day   =   10 – 15 minutes each day

This may be quite different from the way you have read the Bible previously, but it is very helpful for gaining an overview of the redemptive story.

7. Finally, read the Old Testament prayerfully.

Ask Christ, the living Word of God, to reveal himself to you as you read the written Word of God. Remember, it is him you are seeking, not theological knowledge.

Reflection Questions 11

1. What new insights have you gained from reading this chapter?

2. Are there Old Testament stories that you now have a deeper understanding of?

3. Read Luke 24:27 and 24:44-45. Jesus led these disciples in a "Bible study" through the Old Testament. What does this infer about the relationship between the Old Testament and Christ?

4. Read and compare Ephesians 3:3-5, Colossians 1:26-27 and Romans 16:25-26. Why did God deem it necessary to keep the message about Christ "hidden" for so long?

5. Read and compare 2 Corinthians 3:14-16 and John 5:39-40. What is the key to unlocking the meaning of the Old Testament? Explain.

6. Are there aspects of the Old Testament that you find difficult to read or understand?

7. Do you regularly read the historical narrative section of the Old Testament? Why not make a commitment to reading through it? Decide how many chapters each day you would like to read:

I will aim to read .... chapters each day

PART III

HERMENEUTICS

Principles of Biblical Interpretation

CHAPTER 12

HERMENEUTICS

The word *hermeneutics* is derived from the Greek word ἑρμηνεύω (*hermeneuō*), which means *"to interpret"*. In Christian parlance, it refers to the accepted principles for correctly interpreting the Bible. There are some very scholarly, detailed books on the topic of hermeneutics for those who want to study this topic at depth. The following chapters, however, are aimed at providing a basic introduction to the principles of biblical interpretation to ordinary Bible readers, as well as providing some practical examples of those principles in operation.

The term *hermeneutics* is related to three key concepts, which will be explained in detail: exegesis, interpretation and application. Sometimes *hermeneutics* is used to refer to interpretation only, sometimes to exegesis and interpretation, and, at other times, to all three. In this book we will use the term in its more general sense, to refer to all three. The basic process of hermeneutics is illustrated in the diagram below:

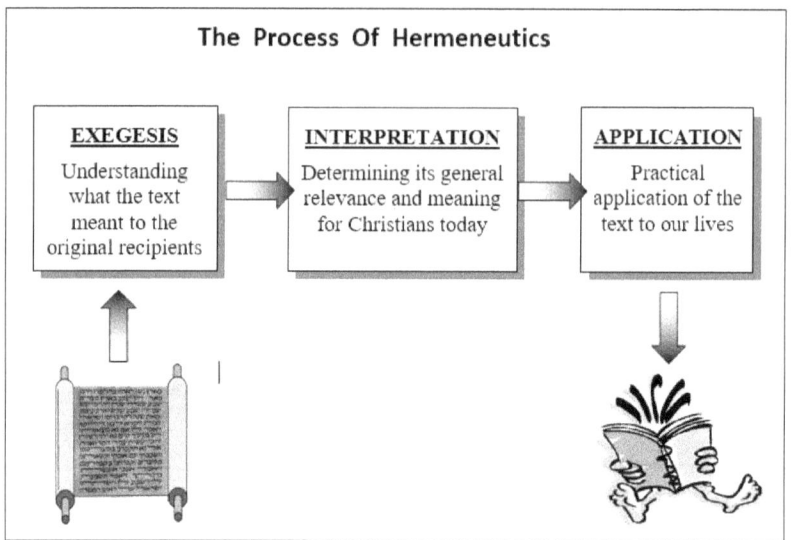

EXEGESIS AND INTERPRETATION

The term *exegesis* comes from the Greek, ἐξηγεῖσθαι, (*exegesthai*),"'*to lead out*". It refers to the process of obtaining the original meaning *out* of the text, as opposed to *eisegesis*, which refers to reading our own meaning *into* the text.

The very real risk of eisegesis has already been identified in Chapter 5. It is almost inevitable that we bring our own bias to any text we are reading. As we read a Bible passage, we tend to filter it through the lens of our preconceptions, our experiences and our already established doctrinal beliefs. The task of exegesis is to, as much as possible, lay aside our natural biases and discover what the text meant to the original writer and recipients. Once we know the original meaning, interpretation then takes over, answering the question, *"In what sense does this text have general relevance for Christians today?"* Once that is established, application helps us "put legs" on a biblical truth, by answering the question, *"How should this truth be applied and lived out in my life?"* Exegesis, interpretation and application are overlapping components of hermeneutics that are essential skills if we are to understand and apply the Bible accurately.

Example: Taking Up Your Cross:

A simple example will illustrate how these three concepts work together. Consider Jesus' statement;

> *"If anyone would come after me, he must deny himself and take up his cross daily and follow me" (Luke 9:23).*

Exegesis

What did this statement mean to Jesus' first century audience? We need to understand something of the culture of first century punishment if we are to make sense of this verse. In Roman colonies in the first century a criminal who was sentenced to crucifixion, was made to walk through all the streets of the town, often naked, carrying his cross on his shoulders before finally being crucified. It was a form of public humiliation, designed to parade his misdemeanours before the entire town and instil a healthy fear of breaking the law among those who witnessed the procession. People would line the streets and jeer at the condemned man, throwing rotten food and stones at him as he walked by. Everyone knew that a man who was carrying his cross was about to die:

- He had lost his freedom: He could no longer go where he wanted, but was chained and dragged around at the end of a rope.

- He had lost his dignity: He was naked, bloody and bruised.

- He had lost his rights: He had lost *all* rights, including the right to life itself. His life was no longer his own; he was a *"dead man walking"*.

When Jesus said that in order to follow him a person must *"take up his cross daily"*, it evoked a powerful, emotive image that would have been very familiar to his audience. They had all seen crucifixion parades. They knew what it meant to *"take up a cross"*. His use of the word *"daily"*, however, made it obvious that he was speaking metaphorically. His listeners would have understood his meaning implicitly. Jesus was saying that becoming his follower is not simply a matter of belief. It means handing control of your life over to him. It means that your life is no longer your own; you have lost the freedom to live as you like. You are now led by Someone else; Christ. You are Christ's captive, and your life belongs to him now.

Interpretation

What relevance does this have to Christians today? Does it apply to us too? There is no doubt that this verse applies across the ages to us as well. Using the principal of interpreting Scripture with Scripture, we find Jesus, in the very next verse saying, *"whoever wants to save his life will lose it, but whoever loses his life for me will save it" (Luke 9:24)*. Similarly, Paul writes, *"You are not your own, you were bought with a price" (1 Cor 6:20)*. Clearly, this is a timeless truth that depicts the cost of commitment to Christ, involving self-denial, sacrifice and obedience to him as Lord.

Application

How does this apply practically to my life? Preachers delivering sermons would at this point attempt to "put legs" on this concept. They would attempt to define what it means to die to self and live for Christ. They would give practical examples of turning from sin to live in holiness; turning from selfish ambition to seek first God's kingdom; being willing to suffer rejection and persecution for the sake of Christ.

In this simple example, you can see the way in which all three elements of hermeneutics - exegesis, interpretation and application - work together to enable you to understand and apply the Bible's message appropriately.

PRINCIPLES OF HERMENEUTICS

Because we are removed from the writing of the Bible in terms of time, language and culture, hermeneutics is essential if we are to understand its message properly. Over the next few chapters we will examine the major accepted principles of hermeneutics:

- Understanding the different literary genres within the Bible

- Revelatory context

- Historical and cultural context

- Literary context (immediate context and wider context)

- Lexical context (the precise meaning of the original Greek and Hebrew words)

- Application principles

Reflection Questions 12

(You may want to combine this chapter and the next in the one study session)

1. What new insight have you gained from this chapter?

2. How does an understanding of first century crucifixion processions help us to understand Christ's injunction to "take up your cross daily" (Luke 9:23)?

CHAPTER 13

LITERARY GENRE

The writers of the Bible employed a wide variety of literary styles to convey God's truth, including historical narrative, poetry, songs, prophecy, wisdom literature, apocalyptic literature, letters, laws, parables and genealogies. Each of these literary forms, or genres, need to be interpreted differently. For instance, the historical narrative of Acts requires a different set of interpretive rules to the didactic (instructional) letters of Paul in the New Testament. Failure to understand the unique aspects of each literary genre can (and often does!) result in poor exegesis (misinterpreting the meaning of the text) and questionable doctrine.

One of the first principles of hermeneutics is to understand the distinctive aspects of each literary genre, and interpret each one appropriately. This chapter provides a basic overview of some of the main literary genres used in the Bible, and the appropriate interpretive approach for each one.

HISTORICAL NARRATIVE

The genre of historical narrative recounts historical events by telling a story. Over half of the Old Testament is comprised of historical narrative (Genesis to Job, plus Daniel). The New Testament contains the book of Acts, which is also an historical narrative. When reading any form of historical narrative, it is important to understand its purpose and its limitations. Failure to do so can, and often does, result in applications being made that were not intended by the writer. The following is a brief summary of the key elements of this literary genre, and some important principles for interpreting it.

1. Historical narrative is descriptive rather than prescriptive.

Historical narrative describes *what* happened, but does not usually give an explanation as to *why* it happened, nor even whether it *should* have happened or should *continue* to happen today. It does not necessarily include moral judgments about whether the actions or events were good or bad, but simply records the facts as they occurred. For instance, Judges 6 records Gideon laying a fleece before God to test his will. The narrative does not say whether this was a wise or unwise action on Gideon's part, it simply records that this is what he did. Many Christians have read this and assumed that "laying a fleece" is an acceptable method of discerning God's will. This, unfortunately, misses the point of the Gideon narrative; that God saved Israel through Gideon *despite* his lack of trust in God. The fact that Gideon had to pre-empt his second "fleecing" by saying to God *"do not be angry with me" (Judges 6:39)* is a subtle clue by the narrator that Gideon's actions were testing God's patience, and that his use of the fleece to test God arose from doubt and fear rather than from faith. It showed a lack of trust in God's clear direction that had *already* been given to him (Judges 6:14-16).

For this reason, Gideon's method of laying a fleece is not ordinarily considered to be an acceptable or mature method of seeking God's will. But this is not explicitly stated in the narrative because historical narratives, by their very nature, do not usually make overt value judgments of this kind; they simply record the facts. Basing our praxis upon historical narrative can be misleading and harmful, because we may well be emulating actions that are unwise or foolish.

2. Historical narrative is documentary rather than doctrinal.

With the exception of a few passages, such as the handing down of the Ten Commandments in Exodus 20, historical narrative does not overtly purport to teach doctrine. This does not mean that historical narrative does not have a theological purpose. Each narrative is constructed with a clear theological purpose in mind. The book of Ruth, for example, has the strong theme of redemption running through it. The writer intends us to see it both as an illustration of God's redeeming grace and, also, of Israel's call to be a light to the Gentiles. These are the two big theological themes underlying the story. Both themes are clearly taught *propositionally* in didactic (instructional) portions of Scripture elsewhere, but they are *illustrated* for us in the story of Ruth. The purpose of historical narrative is not to instruct *propositionally*, but to document *illustratively*.

The theological themes within historical narratives are *implicit* rather than *explicit*. The writer allows the story to speak for itself and assumes a certain level of knowledge within the reader. In the story of Ruth, for example, the concept of Israel being a light for the salvation of the Gentiles is nowhere explicitly stated within the narrative. It is *illustrated* by Boaz, an Israelite, taking pity on Ruth, a Moabite widow, by marrying her and, in so doing, redeeming her and enfolding her into the family of God. In telling this story the writer assumes familiarity with God's *explicit* covenantal declaration to Abraham that *"through your offspring all nations on earth will be blessed" (Gen 26:4)*. This truth is embedded within the story, but not explicitly stated. Such is the nature of historical narrative.

3. Historical narrative is general rather than specific.

Any theological understanding that we glean from historical narrative will be general, rather than detailed and specific. Historical narrative aims to illustrate big theological themes, but does not provide us with a precise treatise of individual doctrines; that is saved for didactic (instructional) Scripture. The book of Acts, for example, illustrates the growth and development of God's church on earth as it was empowered by the Holy Spirit. The big theological themes of Acts are:

- Christ's work on earth continued after his resurrection, through his Holy Spirit.

- The growth of this new movement called Christianity was clearly the work of God, not man.

- Gentiles were intended by God to be included in the church.

These themes are taught *precisely* and *explicitly* in the didactic letters of the New Testament, but are only illustrated *generally* and *implicitly* in the Acts narrative. If we are to understand these doctrines clearly, we must gain that understanding from the didactic letters rather than from the Acts narrative. Exactly how are the Gentiles included in the church? What is their relation to the Jews now that they are all *"in Christ"*? What is to be their relationship to the laws of Moses? How are Jewish and Gentile Christians to function together? These, and many other questions, are only definitively addressed in the propositional teaching of the New Testament letters. Precise doctrinal understanding only comes from didactic Scripture; historical narrative simply paints the big picture. In fact, it is only because of the clear exposition of these doctrines in didactic Scripture that we can perceive them as embedded within the story of Acts.

Historical narrative, therefore, is to be distinguished from didactic Scripture which contains propositional truths whose clear purpose is precise doctrinal instruction. Christian doctrine is to be founded primarily upon these didactic portions of Scripture rather than upon historical narrative.

4. Historical precedent can only be established as normative when it is explicitly stated as such.

In other words, just because something occurred in the book of Acts does not mean that it should *always* happen that way; that it should be considered as "normative" or universally binding upon all future Christians.

Consider the example, in Acts 2, of the fellowship of the early Christians in Jerusalem after the day of Pentecost. Luke states that *"every day they continued to meet together in the temple courts" (Acts 2:46)*. This is a wonderful description of the commitment and enthusiasm of these first Christians, but we cannot infer from this that all Christians must meet together daily. There is no indication, either explicitly stated in Acts or elsewhere in Scripture, that this historical precedent should be considered as normative.

For an historical precedent to be considered normative, there must be a clear statement to that effect, either in the narrative itself or elsewhere in Scripture. For instance, in the evangelistic sermons recorded for us in Acts, the concept of repentance is always strongly preached. We know that this is a normative, essential part of the gospel message because the didactic passages of Scripture elsewhere declare it to be so (2 Cor 7:10; 2 Pet 3;9).

Consider another example; the "choosing of the seven" in Acts 6. The Apostles instructed the newly converted Grecian Jews in Jerusalem to *"choose seven men from among you" (v.3)* to oversee the daily distribution of bread to the Grecian widows. A rift had developed between those who had been converted from the Grecian synagogue (Greek speaking Jews born in other lands) and those from the Hebraic synagogue (Hebrew speaking Jews born in Israel). The widows of the Grecian Jews were being overlooked in the daily distribution of bread. To remedy this problem, the Apostles instructed the church to appoint *"seven men"* to oversee the daily distribution of bread. This would allow the Apostles to devote themselves to the preaching of the gospel. Some Christians have seized upon this passage as an example of the election of deacons, and use it as a proof text to substantiate democratic elections as *normative* for the church. Several points need to be made:

- To view these men as the first deacons may not be entirely accurate, as at least some of them were also involved in preaching the gospel and working miracles (Acts 6:8f).

- To say that they were chosen by democratic election is to go beyond what is written. We are simply told that the Grecian Jews *chose* them. This does not necessarily mean that they *voted*. The men may well have been simply selected and appointed by the elders of the Grecian synagogue. Democratic election is by no means clear.

- Later in the book of Acts we read that *"Paul and Barnabus appointed elders in each church" (Acts 14:23).* This appointment of church leaders contradicts the model of democratic election supposedly illustrated by Acts 6. Not only is democratic election not *clear* in Acts, it is also not *universal.*

- Democratic election of church ministries is not taught propositionally in the New Testament letters. The only clear statement about how people were chosen for ministry is found in Titus 1:5 where Paul instructs Timothy to *"appoint elders in every town".* The concept of democratic election is, therefore, not *substantiated* by didactic Scripture.

The historical narrative of Acts 6 makes no attempt to formulate any type of ecclesiological doctrine, nor does it make any claim for this to be seen as prescriptive; it simply records what took place. Prescribing doctrine is not the purpose of historical narrative. The differing ecclesiological practices recorded in Acts in relation to the appointment of leaders and servants within the church should, if anything, cause us to be wary of formulating any dogmatic doctrines of church practice. This is not to say that democratic election as a form of church appointments is wrong; just that it cannot be substantiated as normative from the book of Acts or from anywhere else in Scripture.

The above example illustrates some important principles for establishing normative precedent in historical narratives. For normative precedent to be established, it must be:

- Clear: There must be no ambiguity about the nature of the behaviour or action. In the case of democratic election in Acts 6, it cannot be unequivocally established that such a process took place.

- Universal: There must be no exceptions or contradictions. In the previous example, there are several contradictory instances of church leaders and officers being *"appointed"* rather than elected (Acts 14:23; Titus 1:5).

- Prescribed in didactic Scripture: Only when it is substantiated by unambiguous propositional teaching can we be sure of a normative precedent.

It is possible for a certain practice to be universal within a historical narrative without it being binding upon all future Christians as normative practice. Take, for example, the Lord's Supper, which seems to have been universally practised as part of a whole meal. This is certainly how Jesus instituted it (Luke 22) and how the early church continued to practise it (Acts 2:46, 1 Cor 11). Yet, this particular manner of celebrating the Lord's Supper as part of a whole meal is not regarded by most Christians as universally binding because it is not prescribed in didactic Scripture as normative. In order to establish normative precedent from historical narrative, the behaviour must be *clear*, it must be *universal* within the narrative *and* it must be explicitly *prescribed* as normative, either within the narrative or in didactic Scripture elsewhere.

THE GIFT OF TONGUES IN ACTS

No issue better highlights the difficulties and inherent dangers of using historical narrative for building doctrines than the issue of the gift of tongues, recorded in Acts. At the risk of being controversial, let us briefly examine this issue to see if we can put our interpretive principles into practice. The starting point is to examine what the book of Acts documents about the occurrences of the gift of tongues.

Rick Walston, a Pentecostal preacher and theologian, makes a very good observation:

> *"The fact that Luke [in Acts] gives three accounts of people who spoke in tongues in association with the baptism with the Holy Spirit is not to be discarded, but neither is it to be elevated to theological dogma. Truth certainly can be gleaned from historical narrative, but one must be careful not to draw universal, conclusive norms based on occasional happenings within the historical narrative. Luke's account seems to indicate that speaking in tongues is a normal Christian experience, but the account does not provide an adequate exegetical basis to make it a norm."* ("The Speaking in Tongues Controversy", Rick Walston, p.152)

At this point it is important to differentiate between *normal* and *normative*. To describe something as *normal* means that it is not strange or out of place. To describe something as *normative* means that it is universal – without exception. Thus, it is *normal* to catch a cold in winter (it is not unusual), but it is not *normative* to do so (because not *everyone* will catch a cold in winter).

The book of Acts indicates that tongue-speaking among the first century Christians was *normal* (falling within the spectrum of normal Christian behaviour) but not *normative* (not universal or essential for every Christian).

The book of Acts records 26 conversion accounts, over a 20-year period, but there are only 3 accounts of people speaking in tongues:

- Tongues in Jerusalem (Acts 2:1-13): Fifty days after Christ's resurrection, on the Day of Pentecost, the Holy Spirit first indwelt believers. About 120 disciples were *"filled with the Holy Spirit and began to speak in other tongues as the Holy Spirit enabled them"* (Acts 2:4).

- Tongues in Caesarea (Acts 10:44-48): Several years later (about 35-38 AD), in the home of Cornelius, a Roman centurion, Cornelius and his whole household were converted as Peter preached to them. They *"received the Holy Spirit"* (Acts 10:47) and began speaking in tongues and praising God. This miraculous outpouring of the Spirit was a sign for Peter and the Jewish Christians that God had made salvation available to the Gentiles as well.

- Tongues in Ephesus (Acts 19:1-7): Thirteen years later (about 51 AD), Paul encountered twelve disciples of John the Baptist, and preached to them about their need to place their trust in Jesus the Messiah. They were *"baptised into the name of the Lord Jesus"* (v.5), after which *"the Holy Spirit came on them and they spoke in tongues"* (v.6). This was another important watershed in the early church development, as it signified the incorporation of John's disciples into the Christian church, and the harvesting of the seeds of repentance that John had faithfully sown.

Apart from these three instances, there is no evidence of tongues-speaking in the remainder of the book of Acts. There is no mention of new converts speaking in tongues in the remaining 23 conversion accounts recorded in Acts. These include the 3,000 on the Day of Pentecost (2:41), the Ethiopian eunuch (8:36-39), Saul (9:1-9), the "great number" in Antioch (11:21), the "multitude" in Iconium (14:1), as well as Lydia, the Philippian jailer, and their households (16:14,15,30-34).

When all the new converts recorded in the book of Acts are estimated and tallied, only about 12% of those converted are recorded as speaking in tongues. An argument for tongues being universal and normative in the New Testament church simply *cannot* be predicated upon the book of Acts.

Speaking in tongues as a normative Christian experience is a doctrine that cannot legitimately be established from the book of Acts. Furthermore, even if every instance of conversion recorded in Acts *did* describe accompanying tongue speaking, insisting upon tongue-speaking as normative experience based upon this evidence alone would be a *non-sequitur* (illogical conclusion). In such a hypothetical scenario (recorded tongue speaking in 100% of conversions), Luke *may* have intended us to view tongue speaking as normative, but he could just as easily have recorded these particular events because they were *exceptional*. The point is, we are not told. Such is the often-ambiguous nature of historical narrative. This is why didactic Scripture is required in order to correctly interpret historical narrative.

Regarding whether speaking in tongues is normative, we are, in fact, given a clear *didactic* statement in 1 Corinthians 12:30; *"Do all speak in tongues? No."* While the word "no" is not printed in all English translations, the inclusion of the implied "no" (in Greek, *"mer"*) is present in the Greek text at the end of each of the rhetorical questions asked by Paul in that passage. This was a common Greek grammatical convention employed when a writer wanted his readers to understand that the answer to a rhetorical question was "no". The International Standard Version Bible renders this passage best:

> *"Not all are apostles, are they? Not all are prophets, are they? Not all are teachers, are they? Not all perform miracles, do they? Not all have the gift of healing, do they? Not all speak in tongues, do they? Not all interpret, do they?" (1Co 12:29-30)*

The clear *didactic* statements of 1Corinthians 12:29-30 enables us to interpret the *historical narrative* of the book of Acts. From this we can conclude that speaking in tongues may be *normal* Christian behaviour, but it is definitely not *normative* (universal).

This example illustrates how *didactic*, prescriptive passages must be used to interpret *historical narrative*, whose purpose is descriptive rather than prescriptive.

DIDACTIC LETTERS

Much of the New Testament comprises letters by Paul and other writers to churches and individual Christians in the first century. Letters contain a more direct, instructional nature than most other literary genres. They contain prescriptive passages of theological truths and authoritative instructions for living the Christian life. Because of their didactic nature, a more direct interpretive approach is possible than with historical narrative. This does not mean, however, that *every* imperative in a biblical letter can be applied directly to us. Some important hermeneutical considerations still need to be employed:

1. Recognise Cultural Relativity

Because letters were written by first century Christians to other first century Christians, they sometimes address historical and cultural issues that were relevant to them but no longer relevant to us. For instance, although Paul commands that women should have their heads covered in church (1 Cor 11:5) we do not accept this as a command that applies today because of our understanding that, in first century Israel, only prostitutes and brazen women went about with their heads uncovered. This cultural situation no longer exists, and so the command is no longer relevant. Similarly, Paul's injunction to *"greet one another with a holy kiss" (Rom 16:16)* arises from the first century cultural practice of kissing as a sign of deferential respect that does not exist today. The New Testament's condemnation of homosexuality (Rom 1:27; 1 Cor 6:9), however, is not a matter of cultural relativity. In fact, the biblical prohibition against homosexuality was *counter-cultural* in the world of the first century, where homosexuality was a widely accepted practice. There is also no hint of cultural relativity in Paul's emphatic statement that *"the wicked will not inherit the kingdom of God ...neither the sexually immoral ... nor homosexual offenders ... will inherit the kingdom of God"* (1 Cor 6:9).

2. Distinguish Between the General Principle and the Application

Even though the New Testament letters sometimes address cultural issues that are no longer relevant, there are underlying principles that are still applicable to us. Paul's discussion of meat offered to idols (1 Cor 8 and 10) deals with a cultural issue that does not exist for most people in the Western world today; whether it is morally acceptable to purchase and eat meat from a butcher that is attached to a pagan temple where the meat being sold was slaughtered as an act of worship to that particular idol. (Such meat, in the ancient world, was often cheaper than meat sold through regular outlets). Clearly this situation no longer applies to Christians living in the Western world. Paul's instructions concerning this matter, however, reveal two general principles that can still be applied:

- Firstly, the issue of food and drink is a matter of indifference to God, in the sense that it does not make us more or less acceptable to him.

- Secondly, we should refrain from an activity that may be a matter of indifference *if* it places another believer in danger of having their faith "destroyed" (1 Cor 8:11).

3. Only Apply the General Principle to Genuinely Comparable Situations

Care needs to be taken to not stretch a general principle to apply to a situation that is significantly dissimilar to the original. For example, the previously mentioned "stumbling-block" principle (1 Cor 8) only applies in situations where the exercise of one's freedom has the potential to *"destroy"* (v.11) another person's faith. This principle does *not* refer to something that merely offends another believer who happens to have a different opinion on the matter. It should not be used, for example, by a Christian who wishes to pressure another Christian to conform to his standard because of his claim to be offended. If the matter is truly one of indifference to God, and the supposedly offended Christian is not in any danger of emulating the action and going against his own conscience, then the one whose conscience is clear in the matter is free to continue his practice. In such a case there is no biblical mandate to force compliance upon Christians in matters of indifference.

4. Distinguish Between Matters of Indifference and Eternal Morals

This is an important distinction that is sometimes not easy to resolve. We have already seen that the New Testament identifies food offered to idols as a matter of indifference. Paul extends this to all food in general (1 Cor 8:8). In other words, there is no food that is wrong for a Christian to eat. In Romans 14, Paul extends this to the drinking of alcohol as well. This is a disputed issue in Christianity, as there are some who maintain that the drinking of alcohol, even in moderation, is a sin. They categorise abstinence from alcohol as a timeless, universal moral rather than a matter of indifference. Yet, at the risk of offending such brethren, this does not seem to be Paul's meaning in Romans 14.

The central theme of the Romans 14 is that we should *not* pass judgment on one another for decisions in matters of indifference to God. In verses 1-8 he states that Christians are free to choose to eat meat or not, and to keep the Sabbath or not, and that we should *not* judge one another for our decisions in these matters. He points out that *"He who eats meat, eats to the Lord ... and he who abstains does so to the Lord" (Rom 14:6)*. In other words, these kinds of issues are matters of indifference; they are for each person to decide for themselves. In verse 17 he extends this to alcohol as well; *"For the kingdom of God is not a matter of eating or drinking, but of righteousness ..."*. Paul then concludes the chapter with the "stumbling-block" principle, *"It is better not to eat meat or drink wine or to do anything else that will cause your brother to fall" (Rom 14:21)*.

The inference of this passage is clear. Drinking alcohol is in the same category as eating meat; both are matters of personal choice that are only to be avoided if, by partaking in their consumption, you will cause another weaker Christian to emulate you and *"destroy"* their faith (1 Cor 8:11).

That abstinence from alcohol is clearly a matter of personal choice and not a mandatory Christian ethic is seen from Paul's instruction to Timothy to *"stop drinking only water and <u>drink a little wine</u> because of your stomach" (1 Tim 5:23),* and also by his statement that *"whether you eat or drink, do it all for the glory of God (1 Cor 10:31).* His injunction, in 1 Timothy 3:8, that deacons be people who *"do not indulge in much wine"* (and also in Eph 5:18 and Titus 2:3) is clearly a prohibition against excess, rather than a command for total abstinence.

The fact that there is still debate and disagreement among Christians on the issue of alcohol, shows how difficult it can be to distinguish between matters of personal preference and eternal moral imperatives. It also reveals our tendency to bring our personal bias and church traditions to our reading of Scripture. Often, when confronted with a verse or passage which challenges a previously held conviction, our immediate, subconscious attitude is, *"How can I explain this passage so that it fits in with my current belief?"* The task of serious Bible students is to approach the Scriptures with a desire to read them with uncluttered vision and a willingness to be shaped by them, rather than to shape them into conformity with our own beliefs.

PRAYERS AND SONGS

Psalms is a book of prayers and songs addressed to God, poetic in form, and written over many centuries. Many of them were used in public worship of God by the people of Israel. They vary greatly in nature; petition, worship, confession, cries of anguish and declarations of faith. They are not didactic in intention. Their purpose was not doctrinal instruction. They were written to assist the ancient Hebrews in the expression of their faith to God. It is a book of prayer and praise, rather than a book of doctrine.

While the book of Psalms certainly contains some beautiful expressions of theological truth, these need to be interpreted carefully, with a clear understanding of Hebrew poetry. Here are some helpful hermeneutic principles:

1. Parallelism

Many of the Psalms incorporate synonymous parallelism, where a single thought or concept is expressed in two lines, with the second line repeating and reinforcing the first. For instance; *"The heavens declare the glory of God; the skies proclaim his handiwork" (Psalm 19:1)*. Understanding parallelism helps us to interpret these verses correctly. Both halves of the verse are saying the same thing in different words. The word *"heavens"* is not a reference to God's dwelling place. It is used in parallelism with *"skies"*, and so it is apparent that they are both speaking of the same thing; the physical firmament of stars and sky.

2. Metaphors

As poems, the Psalms are full of rich metaphors. God is described as a shepherd, rock, shield and fortress. Other examples of metaphors are, *"I am a worm, not a man" (22:6)*, and *"Many bulls surround me ... roaring lions tearing their prey open their mouths wide against me" (22:12-13)* and *"men whose teeth are spears and arrows" (57:4)*. Clearly these cannot be taken literally. The difficulty, of course, lies in determining whether a statement is a metaphor or whether it is literal. For example, there are over 100 Bible verses which refer to either the *"hand of God"* or the *"finger of God"*. To infer from these, however, that God literally has physical hands, would be to define him as a physical being, which would completely contradict his metaphysical nature (*"God is Spirit"*, John 4:24) and his transcendent omni-presence (Psalm 139), taught throughout the Scriptures. Clearly, we must interpret references to God's "hand" or "finger" as being metaphorical depictions of his interventional actions in our world.

Determining whether something is a metaphor or literal can have a significant impact upon doctrine! In many cases, such as the one above, interpreting a specific reference in the wider context of the teaching of Scripture elsewhere is an important principle for determining whether a statement is literal or metaphorical.

3. Expressions of Lament

As well as songs of praise and expressions of joyous celebration, the Psalms also contain expressions of great sadness and grief; the outpouring of raw emotion at times of great distress. At times, this outpouring of emotion can involve hyperbole; exaggerations which should not be taken literally. For example:

> *"How long, O Lord? Will you forget me forever?" (Psa 13:1)*

> *"Why, Lord, do you stand far off? Why do you hide yourself in times of trouble?" (Psa 10:1)*

In these instances, the psalmist is expressing his *feeling* that God is far from him. As expressions of a feeling, these statements are valid and poignant, but they do not represent truth in the theological sense. The New Testament declares that *"God is not far from any of us, since it is in God that we live and move and exist." (Acts 17:27-28)*. Nor does the omniscient (all-knowing) God *"forget"* anything or anyone. We must, therefore, regard these kinds of statements as expressions of the pain of *perceived* separation from God, not necessarily God's *actual* distance from the psalmist. Hyperbole is often used in the Psalms to express extremes of emotion, and we must be careful not to attach literal theological meaning to such statements unless it is clear elsewhere.

WISDOM LITERATURE

The books of Proverbs, Job and Ecclesiastes are a particular genre of writing known as wisdom literature. This genre is unfamiliar to most modern Christians and, because of this, these books are often misinterpreted and misapplied.

Wisdom literature in the ancient world was a genre that sought to express a wise understanding of life by examining the behaviours and choices of people and their corresponding consequences. The wisdom books of the Bible are of this nature. They are not overtly theological, but tend, rather, to focus on the practical side of life. The book of Proverbs is a good example. It is a collection of brief, pithy statements that provide wise reflections on the practical issues of life.

Here are some useful hermeneutical guidelines for interpreting biblical wisdom literature, and proverbs in particular:

1. Some Proverbs Are Generalisations

They state what generally happens, in a simplified form, but we must not think that they are universal truths or that they include every nuance of the truth. For example:

> *"Commit to the Lord whatever you do, and your plans will succeed" (Prov 16:3)*

This is the most commonly misinterpreted kind of proverb. These kinds of proverbs attempt to condense into short, pithy statements, truths that are often very complex. In condensing the truth, the proverb captures the central concept but does not elaborate on the associated contributing factors and conditions. In this case, the proverb is stating that the key to a successful life is living a life that is committed to God. It is *not* saying that if you have a plan you would like to implement, you can simply ask God to help you and he will always make it happen! Clearly, this is not a *carte blanche* licence guaranteeing the success of any harebrained scheme or self-focused desire that we decide to pray about. There are many other biblical conditions that need to be factored in, before we can be assured that God will bless our plans; factors like the will of God (1 John 5:14) and having pure motives (Jms 4:3).

2. Some Proverbs Are Hyperbolic.

Some proverbs speak in exaggerated terms. For example:

> *"If a ruler listens to lies, all his officials become wicked" (Prov 29:12)*

This proverb describes the fact that if someone in authority does not want to be told the truth, those under him tend to oblige by telling him the lies he wants to hear. They join him in his wickedness. While this is certainly true generally, it does not mean that it is impossible to remain truthful if you are under such authority. There are examples of people who have remained truthful and godly while working under dishonest leadership. Hyperbole is used (*"all his officials"*) simply to stress the overwhelming tendency of corruption to spread from the top down.

3. Some Proverbs Are Metaphorical.

For example:

> *"The Lord tears down the house of the proud, but he sets the widow's boundary stones in place" (Prov 15:25)*

Physical metaphors such as this are sometimes used to describe a spiritual truth that is proposed more esoterically elsewhere. In this case, this proverb is expounding the same truth proposed by the Apostle James, *"God opposes the proud but gives grace to the humble" (Jms 4:6)*. Obviously, God is not literally tearing down the homes of every person who is proud. Not only do we have to understand proverbs like this as metaphors, but we also need to combine this principle of interpretation with the principles regarding generalisations and hyperbole. We should not see this proverb as universally true in every circumstance. We cannot assume that it will *always* go well for the humble and that the proud will *always* be somehow thwarted by God in this life. Jeremiah comments that sometimes the opposite seems to happen: *"Why does the way of the wicked prosper? Why do all the faithless live at ease?" (Jer 12:1)*

4. Some Proverbs Are Warnings Couched in The Terminology of Prohibition.

Consider the following:

> *"Do not be the one who shakes hands in pledge, or puts up security for debts; if you lack the means to pay, your very bed will be snatched from you". (Prov 22:26-27)*

Some people have interpreted this to be an absolute prohibition against entering into debt or incurring a mortgage. While this is literally what the words say (*"Do not ..."*) we are not meant to interpret it as a universal, literal prohibition of secured debt. The proverb is a warning against the very real danger of "losing everything" if you enter into debt <u>unwisely</u>. It is a strong warning to make sure you have *"the means to pay"* before incurring contractual debt. The use of prohibitive language in proverbs such as this, needs to be interpreted as another form of hyperbole, rather than as literally and universally prohibitive.

ECCLESIASTES

Ecclesiastes, another example of biblical wisdom literature, is a very difficult book to interpret, even dividing Bible scholars as to its proper interpretation. The view of the majority of scholars is that the book portrays the meaninglessness of life without a relationship with God and without any hope of life beyond the grave. Only at the very end of the book does the writer refer to God at all, in what is clearly a warning of the inevitable judgment that awaits mankind:

LITERARY GENRE

Ecc 12:13-14 "Now all has been heard; here is the conclusion of the matter: Fear God and keep his commandments, for this is the whole duty of man. For God will bring every deed into judgment, including every hidden thing, whether it is good or evil."

The book of Ecclesiastes, therefore, seems to be a vivid portrayal of the dismal worldview of the person without faith and without hope. This view of Ecclesiastes certainly accounts for the many statements contained within it that are the antithesis of the Bible's teaching elsewhere:

ECCLESIASTES	THE REST OF THE BIBLE
Eccl 1:14 "I have seen all the things that are done under the sun, and all of them are meaningless – a chasing after the wind."	**Col 3:23** "Whatever you do, work at it with all your heart, as working for the Lord, not for men" **Col 3:17** "And whatever you do, whether in word or deed, do it all in the name of the Lord Jesus, giving thanks to God the Father through him".
Eccl 2:15 "What do I gain by being wise? This too is meaningless"	**Prov 3:13 & 4:5** "Blessed is the man who finds wisdom, the man who gains understanding, ... Get wisdom, get understanding; do not forget my words or swerve from them".
Eccl 2:24 "A man can do nothing better than to eat, drink and find happiness in his work"	**Luke 12:19-20** "And I'll say to myself, "You have plenty of good things laid up for many years. Take life easy; eat, drink and be merry."' (20) "But God said to him, 'You fool! This very night your life will be demanded from you. Then who will get what you have prepared for yourself?'
Eccl 3:19 "Man's fate is like that of the animals; the same fate awaits them both. Man has no advantage over the animal"	**1Thes 4:17-18** "After that, we who are still alive and are left will be caught up together with them in the clouds to meet the Lord in the air. And so, we will be with the Lord forever. (18) Therefore encourage each other with these words".
Eccl 9:2 "All people share a common destiny- the righteous and the wicked, the good and the bad"	**Matt 25:46** "Then the wicked will go away to eternal punishment, but the righteous to eternal life."

APOCALYPTIC LITERATURE

Although the last book of the Bible, the book of Revelation, contains some sections which are letters and some which are prophecy, it is primarily apocalyptic. There were dozens, perhaps even hundreds, of apocalyptic books written from 200 B.C. to 200 A.D., and they share some common elements:

- They were written during times of hardship or persecution.

- They looked ahead to the end of the world, the judgment and the final triumph of good over evil.

- They contained dreams and visions that were full of fantasy images (beasts with multiple heads, etc.) rather than the common images that Jesus used (salt, bread, vineyards, etc).

- They were full of symbolism involving numbers and patterns.

The non-canonised (not included in the Bible) apocalyptic writings were works of imagination by writers who claimed to have experienced visions of fantastic images depicting the cataclysmic events of the end of the age. Many of the false religions of the ancient world were replete with apocryphal sacred writings of this nature. What sets John's apocalyptic book apart from the others of his time, is his assertion that his visions were directly from God and, more particularly, that it was Jesus himself who directed him to record what he saw and heard.

> *Rev 1:9-11 "I, John, your brother and companion in the suffering and kingdom and patient endurance that are ours in Jesus, was on the island of Patmos because of the word of God and the testimony of Jesus. On the Lord's Day I was in the Spirit, and I heard behind me a loud voice like a trumpet, which said: "Write on a scroll what you see ..."*

The book of Revelation is a difficult book to interpret, because 21st century readers are not familiar with apocalyptic writing. All kinds of conflicting interpretations of Revelation are made because of the lack of understanding of this genre. The people of the 1st century, however, had no such problem, because they understood the conventions of apocalyptic writing.

The following are a few of the more important rules for interpreting apocalyptic literature generally, and Revelation in particular, that might help us navigate through this strange and perplexing book.

1. Apocalyptic literature is like a painting that is meant to be viewed as a whole, rather than examined with a magnifying glass.

The 1st century Christians understood this implicitly and would not have tried to assign specific meaning to every detail of John's visions. What was important was the big picture of God's eventual triumph over evil, his punishment of the wicked, his salvation of the righteous, his renewal of the earth in perfection and the final establishment of his eternal kingdom of peace and joy. It is these major themes of the painting that we are meant to focus upon, rather than attempting to work out what the ten horns on the beast from the sea represent.

For example, the first four horsemen (Rev 6) and the first four trumpets (Rev 8) of God's judgement are best seen as different brushstrokes depicting God's impending judgment on his enemies, rather than trying to interpret them as successive periods of history or separate and distinct waves of judgment.

This principle, of viewing the entire book as one big painting, is the most important principle for its interpretation, yet it is the one that is most commonly ignored. The best way to read the book of Revelation is in one or two sittings, from beginning to end, letting the visions wash over you as you gain a sense of the big picture of the impending ultimate victory of good over evil.

2. The book of Revelation was, firstly, a prophetic word to the churches of the 1st century, before it was a book about the end of the world.

The apocalyptic prophecies that the book of Revelation contains, have a dual fulfilment, the first of which was the imminent fall of the Roman empire and God's judgment upon it for the persecution of his church. The 1st century Christians were suffering at the time of John's writing, and their suffering was about to increase. John himself, at the time of his visions, was incarcerated in a Roman penal colony on the island of Patmos. Many of the images in John's visions relate directly to this more immediate fulfilment and would have been recognisable to the 1st century Christians. Scholars suggest that the original recipients of this book would have seen it as being *primarily* about the downfall of Rome and only *dimly* about the end of the world.

This dual mixture of temporal (near) and eschatological (far) fulfilments of John's visions makes Revelation a difficult book to interpret. The wise reader would do well to avoid dogmatic assertions as to the "correct" interpretation of any parts of it.

3. The only interpretations of which we can be certain are those identified by the book of Revelation itself.

There are six images which are interpreted for us within the book itself:

- The *"one like a son of man"* is Christ (1:13).

- The golden lamp stands are the seven churches (1:20).

- The seven stars are the seven angels of the seven churches (1:20).

- The great dragon is Satan (12:9).

- The seven heads are the seven hills on which the woman sits (17:9).

- The prostitute is the great city (Rome) (17:18).

These are the only interpretations of which we can be certain, because they are revealed for us by the Bible itself. Given the large number of conflicting interpretations of the many other fantastic images within the book of Revelation, it would seem arrogant to become too dogmatic about any single interpretation.

With the previous proviso firmly in mind, there are some images in John's vision which are common images in all or most 1st century apocalyptic writing, and which had standard meanings that were commonly understood:

- White horseman = conquest

- Red horseman = war

- Black horseman = famine

- Pale horseman = death

- Beast out of the sea = world empire (*not* an individual ruler)

These were common images in ancient apocalyptic writing which God apparently incorporated into the vision he gave to John. These elements would have been readily understood by the 1st century readers to whom the book was originally addressed.

4. Attempting to tie any aspects of John's vision to specific world events is pointless and counterproductive.

The plethora of contradictory interpretations of the book of Revelation, and the countless speculative preachers all claiming to have cracked the code, should serve as a warning to us. Not only is this kind of "micro interpretation" of the book almost certainly doomed to failure, but, more importantly, it misses the whole point of apocalyptic literature. It is not a puzzle to be solved or a code to be broken; it is a majestic painting to be admired. The purpose of the book of Revelation is not to provide us with a specific timetable of future events, but to fill us with the assurance that God has the course of human history firmly in his sovereign hands. It assures us that evil will finally be conquered, death will be vanquished, sin will be punished, the redeemed will be perfected, the universe will be restored, Satan will be destroyed, the Son will be glorified, and God's Kingdom will be fully and eternally established on the earth. It is a grand picture.

The best advice I can give you for reading the book of Revelation, is to put away the magnifying glass, step back and admire the painting!

Reflection Questions 13

1. What new insights have you gained from reading this chapter?

2. Has this chapter changed your view of any of the books of the Bible?

3. This chapter has indicated that historical narratives describe, but do not prescribe. What does this mean?

3. What is the difference between something being "normal" and "normative"?

4. How should a proper understanding of the nature of historical narrative impact our view of some of the events described in the book of Acts? Take, for example the issue of speaking in tongues. Compare Acts 10:44-46 (historical narrative) and 1 Corinthians 12:29-30 (didactic Scripture). Note, also, the apparent absence of tongue speaking in the conversion of the 3,000 on the day of Pentecost (in Acts 2:38-41), yet verse 4 indicates that the disciples in the upper room spoke in tongues as they were filled with the Holy Spirit.

5. Read Romans 14. This entire chapter deals with "questionable matters" such as drinking alcohol. What principles does it teach? Are there any universal standards that can be applied to everyone? In deciding whether to drink alcohol or not, what, according to verses 20-21, should be our primary consideration?

CHAPTER 14

HISTORICAL AND CULTURAL CONTEXT

God did not communicate his Word as a list of propositional statements dictated directly from heaven. Instead, he communicated his eternal truth through people who wrote with historical and cultural particularity. Each book of the Bible is shaped by the language, culture and historical events of its time, and needs to be understood within that context. The society of two thousand years ago was, in many ways, incommensurable with our own. Societal structures, social conventions, and the way words and concepts were employed, were significantly different to those of today. We are separated from the world of the New Testament by a vast gulf of language, time and culture, and from the world of the Old Testament by an even wider gulf. Yet, we must come to a reasonable understanding of these ancient cultures, if we are not to misinterpret the Bible's message.

In the case of the New Testament epistles, the doctrines contained within a particular letter were almost always developed and articulated in response to specific circumstances at the time. Understanding the *precipitating circumstances* of a book of the Bible, as well as its general *historical and cultural context*, is vital for correctly interpreting its message. These are the two contextual factors that we will examine in this chapter. For the average Bible reader, Bible commentaries and study Bible notes are an extremely helpful tool for discovering this important background information for understanding a book of the Bible or a particular passage.

In this chapter we will examine several examples of how an understanding of the *precipitating circumstances* of a book, as well as the *general historical and cultural context*, significantly improves our interpretation of its message.

PRECIPITATING CIRCUMSTANCES

On occasions, there were very specific issues that prompted the writing of a New Testament letter or part of a letter. Most of Paul's letters, for example, were addressed to specific churches, and they often contained precise instructions regarding a particular situation that had arisen in that church. Gaining an understanding of the precipitating events that prompted the writing of a portion of Scripture will often provide a richer, deeper appreciation of its message and help prevent you from misinterpreting its meaning. The following examples demonstrate how an understanding of precipitating circumstances can enrich our understanding of the Bible's message.

1 Thessalonians

Precipitating Circumstances: The Thessalonians were extremely new Christians who were without any mature leadership, because Paul had been forced to flee from their city after preaching the gospel to them for only three weeks. These new Christians were facing intense persecution from the hostile Jewish community and were asking Paul, via Timothy, who had visited them briefly (1 Thess 3:2), about the fate of those in their midst who died before Christ returned. Because of their expectation that Christ was about to return any day, some of them had stopped work and were simply waiting for him to appear.

Message: Paul's instructions about the coming of the Lord, and the fate of those who die beforehand, in 1 Thessalonians 4 & 5, are not abstract theological ideas, but are intensely pastoral in nature. Paul writes to a people who are suffering terribly and who are desperate to be assured that Christ will, indeed, return and that those who die beforehand will not miss out on a place in his kingdom. He also encourages them to go on with their lives as they await his return, and not sit around idly, looking up to the sky (1 Thess 4:11-12).

2 Thessalonians

Precipitating Circumstances: After receiving Paul's first letter, a rumour had reached the Thessalonian Christians that Christ had already returned, and that they had missed out on the resurrection to his eternal Kingdom.

Message: Paul wrote this second letter not long after the first, to assure the Thessalonians that they had not missed the return of Christ. His explanation, in 1 Thessalonians 2, of the events yet to be fulfilled prior to Christ's return, arise, not from cold theological speculation, but in response to a pastoral need in the recipients.

There are many circumstantial particulars, such as these, that a Bible commentary or study Bible can point out, to help you understand the significance of a passage, and which can provide added nuances to its meaning. For every New Testament letter, there are specific circumstances that prompted its writing as a whole, as well as specific circumstances that prompted the writing of different sections within it. Understanding those particular circumstances will provide a much deeper appreciation of its message.

GENERAL HISTORICAL AND CULTURAL CONTEXT

Our understanding of the general historical and cultural background of the ancient world can significantly impact our interpretation of a passage as well. In the remainder of this chapter we will examine two examples; women's head covering and male headship.

Women's Head Covering

Consider Paul's instructions, in 1 Corinthians 11, that women should have their heads covered in church. On the face of it, Paul's instructions seem absolute and irrevocable:

> *1Cor 11:3-16 "Now I want you to realize that the head of every man is Christ, and the head of the woman is man, and the head of Christ is God. (4) Every man who prays or prophesies with his head covered dishonours his head. (5) And every woman who prays or prophesies with her head uncovered dishonours her head—it is just as though her head were shaved. (6) If a woman does not cover her head, she should have her hair cut off; and if it is a disgrace for a woman to have her hair cut or shaved off, she should cover her head. (7) A man ought not to cover his head, since he is the image and glory of God; but the woman is the glory of man. (8) For man did not come from woman, but woman from man; (9) neither was man created for woman, but woman for man. (10) For this reason, and because of the angels, the woman ought to have a sign of authority on her head. (11) In the Lord, however, woman is not independent of man, nor is man independent of woman. (12) For as woman came from man, so also man is born of woman. But everything comes from God. (13) Judge for yourselves: Is it proper for a woman to pray to God with her head uncovered? (14) Does not the very nature of things teach you that if a man has long hair, it is a disgrace to him, (15) but that if a woman has long hair, it is her glory? For long hair is given to her as a covering. (16) If anyone wants to be contentious*

about this, we have no other practice—nor do the churches of God".

Not only is Paul adamant that a woman should have her head covered in the public gatherings of the church, but he appeals to theological truths to substantiate his stance (vv.1, 8-10). Furthermore, his final statement leaves us in no doubt that this is to be a universal practice among all the New Testament churches (v.16). What are we to make of this? Must I rush out to the shops and buy my wife a hat for church on Sunday, so that she will no longer be sinning by allowing our fellow worshippers to see her beautiful long hair?

There are three important cultural issues underlying this passage:

- **Firstly,** ancient Palestine was a highly patriarchal society. Women were not given an education, because they were expected to marry and assume "wifely" duties. They were seen as inferior to men in every way, and were completely under male authority. A common Jewish prayer was, *"Lord, I thank you that you did not make me a woman or a Gentile"*.

- **Secondly,** a woman always wore some form of head covering when in public, as a sign of her submission to her husband, or her father if she was unmarried. It was a sign of her acquiescence to the place allotted to her by society. Failure to do so was a disgrace.

- **Thirdly,** only prostitutes and brazen, immoral women went out in public without their heads covered. In fact, the lack of a head covering was how a man could identify a prostitute if he was looking for one!

Apparently, in Corinth, some women converts were exercising their new-found freedom in Christ by not wearing head coverings in church. Visitors attending such church gatherings would assume that the women with uncovered heads were either brazen prostitutes (effectively advertising their availability) or that they were scornfully disrespecting their husbands and fathers. Either way, the gospel would be brought into disrepute. Therefore, Paul writes in response to this situation and insists that women must wear a head covering in church.

In determining whether a New Testament practice such as this is applicable to us, we must ask ourselves whether the same factors that required its implementation in the first century are still in place today. In this case, we can, emphatically, say that they are not:

- We do not live in a patriarchal society where women are not educated, not employable and treated as inferior and completely under the authority of men (although some feminists may want to debate that point!).

- We do not live in a society where women must wear head coverings to symbolise their submission to men and their place in society.

- We do not live in a society where a woman without a hat is regarded as a prostitute.

To insist on head coverings in church today would be *incongruent* with the rest of society. In fact, this is the whole point. It was because the wearing of head coverings was the practice of their *whole society* that Paul insisted that it be their practice in church. To do otherwise would be to invite all sorts of scandalous accusations against them and bring the gospel into disrepute.

Clearly, this is not the case today. Leaving heads uncovered in church will not bring the gospel into disrepute, because it is in keeping with the social conventions of our time. In fact, an argument could be made that if we were to insist that women wear hats or scarves in church, we would be creating an unnecessary barrier for the proclamation of the gospel by placing ourselves *out of step* with society, which could cause the gospel to be seen as antiquated and irrelevant.

Of course, this argument of cultural particularity must never be used to discard biblical principles that are moral and eternal. The church must, for example, maintain our abhorrence of all forms of sexual immorality, no matter how our society evolves to embrace such practices as normal and acceptable. The principle of cultural particularity only applies to peripheral issues of taste and convention, rather than to issues that are central to the gospel or part of God's timeless moral standards.

A question may well arise at this point: If the issue of head coverings is one of cultural particularity, why does Paul appeal to timeless, absolute theological truths to support it? (vv.1,8).

- **Firstly**, it is important to stress that Paul's teaching *does* arise from the cultural conventions of his day: *"Judge for yourselves: Is it proper for a woman to pray to God with her head uncovered? Does not the very nature of things teach you that if a man has long hair, it is a disgrace to him"* (1 Cor 11:13-14). Here Paul is clearly appealing to a commonly held set of cultural standards, with which his hearers were very familiar, but which no longer exist in our society.

- **Secondly,** we must distinguish between the timeless principle and the cultural application. In this case the timeless principle is the spiritual headship of man over woman, whereas the first century cultural application was the wearing of hats.

Male Headship

The issue of male headship will be discussed in detail in Chapter 17. Some brief preliminary comments, however, are helpful for our discussion of cultural and historical context. While it is entirely appropriate to discard the obsolete cultural application of head coverings, the issue of male headship is not as easily dismissed. Paul, in writing to the church in Corinth, states;

"The head of every man is Christ, and the head of the woman is man, and the head of Christ is God" (1 Cor 11:3).

Liberal Christians do not regard this statement concerning the headship of man over woman as a timeless truth. They regard it as another outdated cultural viewpoint of the first century patriarchal society. Many evangelical Christians, however, regard the headship of man over woman as a timeless truth. This is because Paul refers to the created order of men and women as the basis for this doctrine:

"For man did not come from woman, but woman from man; neither was man created for woman, but woman for man" (1 Cor 11:8-9).

In substantiating the doctrine of male headship, Paul does not appeal to particular cultural practices or beliefs of the 1st century, but to intrinsic differences between man and woman, set in place by God from the beginning of creation. This may not be a particularly popular teaching in our modern, liberated world, and many people would like to dismiss it as an obsolete cultural belief from an uninformed, sexist patriarchal society. But the passage itself does not allow us to dismiss it so easily. Paul's appeal to both the order of creation and the distinctive roles assigned to men and women by God in the very beginning, leave us in no doubt that Paul was convinced that this doctrine is a timeless truth rather than a temporary cultural belief. Furthermore, in 1 Corinthians 11, the headship of man over woman is compared to the headship of God the Father over Christ. Furthermore, in Ephesians 5, male headship is compared to the headship of Christ over the church. These two passages make it extremely difficult to dismiss this as a temporary cultural teaching.

Significantly, the fact that the headship of man over woman is compared to the headship of Christ over the church and of the Father over Christ, tells us two important things:

1. It is a hierarchy of **function** not of value (the Father and Son are equally divine).

2. Male headship involves some degree of leadership, for Christ clearly has such a role over the church, as does the Father over the Son. (Jn 4:34; 6:38-39; 5:19; 11:41-42).

How male headship ought to work in practice within the marriage relationship is spelt out for us in Ephesians 5. This passage speaks of the husband taking the lead in laying down his life for his wife, and putting his wife's needs before his own, just as Christ laid down his life for the church (Eph 5:25). The husband is to take the lead in loving and serving his wife. Furthermore, the whole passage on headship in Ephesians 5 begins with the contextualising statement, *"Submit to one another out of reverence for Christ" (Eph 5:21)*. Rather than a domineering relationship, the headship of the husband over the wife, as prescribed in the Bible, is a headship of selfless, sacrificial love, within the context of mutual submission to each other and ultimate submission to Christ. Surely no wife could object to this kind of headship!

The 1st century church acknowledged the timeless truth of male headship with a cultural practice that is no longer relevant or necessary; the covering of women's heads. Learning to distinguish between universal, timeless truths and issues of cultural particularity is essential as we seek to apply the biblical writings to our own culture and time.

Other examples of New Testament teaching and practice that are widely considered to be issues of cultural particularity, and therefore no longer applicable, are:

- It is disgraceful for a man to have long hair (1 Cor 11:14)

- It is disgraceful for a woman to have short hair (1 Cor 11:6)

- We should greet one another with a holy kiss (Rom 16:16)

- Foot washing (John 13:1-16; 1 Tim 5:10)

Distinguishing between cultural application and universal truth, however, is not always simple. Some issues continue to be widely debated among Christians. The role of women in ministry within the church is a prime example, and this will be covered, in detail, in Chapter 17.

HELPFUL TOOLS FOR INTERPRETING THE BIBLE

Study Bibles have helpful notes which give very basic summaries of the most important aspects of historical and cultural context. For more serious Bible students, Bible commentaries can be helpful tools to provide you with the context necessary to correctly interpret a verse or passage. We must realise, however, that commentaries are not infallible. Even scholars can err, and their deliberations should not be granted the same authority as Scripture.

For example, consider the verse in Mark 10:25;

> *"How hard it is for the rich to enter the kingdom of God. It is easier for a camel to go through the eye of a needle than for the rich to enter the kingdom of God" (Mark 10:25)*

Some commentators postulate that there was a gate in Jerusalem known as the *"Needle's Eye"*, through which camels could squeeze only by having their loads unpacked. The point of this "interpretation" is that camels could go through the eye of the needle, but only with great difficulty. The trouble with this exegesis is that it has no basis in recorded history. There never was a gate like this in Jerusalem. No such gate has ever been uncovered by archaeology, nor is there any reference to such a gate in any historical document. (No respected historian or historical website supports the view of a gate with this name, and even common web-based encyclopedias such as Wikipedia point out the fallacy of this belief). In fact, the idea originated in the speculations of an 11th century Greek commentator, named Theophylact, who struggled with the apparent harshness of this text. It was speculation only, with no historical evidence, but the idea has taken root with some commentators and preachers who have not bothered to check the historical facts.

If you are going to read a commentary, it is important to make sure it is the work of a respected scholar and publisher. It is also a good idea to read more than one commentary, in order to obtain more than one perspective. For the average Bible reader, however, Study Bibles, with helpful background notes and explanatory comments, are an excellent starting point, with the NIV and TNIV Study Bibles representing the most up-to-date scholarship.

Reflection Questions 14

1. What new insights have you gained from reading this chapter?

2. Do you regard the headship of man over woman as a timeless truth or an out-dated cultural precept? Why?

3. Read 1 Corinthians 11:3-36. In this passage, what are timeless truths and what are outdated cultural applications? Do you regard the instruction for a woman to cover her head in worship as a timeless truth or an outdated cultural application? Why?

4. Read Mark 10:17-1-27. Why is it so difficult for a rich person to "enter the kingdom of heaven" (v.23)? What makes it so difficult?

5. Jesus' statement in Mark 10:27 indicates that God is able to save even those who are wealthy. What kinds of changes might God need to bring about in such a person's heart in order for them to be saved? What application does this have for those of us in the western world who are so wealthy in comparison to poorer nations?

6. Read mark 10:29-31. What promises are we given in this passage? Do you think this promises financial prosperity in this life? How should this passage shape the way we live?

CHAPTER 15

LITERARY and LEXICAL CONTEXT

It is often said that *"a text without a context is a pretext for a proof text"*. In other words, if we lift a verse or passage directly out of the Bible, ignoring the moderating meaning of the verses surrounding it, we are very likely to misinterpret its message and inappropriately apply it. Every verse of the Bible can only be properly understood in the context of its immediate passage, chapter and book. It is also essential that we correctly understand the meaning of the words used in the Bible. This is referred to as "lexical" context. These two principles are the simplest, most fundamental hermeneutical principles, yet they are often either overlooked or handled very poorly. Failure to adequately consider the literary and lexical context of a verse or passage is arguably the most common cause of misinterpretation and erroneous doctrines.

C. S. Lewis once wrote,

"We must not use the Bible as a sort of Encyclopedia out of which texts (isolated from their context and read without attention to the whole nature and purport of the books in which they occur) can be taken for use as weapons." [1]

In this chapter we will investigate several examples of verses that are commonly taken out of context. By examining the context of these verses, it will become apparent that the true meaning of these verses is very different from the one that is commonly proposed.

EXAMPLE 1:

READ THE REST OF THE VERSE AND UNDERSTAND THE LEXICAL CONTEXT

PROVERBS 29:18

"Where there is no vision, the people perish." (KJV)

This verse is commonly cited to establish the belief in the importance of having long term goals and strategies for the future. It is often quoted by church leaders as they seek to convince congregations of the necessity to formulate plans for the future and to construct catchy vision statements.

The King James Version (above) is the most commonly cited version of this verse, because it uses the word *"vision"*. However, there are two problems with the way this verse is often quoted. Firstly, the second half of the verse is usually ignored. Secondly, the word "vision" is not considered to be the best translation of the Hebrew (chazon: "חָזוֹן"), according to the most recent scholarship. The NIV provides us with a more accurate lexical rendering:

"Where there is no <u>revelation</u>, people cast off restraint;

but blessed are those who heed wisdom's instruction"

This proverb is written using classic Hebrew parallelism. In parallelism, the two halves of a proverb describe the same truth, either by similarity or by contrast. In this case, the conjunction "but" indicates that contrast is intended. When God's *"revelation"* is absent or not heeded, people's behaviour degenerates, but when *"wisdom's instruction"* is heeded, people are blessed. In this parallelism, therefore, we are meant to understand that *"revelation"* and *"wisdom's instruction"* are one and the same thing. When it is heeded things go well; when it is not heeded, things go badly. What is being described here is not some esoteric vision of the future, not some concocted imagining by an individual or a church of what they would like to see happen one day, but the publicly revealed words of God that he gives us to guide our behaviour. It is speaking of God's Word: His revelation to mankind! This proverb, therefore, is articulating the importance of regularly reading God's word in order to live a wise, godly life. It is *not* speaking about the importance of constructing clever plans and strategies for the future.

To quote this verse as a justification for the contemporary philosophy of visioning the future is lifting half of the verse out of context and completely ignoring the most basic principle of hermeneutics. All we have to do is read the second half of the verse to determine its true meaning! It is staggering that many Bible teachers have not even bothered to do this, resulting in completely misrepresenting this verse to their congregations.

EXAMPLE 2:

READ THE REST OF THE BOOK!

MALACHI 3:10

> *"Bring the whole tithe into the storehouse, that there may be food in my house. Test me in this," says the LORD Almighty, "and see if I will not throw open the floodgates of heaven and pour out so much blessing that there will not be room enough to store it."*

Here is a verse that is extremely popular today and is used to teach the concept of blessing in return for tithing. We have discussed previously how the command to tithe was part of the old covenant. It was not renewed in the new covenant, nor is there any indication in the New Testament that tithing was practised by the early church. We also discussed how Old Testament blessings and curses were intrinsically linked to the old covenant laws, all of which are now rendered *"obsolete"* by the new covenant in Christ (Heb 8:13).

Despite this, however, verses such as Malachi 3:10 continue to be inappropriately applied to Christians today, usually by those whose income is derived from church giving. This modern-day prosperity application is characterised by two misguided beliefs.

The first, is that tithing is the obligatory minimum requirement for Christians. This is not founded upon any New Testament Scriptures that teach tithing, because there are none! Instead, it is based upon a form of twisted logic that says that if God required tithing of people in the Old Testament then, surely, he must require *at least* that from us today, and *probably more*. Underlying this is the disturbing concept that because we have been more blessed than those in the Old Testament, we should pay God more money than they did, or at least as much as they did. Of course, money preachers do not express it as crudely as this; their message is delivered with persuasive and emotive eloquence, but the concept should disturb us because it represents a subtle undermining of the gospel of grace. Of course, the New Testament exhorts us to give *"generously"* to God's kingdom (2 Cor 6:9-15), and many Christians freely choose to give *more* than 10% of their income to the work of the church as an expression of that generosity. But to legislate 10% as the minimum requirement is a legalistic stricture that has no basis in the New Testament.

The second misguided belief is that verses such as Malachi 3:10 promise us material prosperity and blessing in return for tithing. This represents a serious lack of appreciation for the ***literary context*** of this Old Testament passage. Malachi 3:10 is a plea by God for his people to return to him and worship him wholeheartedly. Israel had strayed from God and, consequently, had been cursed by him:

> *"You are under a curse, the whole nation, because you are robbing me" (Mal 3:9)*

The problem was much more than simply neglecting their tithes. Malachi Chapter 1 tells us that the Israelites were worshipping other gods. They were giving their finest offerings to those false gods and were bringing sick and injured animals to the temple as an offering to the true God - animals that would probably have died or needed to be put down anyway:

> *"You bring injured, crippled or diseased animals and offer them as sacrifices" (Mal 1:13)*

This offended God:

> *"I am not pleased with you, says the Lord Almighty, and I will accept no offering from your hands. For my name will be great among the nations…" (Mal 1:10)*

God declared that this was a symptom of a deeper spiritual sickness; his people had turned away from him in their hearts:

> *"You have not set your hearts to honour me" (Mal 2:2)*

This spiritual sickness resulted in a multitude of other sins, for which God was judging them:

> *"So I will come near to you for judgement. I will be quick to testify against sorcerers, adulterers and perjurers, against those who defraud labourers of their wages, who oppress the widows and the fatherless, and deprive aliens of justice, but do not fear me" (Mal 3:5)*

Therefore, God had cursed the entire nation by sending a drought upon the land, resulting in a severe famine:

> *"I will send a curse upon you, and I will curse your blessings"* (Mal 2:2)

The whole book of Malachi is a plea from God towards his adulterous people, summarised by the simple statement in Malachi 3:7:

> *"Return to me, and I will return to you," says the Lord Almighty. (Mal 3:7)*

With this context in mind, Malachi 3:10 contains a command and a promise:

The command:

> *"Bring the whole tithe into the storehouse"*

Their meagre, diseased offerings, which were symptomatic of their spiritual malaise, were to be replaced with whole-hearted giving, as a sign of their renewed commitment to God.

The promise:

God promised that he would send rain upon the land again, to end the drought:

> *"I will throw open the floodgates of heaven"*

He promised to end the famine and bless them again with food in abundance:

> *"and pour out so much blessing that you will not have room enough for it"*

Malachi 3:10 must be interpreted in the context of the *whole book* of Malachi, which is the historical account of God's punishment of a sinful, idolatrous nation, and his promise to remove that punishment if they repent.

How can we apply this verse to ourselves today?

1. We can't *directly* apply this verse to ourselves at all!

This prophecy was given to an unregenerate, pre-Christian people who were cheating God, swindling the poor, intermarrying with pagan nations, indulging in sorcery and committing spiritual adultery, which resulted in them being cursed by God. If you think this applies to you, then you have a big problem!

2. We can, however, make two general applications:

- God disciplines those he loves

- God removes his discipline and restores us when we repent

The reason we can make these applications is because

1. This is the actual historical meaning of this passage, and;

2. These are clearly articulated New Testament principles. Just as God disciplined these pre-Christian people in the Old Testament, he continues to discipline his people in the New Testament era.

Malachi 3:10 is *not* a spiritual guide to prosperity and wealth. It is *not* a promise by God to give us more money in the bank if we give 10% to church. It describes God's desire to bring a sinful, adulterous people to repentance so that he might then heal their land. In particular, God's promise to *"throw open the floodgates of heaven"* was quite literally a promise to send rain to a land in drought. It should *not* be allegorised to infer a flow of money into our bank accounts. It was God's promise to *cease his punishment* of his people. For the Israelites, this passage literally meant the promise of restored crops and food in abundance. It did not infer, *in any way*, that they would be made wealthy with silver or gold.

Why is this verse so often quoted to teach the principle of financial prosperity for those who tithe?

This verse is commonly misinterpreted because it is taken out of its *immediate literary context*. People jump straight into application, without first engaging in exegesis. We must never start with the question, *"What does this mean for me?"* We must always begin with the question, *"What did this mean for them?"* A text can never mean *now* what it never meant *then* (although, in the case of prophecies, it possible for enlightened New Testament Christians to perceive a subsequent, further fulfilment that would not have been obvious to the ancient Israelites).

We cannot lift a verse straight out of the Old Testament and treat it as if it is a word from God for us today. This was a prophetic word from God for a pre-Christian nation 2,500 years ago. It was a very specific word for a very specific situation. Only when we fully understand the historical context can we then hope to apply a passage accurately and appropriately to ourselves.

How do we discover the literary context of a verse or passage?

Very often the simplest and best way of properly understanding a verse is to read the rest of the book. That is all we needed to do in order accurately interpret Malachi 3:10. Once again, it is staggering that many Bible teachers fail to do this. By ignoring this most fundamental of all hermeneutic principles, a gross misinterpretation of Scripture results, and a harmful false doctrine is perpetuated.

EXAMPLE 3:

IMMEDIATE AND COVENANTAL CONTEXT

JEREMIAH 29:11

"For I know the plans I have for you," declares the LORD, "plans to prosper you and not to harm you, plans to give you hope and a future."

This is one of the most quoted verses in the Bible. It has given rise to more fridge magnets, posters, wall hangings, bookmarks and other Christian paraphernalia than any other verse in the Bible. This verse is commonly cited by Christians to indicate a belief in God's wonderful plan for their life and his desire to bless them with prosperity. Unfortunately, this interpretation fails to understand two important elements of context; the context of the whole book of Jeremiah, and the context of its place in covenantal history.

1. The Context of The Book of Jeremiah.

The latter part of the book of Jeremiah contains a prophecy sent from the prophet Jeremiah in Jerusalem to the exiled Jews in Babylon:

> <u>Jeremiah 29:1</u> *"This is the text of the letter that the prophet Jeremiah sent from Jerusalem to the surviving elders among the exiles and to the priests, the prophets and all the other people Nebuchadnezzar had carried into exile from Jerusalem to Babylon."*

The Jews had been taken into exile because of their idolatry and rebellion against God. **They were currently under a curse because of their wickedness**. They were captives in a foreign land, often struggling to survive with minimal food and provisions. But God spoke through Jeremiah to assure them that the time was coming when their punishment would end; when God would restore them to the promised land, where they would once again be blessed with abundant provisions. This verse was written to a disobedient people who were currently cursed by God and being punished for their idolatry and wickedness. It represents God's announcement that their punishment was soon to end.

Whenever I am asked whether Christians can claim this verse for themselves, I answer, *"Certainly! Provided you believe you are an idolatrous, wicked person who is currently cursed by God and being punished for your sins, and that God is about to end your punishment!"*

2. Covenantal Context

The word translated *"prosper"* here is the Hebrew word *"shalom"*. This is a word rich with meaning; implying peace, happiness, health, well-being and prosperity. This accords with God's mode of rewarding his people in the old covenant: with rewards that were immediate and tangible. We have previously noted that God's mode of rewarding new covenant Christians is very different to this (see Chapter 8). In the old covenant, God dealt with the Israelites as immature infants. He motivated and disciplined them in more immediate, tangible ways than he does with Christians in the new covenant. This passage in Jeremiah, where God tells them of his imminent plan to cease their punishment and reward them with abundant provisions, is the classic use of the old covenantal "carrot and stick". In the new covenant, instead of immediate punishments, people today are *"storing up wrath against yourself for the day of God's wrath, when his righteous judgment will be revealed." (Romans 2:5).* And instead of immediate, tangible rewards, we are now motivated to *"store up for yourselves treasures in heaven, where moth and rust do not destroy." (Matthew 6:19-20).*

It must also be stressed that this promise of "Shalom" in Jeremiah was not addressed to the whole nation, but only to those who were in Babylon. To the Jews remaining in Jerusalem, God promised to curse them with death, disease, sword, famine and plague (Jer 29:16-19). I don't hear many Christians claiming this promise for themselves today!

We must be very careful not to apply verses to ourselves that were never intended for us. This was a prophecy given to a group of people 2,500 years ago who were exiled by God because of their idolatry and wickedness. It promises an end to their punishment, an eventual restoration to their promised land and the granting of the manifold blessings of "Shalom". This is entirely consistent with God's system of rewarding his people under the old covenant; a system that is vastly different to the eternal spiritual rewards we are promised under the new covenant.

Christians are not promised a physical promised land in this life. In fact, Jesus told us that *"in this life, you will have many troubles"* (John 16:33). Instead of temporal rewards that will not last, Christians are promised a much greater inheritance: the eternal promised land of Revelation 21. Christians would do well to remove their Jeremiah 29:11 fridge magnets, and replace them with verses that proclaim the gospel rather than verses that inappropriately seek prosperity and personal gain!

CONCLUSION

Taking note of the immediate context of a verse is the most fundamental of all hermeneutic principles. Reading the surrounding verses, chapters, and book will significantly diminish the possibility of misinterpretation. This is one reason why reading whole chapters of the Bible in one's daily reading schedule is recommended.

Chapter Footnotes

1. C. S. Lewis, "Collected Letters of C. S. Lewis", Letter to Mrs Johnson, written on November 8th, 1952.

Reflection Questions 15

1. What new insights have you gained from reading this chapter?

2. Consider the examples cited in this chapter. Have the explanations caused you to change your interpretation of any of these passages?

3. Is there anything in this chapter that you are struggling with?

4. Read Malachi 1:1-12. How does this chapter (and, indeed, the entire book of Malachi) modify the interpretation of Malachi 3:10? What are the particular circumstances that God is addressing here? What, if any, application can we make for ourselves?

5. Read Jeremiah 29:10-14. What is the context of the promise of verse 11? Where are the Israelites; what has happened to them and why? How does this impact our interpretation of verse 11?

6. Read Matthew 6:19-20. How does this teaching by Jesus moderate our understanding of the promise of Jeremiah 29:11?

7. Read 2 Corinthians 6:9-11. This New testament promise is read, by some, to be a promise of financial blessing. While financial blessing may, at times, be given to some people, what appears to be the main blessing that is promised in this passage?

CHAPTER 16

INTERPRETING SCRIPTURE WITH SCRIPTURE

Most doctrines in the Bible are not completely encapsulated within a single passage. If we are to gain a comprehensive understanding of a particular teaching, we must take into account references to that topic across numerous passages of Scripture. Each individual Bible passage will usually provide a single perspective on a particular truth, and it is only when these individual passages are considered together, that a more complete explanation of the doctrine emerges.

In many cases, if we read a single passage in isolation, it is possible to develop a skewed understanding of a doctrine. For this reason, an important principle of hermeneutics is to always interpret Scripture with Scripture. In other words, it is vital that we don't derive our understanding of a biblical doctrine from a single verse or passage, but that we take into account other Bible passages which may moderate, qualify or add to our understanding of that doctrine. In this chapter we will examine three examples which demonstrate the importance of interpreting Scripture with Scripture; salvation, answered prayer and healing. In each example, failure to follow this interpretive principle can, and often does, lead to a skewed understanding of the doctrine.

1. SALVATION: WHAT MUST I DO TO BE SAVED?

What must I do to be saved? Upon first consideration, this might seem a simple issue, but consider the variety of answers to this question that the New Testament provides.

- Sell your possessions and give to the poor (Matt 19:21)

- Believe in Jesus (Acts 16:30-31)

- Believe and declare your faith publicly (Rom 10:9-10)

- Call on the name of the Lord (Rom 10:13)

- Repent and be baptised (Acts 2:38)

- Be baptised and call on Jesus' name (Acts 22:16)

- Believe and be baptised (Mark 16:16)

- Hear and believe (John 5:24)

- Receive Jesus and believe in his name (John 1:12)

- Have the Son (1 John 5:12)

- Be baptised (1 Peter 3:21)

BIBLE VERSE	ANSWER
Matt 19:21 "Sell your possessions and give to the poor, and you will have treasure in heaven. Then come, follow me"	Sell your possessions and give to the poor
Acts 16:30-31 "He asked, 'Sirs, what must I do to be saved?' They replied, 'Believe n the Lord Jesus, and you will be saved – you and your household'."	Believe
Rom 10:9-10 "If you declare with your mouth 'Jesus is Lord' and believe in your heart that God raised him from the dead, you will be saved. For with the heart one believes and is justified, and with the mouth one confesses and is saved."	Believe and declare your faith publicly
Rom 10:13 "Everyone who calls on the name of the Lord will be saved"	Call on the name of the Lord
John 3:16 "For God so loved the world that He gave His only Son, that whoever believes in Him should not perish but have eternal life"	Believe
Acts 2:38 "Repent and be baptised, every one of you, for the forgiveness of your sins."	Repent and be baptised
Acts 22:16 "Be baptised and wash away your sins, calling on His name"	Be baptised and call on His name
Mark 16:16 "Whoever believes and is baptized will be saved, but whoever does not believe will be condemned".	Believe and be baptised
John 5:24 "Truly, truly I say, whoever hears my words and believes Him who sent me has eternal life and will not be judged, but has crossed over from death to life"	Hear and believe
John 1:12 "To all who received, Him, to those who believed in His Name, he gave the right to become children of God"	Receive Jesus and believe in His Name
John 3:36 "Whoever believes in the Son has eternal life, but whoever rejects the Son will not see life"	Believe
John 6:47 "Truly, truly I say to you, whoever believes has eternal life"	Believe
1 John 5:12 "Whoever has the Son has life, whoever does not have the Son does not have life"	Have the Son
1 Peter 3:21 "this water symbolises baptism which now saves you"	Be baptised
2 Cor 7:10 "Godly sorrow brings repentance that leads to salvation"	Repent

The above table beautifully illustrates the point that no single verse or passage of the Bible explains a particular doctrine in its entirety. Each verse illuminates a different aspect of the truth, and if we are to reach a comprehensive understanding of the topic, we must embrace the totality of the Bible's teaching on that issue. In the case of salvation, each of the above verses focuses on a particular aspect of the response that God requires. Some focus on the necessity of faith, while others focus on the need for repentance. If we were to base our theology on just one or two verses, it is possible we could develop a theology that is unbalanced. Only by interpreting Scripture with Scripture, embracing complementary perspectives from other passages, are we able to reach a balanced understanding.

2. ANSWERED PRAYER

The Gospels record several seemingly unconditional promises of answered prayer by Jesus:

> *John 14:13-14.* *"I will do <u>whatever you ask</u> in my name, so that the Father may be glorified in the Son. If you ask me for <u>anything</u> in my name, I will do it"*

> *John 15:16.* *"<u>Whatever you ask</u> in my name the Father will give you"*

> *John 16:23-24.* *"Truly, truly, I say to you, if you ask the Father for <u>anything</u> in my name, he will give it to you. Until now you have asked for nothing in my name; ask and you will receive, so that your joy may be made full."*

> *Matt 7:7-8.* *"Ask, and it will be given to you; seek, and you will find; knock, and it will be opened to you. For everyone who asks receives, and he who seeks finds, and to him who knocks it will be opened."*

> *Luke 11:9.* *"So I say to you, ask, and it will be given to you; seek, and you will find; knock, and it will be opened to you."*

Upon first reading, these promises appear to be unconditional and absolute. Jesus and the Father will apparently grant you *"whatever you ask" (Jn 14:13)*. You may *"ask the Father for anything"* and *"he will give it to you" (Jn 16:23)*. If these are the only Bible verses that we read about prayer, we could easily become convinced that God has given us a carte blanche promise to grant us whatever we ask for in prayer. We could believe that God has provided us with an unlimited heavenly credit card (that we never have to repay)! Unfortunately, there are some preachers who proclaim precisely this kind of message. This "heavenly credit card" interpretation of these verses can seem very convincing because it has the appearance of being based upon the Scriptures. It is a completely erroneous interpretation, however, because it disregards two important hermeneutic principles:

    A. Exegete *every* part of a verse or passage.

    B. Interpret Scripture with Scripture.

A. Exegete *Every* Part of a Verse or Passage.

The "unlimited heavenly credit card" interpretation of these promises by Jesus does not give due attention to the crucial phrase *"in my name"*. This phrase occurs 5 times in the above verses and serves to qualify Jesus' promises. The only prayers that are guaranteed to be answered are those that are prayed *"in my* [his] *name"*. This is a crucial moderator.

What does it mean to pray in Jesus' name? It *doesn't* mean simply appending our prayers with the words, *"in Jesus' name, Amen."* These are not a set of magic words or a secret code for opening the door into God's throne room. When Jesus exhorted us to pray *"in my name"*, he was not simply instituting a liturgical formula. To pray in Jesus' name refers to both the attitude of the supplicant and the content of the prayer:

Firstly, it means asking in Jesus' merit. (This refers to our attitude as we pray). We come to God in prayer, not trusting in our own righteousness, not relying upon any merit of our own, but wholly trusting in the One who has paid for our sins and has opened the way back to God. As we pray, we are to do so with an attitude of complete trust in the saving work of Christ, through whom we can *"approach the throne of grace with confidence [believing] that we may find grace and mercy to help us in our time of need" (Heb 4:16).*

Secondly, it means praying in accordance with Jesus' character and will. (This refers to the <u>content</u> of our prayers). This concept would have been universally understood in the world of the 1st century. A servant who conducted business *"in the name of"* his master, did so according to the specific instructions given by the master. The servant's actions and words reflected the precise will and character of his lord; in fact he was not at liberty to express his own will and wishes at all. To pray in Jesus' name, therefore, means that we are to offer prayers that reflect the will and character of *our* Lord. The prayers that Jesus is promising to answer are those that reflect the values of his kingdom and the concerns of his heart. Prayers that are motivated by greed and selfishness cannot be said to be prayed in Jesus' name, for they contradict the values of his kingdom.

B. Interpret Scripture with Scripture.

The strong promises made by Jesus regarding prayer, focus upon God's willingness to answer our prayers. These promises, however, must not be read in isolation. There are many other references to prayer in the Bible which describe the kind of prayers that God wants us to pray and the specific conditions for answered prayer. These modifiers need to be incorporated into our understanding, in order to develop a comprehensive doctrine of prayer. They include:

Selfless Motives

Selfish prayers will not be answered:

> *James 4:3.* "You ask and do not receive, because you ask wrongly, to spend it on your passions."

According to God's Will

Only prayers that are in accordance with God's will can be assured of a positive answer:

> *1 John 5:14-15.* *"And this is the confidence that we have toward him, that if we ask anything <u>according to his will</u> he hears us. And if we know that he hears us in whatever we ask, we know that we have the requests that we have asked of him."*
>
> *John 15:7.* *"If you abide in me, and my words abide in you, ask whatever you wish, and it will be done for you."*

The exhortation to *"abide in me and my words abide in you"*, in John 15:7, is an exhortation to walk in fellowship with Jesus and be shaped by his teaching and his will. Only then can we expect to have our prayers answered.

Faith

Many Bible verses discuss the essential nature of faith if our prayers are to be answered:

> *James 1:6.* *"But when you ask, <u>you must believe and not doubt</u>, because the one who doubts is like a wave of the sea, blown and tossed by the wind. That person should not expect to receive anything from the Lord"*
>
> *Matt 21:22.* *"If you <u>believe</u>, you will receive whatever you ask for in prayer"*
>
> *Mark 11:24.* *"Therefore I tell you, whatever you ask in prayer, <u>believe</u> that you have received it, and it will be yours."*

Persistence

Jesus' parable about the persistent widow, in Luke 18, is a powerful indicator that God does not always answer our prayers the first time we utter them. Rather, he desires that we pray persistently, in order to demonstrate our sincerity and our faith:

Luke 18:1-8. *"Then Jesus told his disciples a parable to show them that they should always pray and <u>not give up</u>..."*

Without Unconfessed Sin

The Bible is also clear that God will not answer our prayers if we are currently flagrantly disobeying him in an area of our lives:

James 5:16. "Therefore, confess your sins to one another, and pray for one another so that you may be healed. The effective prayer of a righteous man is powerful and effective."

Psalm 66:18. "If I had cherished sin in my heart, The Lord would not have listened."

All of these conditions for answered prayer need to be understood together. Each of these verses deals with one aspect of prayer. Only by considering them together, by interpreting Scripture with Scripture, can we arrive at a comprehensive understanding of the pre-requisites for answered prayer.

3. HEALING

Another biblical doctrine where it is essential to interpret Scripture with Scripture is the topic of healing. James chapter 5 contains a strong, and seemingly prescriptive, statement of faith in the healing power of God:

"Is anyone among you sick? Let them call the elders of the church to pray over them and anoint them with oil in the name of the Lord. And the prayer offered in faith will make the sick person well; the Lord will raise them up." (James 5:14-15)

What are we to make of this seemingly absolute promise of divine healing? Is this a universal promise that God will heal *every* Christian of *every* disease on *every* occasion? Is healing to be regarded as normative (universally available) or exceptional (an occasional, merciful act of God)?

Many Christians have seized upon this verse to advocate that healing is universally available and normative for Christians. But this position simply cannot be upheld when these statements by James are interpreted in the light of other passages of Scripture.

Firstly, there are clear examples in the Bible of Christians **not** being healed of their illnesses. In 2 Timothy 4:20, Paul states that *"Erastus stayed in Corinth and I left Trophimus sick in Miletus."* If healing is universal and normative, Paul would have simply prayed over Trophimus and healed him. The fact that he didn't do this, tells us that Paul did not have a universalist view of healing. Similarly, in 1Timothy 5:23, Paul advises Timothy to *"stop drinking only water, and use a little wine because of your stomach and your frequent illnesses."* Timothy apparently suffered from an ongoing, debilitating stomach condition. If healing is universal and normative, Paul would have simply advised Timothy to seek prayer for healing. But he *didn't* advise this. Instead, he gave some practical advice for *managing the symptoms* of Timothy's ongoing illness.

Paul's failure to advise the implementation of a normative healing protocol in these instances is all the more remarkable when one considers that Paul has previously been involved in some miraculous healings. In Lystra, Paul healed a man who had been lame since birth with just a few words (Acts 14:8-10), which caused a huge commotion in the city. In Malta, Paul prayed over the father of Publius (a chief official on the island) who was suffering from fever and dysentery, and raised him from his sick bed (Acts 28:7-9). Immediately following this, we are told that *"the rest of the sick on the island came and were cured" (v.9)*. Clearly, Paul believes in God's healing power! Yet, just as clearly, he does not believe that healing is normative.

This is evident in Paul's own life. In Galatians 4:13, Paul writes;

> *"As you know, it was because of an illness that I first preached the gospel to you, and even though my illness was a trial to you, you did not treat me with contempt or scorn."*

This is an important passage for our understanding of healing. Paul suffered an illness for a *protracted period of time*, that apparently forced him to convalesce in Galatia and postpone his missionary plans to travel elsewhere. The fact that God used this illness to bring the gospel to Galatia is indicative of the sovereign way God works through our weaknesses and sufferings. But the important point for us to grasp here, is that even in Paul's own life, he did not experience healing as normative.

This is further evidenced by Paul's well-known reference to his "thorn in the flesh":

> *"In order to keep me from becoming conceited, I was given a thorn in the flesh, a messenger of Satan, to torment me. Three times I pleaded with the Lord to take it away from me. But he said to me, 'My grace is sufficient for you, for my power is made perfect in weakness'."* (2 Cor 12:7-9)

Much has been written about these two verses, not all of it adhering to rigorous hermeneutic principles. The clearest and simplest interpretation of Paul's thorn in the flesh is that it was a physical illness of some kind. This interpretation arises both from the immediate context of chapters 11 and 12, where Paul is talking about his *"weaknesses"*, as well as the lexical understanding of the word "flesh" ("σάρξ"), which literally referred to the physical body. Attempts by healing universalists to explain Paul's thorn in the flesh as an allegorical reference to some kind of spiritual opposition ignore the simplest and clearest interpretation of this passage. Paul's thorn in the flesh is yet another example of a prolonged, debilitating illness suffered by Paul, with prayers for healing not being granted.

These many biblical examples of God's people suffering from ongoing diseases and illnesses must be taken into account when interpreting James 5:14-15. Whatever interpretation we decide upon, it *cannot* contradict the many clear instances of Christians in the Bible who were sick and remained unhealed; for God is not a God of contradictions.

Before we settle upon an interpretation of this passage in James, however, we need to take note of a second category of scriptural references that provide a broader context. These are the propositional passages of the New Testament that make clear, prescriptive statements about healing and sickness. Has Christ's redemption made healing normative? Does the New Testament promise that Christians no longer have to suffer sickness? The answer is a resounding "No"! In fact, quite the contrary. Revelation 21 indicates that it is only after the final resurrection and the creation of a new heaven and earth that there will be no more sickness for God's people:

> *"God will wipe away every tear from our eyes. There will be no more death or mourning or crying or pain, for the old order of things has passed away." (Rev 21:4).*

In the meantime, Christians are not exempt from the common experience of humanity. We continue to live in a fallen world, with imperfect bodies that are subject to frailty, infirmity and disease:

> *"We groan inwardly as we eagerly await our full adoption as sons and daughters, the redemption of our bodies. For in this hope we were saved. But who hopes for what they already have? But if we hope for what we do not yet have, we wait for it patiently." (Rom 8:23-25).*

Christ does not place a protective bubble around his followers. We continue to live with the universal consequences of the Fall (Genesis 2-3). Work is hard. Weeds grow in our gardens. Childbirth is painful. We stub our toes. We fall and break bones. We catch colds. We get headaches. We ingest bacteria and suffer various gastric ailments. We inhale viruses and catch influenza. Cellular DNA is sometimes damaged in replication and our bodies gradually decline in functionality as the years progress. This will be our experience, along with the rest of humanity, until Christ returns. Until then, we *"groan inwardly as we eagerly await our full adoption as sons and daughters, the redemption of our bodies" (Rom 8:23).* This passage indicates that the redemption of our bodies from sickness and infirmity is ours as an inheritance, but we do not have it yet. We must wait for it. *"For in this hope we were saved. But who hopes for what they already have? But if we hope for what we do not yet have, we wait for it patiently." (Rom 8:25).*

It is this **future** inheritance that is referred to in the commonly cited passage in Matthew's Gospel: *"This was to fulfil what was spoken of through the prophet Isaiah; "He took up our infirmities and bore our diseases"." (Matt 8:17).* This is a verse that is often misunderstood. Interestingly, Matthew is quoting Isaiah 53:4, but his quote differs from the original; *"Surely he took up our pain and bore our suffering" (Isaiah 53:4).* This probably indicates that Matthew was quoting from the first century Septuagint version of the Old Testament (a Greek translation of the Hebrew Scriptures). Matthew, however, is writing under the inspiration of the Holy Spirit, and under the Spirit's guidance he is uses this translation to broaden our understanding of our future inheritance. When we combine these two passages, Matthew 8:17 and Isaiah 53:4, we find that the work of Christ on the cross has purchased our future deliverance from three physical things: infirmities, diseases and pain/suffering.

Do we get this inheritance now, or must we wait for it? Some Christians claim that this is our inheritance now; that the cross of Christ has purchased our complete redemption from sickness *in this life*. But this view fails to interpret these verses consistently. If we are to claim complete deliverance from *"diseases"*, based upon these verses, we must also claim complete deliverance from *"infirmities"*. What are infirmities? The Greek word *"infirmities"* (ἀσθενείας; astheneias) is a much broader term than mere sickness. It refers to the normal deterioration of the body due to ageing; grey hair, wrinkling skin, fading eyesight, arthritis, brittle bones, calcification of cartilage, diminishing of height etc. If you are going to claim complete deliverance from disease in this life, based upon this passage of Scripture, you must also claim complete deliverance from growing old! This of course, would be nonsensical! Similarly, you would also have to claim complete deliverance from pain; that you would never again stub your toe or fall and hurt yourself or jam your finger in a door or burn your hand on a hot utensil.

Clearly, the only sensible, logical interpretation of Matthew 8:17 and Isaiah 53:4, is that these verses refer to our future inheritance: the complete deliverance from pain, infirmity and sickness that will be received after final establishment of God's perfect Kingdom at the end of the age. Until then, we must *"wait for it patiently" (Rom 8:25).*

Now, at last, we can return to James chapter 5. We have all the necessary contextual background to guide us in our interpretation. Given the significant biblical examples of Christians who were not healed, together with the prescriptive passages that indicate that we will not be completely delivered from sickness in this life, we must interpret James 5 in a way that is not contradictory. How, then, are we to view this passage that strongly advocates prayer for healing? Let us remind ourselves of the precise wording:

> *"Is anyone among you sick? Let them call the elders of the church to pray over them and anoint them with oil in the name of the Lord. And the prayer offered in faith will make the sick person well; the Lord will raise them up." (James 5:14-15a)*

At first glance this appears to be a universal, unequivocal promise. *"The prayer offered in faith will make the sick person well"*. But we have already seen that this cannot be a universal promise, otherwise Scripture would be contradicting itself. Is there anything else in the immediate context of this passage which might suggest an alternate interpretation? Yes, there is. The verses that immediately follow, introduce another element to the scenario:

> *"If they have sinned, they will be forgiven. Therefore, confess your sins to each other and pray for each other so that you may be healed." (verses 15b and 16).*

This changes everything! James is apparently not referring to general sickness here, but to sickness that has been inflicted upon church members by God as a disciplinary measure for their sinful behaviour. That God sometimes disciplines Christians in this way is corroborated by Paul's denunciation of the Corinthian church's abuse of the Lord's Supper, when he says,

> *"Those who eat and drink without discerning the body of Christ, eat and drink judgment on themselves. That is why many among you are weak and sick, and a number of you have fallen asleep. But if we were more discerning with regard to ourselves, we would not come under such judgment. Nevertheless, when we are judged in this way by the Lord, we are being disciplined so that we will not be finally condemned with the world." (1 Cor 11:29-32).*

There is a lot more to be said about the role of sickness as a means of God's judgment, and it must be stressed that not all sickness is God's judgment. But this passage in 1 Corinthians establishes the fact that God sometimes uses sickness to discipline wayward Christians, in order to restore them to himself when they repent.

It is *this* kind of sickness that James is referring to in chapter 5 of his letter. Apparently, there were some in the church who had sinned and had fallen sick as a result of God's loving discipline. To these people, James issues the unequivocal promise of forgiveness, restoration and healing if they *"confess your sins to each other and pray for each other so that you may be healed" (verse 16).* It is only in this context that James promises that *"the prayer offered in faith will make the sick person well; the Lord will raise them up." (verse 15).* In fact, the phrase, *"the Lord will raise them up",* describes not just being raised up physically from their sick beds, but being restored in their relationship with God and in their fellowship with their fellow believers.

This passage in James 5:14-16 is a classic example of the crucial need to always interpret Scripture with Scripture. It also further illustrates the importance of taking careful note of the immediate context of a verse or passage. Often the interpretive key to a verse is already in plain sight in the surrounding verses, and only requires that we read a little wider. Failure to follow these important hermeneutic principles can, and often does, lead to interpretations that are misleading and even harmful.

Reflection Questions 16

1. What new insights have you gained from reading this chapter?

2. Read John 14:12-14. What do you think is meant by "even greater works than these" in verse 12? How can we expect to do greater works than Jesus?

3. How is the promise of answered prayer, in verses 13 and 14, moderated by the phrase at the end of verse 13? What sorts of prayers should this preclude?

4. Read Mark 11:22-26. This passage outlines two important conditions for answered prayer (verses 23-24, and then verse 25). Discus both, including how they might apply in practice.

5. Read James 5:13-20. The promise of healing in verses 14 and 15 is very strong. What contextual information is provided in the surrounding passage that might moderate these verses? (See the end of verse 15 and verse 16).

6. We must also moderate this verse in the light of the many references in the New Testament to Paul and others experiencing sickness and not being healed. Briefly read back over these references in this chapter.

What kind of doctrinal summary can we, therefore, make on the topic of healing?

7. If you are studying this book in a group, take some time to pray for those in the group, or others who are close to you, who may be sick and in need of healing. It is appropriate to ask God for healing, while also acknowledging that his will may, at times, differ from our own.

CASE STUDY: WOMEN IN THE CHURCH

CHAPTER 17

A CASE STUDY IN HERMENEUTICS:
THE ROLE OF WOMEN IN THE CHURCH

To this point, we have examined some of the most important hermeneutical principles for interpreting the Bible:

- Literary Genre
- Cultural Context
- Historical Precipitating Events
- Immediate Literary Context
- Lexical Context
- Interpreting Scripture with Scripture

Often, a combination of these principles will need to be embraced if we are to accurately interpret a single passage of Scripture. It becomes even more necessary when we are attempting to analyse and correctly interpret a complex doctrine that is developed across a range of passages. The role of women in the church is one such example. In this chapter, we will examine this complex issue exclusively, and demonstrate how several hermeneutical principles come into play.

Before we dive in, however, it is important to acknowledge that this is a complex issue which continues to be hotly debated by biblical scholars and church leaders. While it is true that some participants in the debate are strongly influenced by either feminist or chauvinist philosophies, there are also many sincere scholars on both sides of the debate who have arrived at their positions as a result of rigorous study of the Scriptures.

Given the fact that respected scholars continue to disagree on this topic, it would be arrogant for any person or church to assert that they have arrived at an irrefutable, definitive resolution of the issue. On the other hand, the complexity of the issue should not paralyse us. It is essential that individual churches arrive at a clear theological stance on the matter, in order to determine their own policies regarding the ministry of women in their midst.

This chapter proposes an interpretive approach which is hermeneutically rigorous and affirms the theological inerrancy of the Bible. As the various hermeneutical principles come into play, these will be indicated in [SQUARE BRACKETS] at the start of each section.

THE ROLE OF WOMEN IN THE CHURCH

A comprehensive treatment of this topic requires that we deal with two questions:

    1. Is there any biblical evidence for women in leadership amongst God's people?

2. How should we interpret Paul's seemingly prohibitive statements?

1. IS THERE ANY BIBLICAL EVIDENCE FOR WOMEN IN LEADERSHIP AMONGST GOD'S PEOPLE?

....

[Principle: INTERPRET SCRIPTURE WITH SCRIPTURE]

Before we attempt to interpret any prescriptive statements in the New Testament regarding the role of women in the church, we need to approach the Scriptures with a wide-angle lens to discover whether there are any instances of women being used by God in leadership or teaching roles. This will have a significant impact upon how we interpret Paul's seemingly prohibitive injunctions.

DEBORAH

The clearest example of a woman in leadership is Deborah who, in Judges 4:4, is said to be *"leading Israel"*. The Hebrew word for *"leading"* that is used here is *"shaphat"* which, according to Strong's Exhaustive Concordance Of The Bible, means *"to judge; to govern"*. Clearly the people perceived Deborah as their leader and God was using her in this position, for the next verse tells us:

> *"She held court under the Palm of Deborah between Ramah and Bethel in the hill country of Ephraim, and the Israelites came to her to have their disputes decided." (Judges 4:5)*

The next verse (v.6) sees her summoning the military leader, Barak, and giving him commands. In all of this, she appears to have exercised the same kind of godly authority among the people as did the male judges of her era.

Some critics of this view draw attention to Deborah's song of praise in Judges 5, where, after Israel's victory in battle, she proclaimed, *"the princes of Israel take the lead"*. This, it is claimed, is an indication of Deborah's subservience to the male leaders of Israel. Two things must be said at this point:

....

[Principle: HISTORICAL / CULTURAL CONTEXT]

1. The *"princes of Israel"* were a class of nobility within the nation; a wealthy aristocracy by virtue of their birth, rather than as a result of any call of God.

2. Traditionally it was these princes who captained the armed forces in battle. This was true not only in Deborah's time, but also during Moses' leadership and right throughout Israel's history.

Deborah's praise of the *"princes of Israel"* is, therefore, simply a recognition of their front position in the battle lines, and does not undermines her God-given authority as Israel's leader.

Some critics also point to the fact that there is no specific mention of God having appointed Deborah as leader, and suggest that she is in such a position illegitimately.

....

[Principle: LITERARY CONTEXT]

It needs to be said, however, that several of the male judges are also mentioned without any documented call of God (Shamgar; Abimelech; Tola; Jair; Ibzan; Elon; Abdon;). The omission of a recorded call cannot be used to infer that they were not appointed by God. In fact, the whole narrative of the book of Judges clearly infers that ALL the judges were raised up and used by God. The overwhelming theme of the book is the sovereignty and compassion of God in raising up leaders to deliver the nation. Deborah is one such leader, and the fact that her narrative is one of the longest in the book shows in what high regard she was held.

PHOEBE

In Romans 16:1 Paul refers to Phoebe as a *"diakonos"*.

....

[Principle: LEXICAL CONTEXT]

This term was used in two ways in the New Testament. Firstly, it referred to the office of deacon, whose task was to supervise and co-ordinate some of the practical and pastoral ministries of the church (Acts 6:1-7). The importance of their role is indicated by the qualifications required in order to be appointed to such a role; deacons had to be *"full of the Spirit and wisdom"* (Acts 6:4).

The second usage of the term *"diakonos"* was a more general reference to the ministry of God's Word. Paul regularly applied the term to himself as a minister of the true gospel (1 Cor 3:5; 2 Cor 3:6; 6:4; 11:23; Eph 3:7; Phil 1:1; Col 1:23,25) and also used it for his colleagues in the proclamation of the gospel (2 Cor 11:23; Eph 6:21; Col 1:7; 4:7; 1 Thess 3:2; 1 Tim 4:6).

....

[Principle: IMMEDIATE LITERARY CONTEXT]

Which of these two usages Paul has in mind in Romans 16:1 is not entirely clear. However, his statement in the very next verse, urging the church in Rome to hold Phoebe in high regard and treat her with honour, seems to indicate her prominence in Christian ministry: *"I ask you to receive her in the Lord in a way worthy of the saints and to give her any help she may need from you, for she has been a great help to many people, including me" (Rom 16:2).* The most logical explanation of this verse is that Phoebe was engaged in some form of itinerant gospel ministry, based at Cenchrea, but involving visits to other cities. Paul is here asking for the church at Rome to support her in her forthcoming visit to them.

PRISCILLA

In Acts 18:18 we find Priscilla and Aquilla (her husband) travelling in the company of Paul, apparently sharing the gospel ministry with him. Paul left them in Ephesus (v.19) where they continued the work. In verses 24-26 Priscilla and Aquilla took Apollos (a fellow-preacher of the gospel) aside and instructed him further in the faith. Significantly Priscilla is mentioned first in these passages, before her husband, perhaps indicating that she came from a higher social status, but more likely (given the spiritual tone of the book of Acts) because she was more prominent in Christian ministry. In this instance she appears to have been instrumental in discipling and teaching Apollos.

....

[Principle: IMMEDIATE LITERARY CONTEXT]

Critics of this view argue that Priscilla's ministry to Apollos was not teaching, but evangelism. Yet the immediate literary context clearly indicates that Apollos was *already* a Christian before his encounter with Priscilla and Aquilla, because he *"he [already] taught about Jesus accurately"* (v.25). Others argue that Priscilla must have been under her husband's headship during their joint ministry to Apollos and perhaps didn't do any of the teaching herself. This is purely conjecture and disregards the fact that she is always mentioned first, before Aquilla.

JUNIA

In Romans 16:7 Paul speaks of *"Andronicus and Junia...who are outstanding among the Apostles".*

CASE STUDY: WOMEN IN THE CHURCH

....

[Principle: HISTORICAL AND LEXICAL CONTEXT]

Junia was a female name. In fact, it was a very common female name. The male version was Junianus or Junias. While it is true that "Junias" appears in some later variant manuscripts of this passage, the Anchor Bible Dictionary points out that *"without exception, the Church Fathers in late antiquity identified Andronicus' partner in Rom 16:7 as a woman, as did minuscule 33 in the 9th century which records "iounia" (Junia) with an acute accent. Only later medieval copyists of Rom 16:7 who could not imagine a woman being an apostle wrote the masculine name 'Junias'."* (Freedman, David Noel, ed., The Anchor Bible Dictionary, (New York: Doubleday) 1997, 1992)

....

[Principle: IMMEDIATE LITERARY CONTEXT]

Some critics argue that Andronicus and Junia were not actually Apostles, but simply had an outstanding reputation *among* the Apostles. This, however, is not the most natural way to read the text, and certainly disregards the evidence of verse 7, which tells us that they *"have been in prison with me"*. The most natural reading of this passage is that Junia was an outstanding woman Apostle who had been imprisoned for her gospel preaching.

EUODIA AND SYNTYCHE

....

[Principle: LEXICAL CONTEXT]

In Philippians 4:2-3 Paul mentions Euodia and Syntyche and describes them as his *"loyal fellow workers"* who have *"contended at my side in the cause of the gospel"*. The majority of evangelical scholars agree that this statement by Paul is best interpreted to mean that these women had actively participated in the preaching of the gospel. Paul would not have used such athletic vocabulary to describe their ministry had they simply been his cooks or handmaids!

....

[Principle: IMMEDIATE LITERARY CONTEXT]

Verse 1 also suggests that Euodia and Syntyche held a position of prominence within the church at Philippi. They were apparently in disagreement, causing Paul to exhort them to *"agree with each other in the Lord"*. The fact that their dispute was public enough for Paul to have heard of it, seems to suggest that they exercised some form of influential teaching or leadership role within the church at Philippi.

WOMEN PROPHETS

There existed within the New Testament church a number of women prophets. For example, in Acts 21:7-9, Paul describes his visits to various churches on his journey, and, in the course of this description, he mentions four women in the church at Caesarea who exercised a prophetic ministry:

> *"We continued our voyage from Tyre and landed at Ptolemais, where we greeted the brothers and sisters and stayed with them for a day. Leaving the next day, we reached Caesarea and stayed at the house of Philip the evangelist, one of the Seven. He had four unmarried daughters who prophesied." (Acts 21:7-9)*

Similarly, in 1 Corinthians 11, Paul issues specific instructions to the church in Corinth regarding the proper functioning of their church gatherings. In verse 5, he indicates that in these gatherings, women who prophesy must have their heads covered:

"Every woman who prays or prophesies with her head uncovered dishonours her head" (1 Cor 11:5).

....

[Principle: HISTORICAL CONTEXT]

The existence of women prophets in the New Testament church is notable, particularly in light of the significant role that prophets played prior to the completion and canonisation of the New Testament. During this period, prophets played a crucial role, being used by God to authoritatively declare his will and his words to the church. In the case of the church in Antioch, prophets were listed as part of the leadership team, through whom God directed the church to set apart Paul and Barnabas for missionary work (Acts 13:1-4).

....

[Principle: INTERPRETING SCRIPTURE WITH SCRIPTURE]

The authoritative and revered role of prophets is further reflected by Paul in 1 Corinthians 12:29, where he expressly ranks prophets higher than teachers. In 1 Corinthians 14:31, Paul commends prophecy as the most useful of gifts and says that those who listen to it will *"learn"*, thereby inferring a teaching component to their ministry. The fact that God gifted and called women into such an authoritative prophetic role in the New Testament church adds further weight to their partnership in all aspects of Christian ministry and leadership.

CONCLUSION

There is strong evidence that God called women into varying types of leadership amongst his people, in both the Old and New Testaments. Negating these clear, scriptural examples would require major hermeneutical gymnastics. There remain, however, some statements by the Apostle Paul in the New Testament that appear severely prohibitive regarding the role of women. What are we to make of these?

2. HOW SHOULD WE INTERPRET PAUL'S SEEMINGLY PROHIBITIVE STATEMENTS?

1 TIMOTHY 2:11-14

"A woman should learn in quietness and full submission. [12] I do not permit a woman to teach or to have authority over a man; she must be quiet. [13] For Adam was formed first, then Eve. [14] And Adam was not the one deceived; it was the woman who was deceived and became a sinner."

Much of the debate concerning the role of women in the church centres around this strongly worded injunction by Paul. What are we to make of it? Firstly, we must affirm that this is indeed God's Word. We cannot dismiss it, as some attempt to, as uninspired and, therefore, unauthoritative.

....

[Principle: LEXICAL CONTEXT]

Secondly, it is not just teaching with authority that is prohibited (as if there can be any other form of teaching!), but any and all teaching; for *"teaching"* and *"authority"* are completely separate elements of this sentence in the Greek text. This is correctly rendered in our English translations *"teach OR have authority"* (rather than "teach *with* authority").

The word *"authority"* is not one of the more common Greek words for authority (*exousia, epitage, huperoche, or dunastes*), but the more unusual word *"authentein"*. This word means to usurp authority or to domineer. It cannot, therefore, be taken to prohibit the *general* exercise of authority, but simply the *wrongful* use of authority in a manner which lords it over others.

....

[Principle: HISTORICAL CONTEXT]

The prohibition against a woman teaching a man, however, cannot be explained as easily. Historically, scholars are convinced that there was, at this time in Ephesus, a false teaching with a Gnostic flavour being spread throughout the church, and that much of it was being spread via the women in the church. (Gnosticism was a false religion that purported to endow its followers with secret knowledge and initiate them into secret rituals). In 1st century culture, the uneducated women seem to have provided the network that the false teachers could use to spread their falsehoods throughout the congregation (see 1 Tim 5:13 and 2 Tim 3:6-7). For this reason, some biblical scholars interpret Paul's prohibition against a woman teaching a man (in 1 Tim 2:12) to be applicable only to *that* church at *that* specific time.

....

[Principle: IMMEDIATE LITERARY CONTEXT]

Paul actually provides us with his reasons for this prohibition in verses 13 and 14, and, at first glance, those reasons seem to negate this "cultural" interpretation and propose a universal application:

> *"For Adam was formed first, then Eve. And Adam was not the one deceived; it was the woman who was deceived and became a sinner."*

Many argue that Paul is proposing that the ministry subordination of women is a part of God's created order for mankind. Yet this directly contradicts the clear biblical examples of women in authoritative ministry and leadership among God's people that we have already examined.

....

[Principle: INTERPRET SCRIPTURE WITH SCRIPTURE]

Is there any other way of interpreting verses 13 and 14, which respects the inspired nature of the text and does not contradict the clear teaching and leadership role of women elsewhere in the Scriptures?

....

[Principle: LEXICAL CONTEXT]

The "*for*" can be understood either as the *cause* of the prohibition against women teaching men or as an *illustration* of it. If we take it as an illustration rather than a cause, Paul could simply be drawing an analogy rather than making a universal statement.

....

[Principle: IMMEDIATE LITERARY CONTEXT]

In 1 Timothy 2:13-14, Paul refers to two important facts in the creation narrative: that Eve was created second (v.13), and that she was the one deceived, not Adam (v.14). Paul's argument here could well be that he intends to connect these two facts; that Eve was not present when God gave the commandment and was therefore dependent on Adam for the teaching. In other words, she was inadequately educated - like the women in Ephesus - and more likely to be led astray.

....

[Principle: INTERPRET SCRIPTURE WITH SCRIPTURE]

This kind of analogy is not uncommon in Paul's writings. For instance, in 2 Corinthians 11:3, Paul uses this same story of Eve's deception by the serpent as an *illustration* of the gullibility of the whole church at Corinth (not as a *cause* of their gullibility).

This interpretation of verses 13 and 14 still supports the inspired nature of the text, is consistent with Paul's style elsewhere, and fits with the events in the church at Ephesus at the time of writing. It also provides an interpretation which accords with the evidence of women in teaching roles elsewhere in Scripture. We must always interpret Scripture with Scripture. To interpret this passage as being a universal prohibition would be to directly contradict the clear biblical examples elsewhere of women in teaching and leadership ministry.

1 CORINTHIANS 14:34-35

"As in all the congregations of the saints, women should remain silent in the churches. They are not allowed to speak, but must be in submission, as the Law says. If they want to enquire about something, they should ask their own husbands at home; for it is disgraceful for a woman to speak in the church" (1 Cor 14:33-35).

Must women remain silent in church? Is this a universal truth for today, or an obsolete cultural practice from the 1st century? Was it even a universal injunction back then, or a specific instruction to a specific church in response to a particular circumstance? This is another hotly debated passage which continues to polarise Christian opinion. There are some historical and cultural issues, however, that we must consider as we seek to interpret this seemingly prohibitive statement by Paul.

....

[Principle: HISTORICAL / CULTURAL CONTEXT]

In 1st century Jewish society, women were viewed as inferior and ignorant, and were kept that way through lack of access to education.

Only boys were educated. Women were, therefore, not allowed to speak in synagogues or any other public meetings, because they were regarded as having nothing worthwhile to say; their uneducated opinions were not welcome. A woman's silence in a public meeting was also a symbol of her subservience to her husband. A woman who spoke in a public meeting was considered brazen and disrespectful; she brought disgrace upon herself and dishonour upon her husband, because she was not *"in submission"* to him (v34).

Paul is referring to these entrenched cultural standards when he says, *"it is a disgraceful thing for a woman to speak in the church" (1 Cor 14:35)*. By insisting on women's silence in church he is demanding that Christian gatherings conform to accepted societal conventions. He is calling for cultural congruity so that there may be no impediment to the proclamation of the gospel. For us to insist on women's silence in church today would be *incongruous* with our society and would create a cultural barrier to the proclamation of the gospel.

....

[Principle: INTERPRET SCRIPTURE WITH SCRIPTURE]

We must also interpret Scripture with Scripture. What exactly does Paul mean by saying that women should *"remain silent" (v.33)* and not *"speak" (v.35)*? Three chapters earlier, in 1 Corinthians 11, he has already indicated that women can *"pray or prophesy"* in church (v.4), which clearly involves speaking! His demand for women's silence, therefore, cannot be interpreted as a prohibition of orderly public ministry, but, instead, appears to be an injunction against disorderly interjection.

....

[Principle: IMMEDIATE LITERARY CONTEXT]

This interpretation is corroborated by Paul's recommendation to wives that *"if they want to enquire about something, they should ask their own husbands at home" (v.35)*.

....

[Principle: INTERPRET SCRIPTURE WITH SCRIPTURE]

Elsewhere, Paul recognises the valuable contribution of women in public ministry: Phoebe, a deacon of the church in Cenchrea (Rom 16:1-2), Junia, a female apostle (Rom 16:7), Priscilla, Paul's co-worker in the gospel (Rom 16:3), and Euodia and Syntyche, whom Paul described as his *"loyal fellow-workers"* who *"contended at my side in the cause of the gospel" (Phil 4:2-3)* – expressions recognised by most evangelical Bible scholars as referring to gospel preaching.

Taking all of these factors into account, Paul's instruction, in 1 Corinthians 14, concerning women's silence in church appears to be:

- A product of first century cultural standards which are now obsolete.

- Limited to disruptive behaviour specifically, rather than to public ministry generally.

Of course, there are those who disagree with this interpretation. They view the call for women's silence in church (1 Cor 14:33-35) to be universally binding. Strangely, many of these same people choose to interpret everything else in chapter 14 as culturally obsolete and no longer applicable: That everyone who comes to church should be allowed to share *"a word of instruction, a revelation, a tongue or an interpretation" [v.26]*; that two or three should be allowed to speak in a tongue provided there is an interpreter [v.27]; that two or three prophets should speak [v.29]; that they should not forbid the speaking of tongues [v.39]. On what basis are these instructions discarded as culturally or theologically obsolete, yet the demand for women's silence is retained?

1 CORINTHIANS 11:2-16

"I want you to realise that the head of every man is Christ, and the head of every woman is man, and the head of Christ is God..." (v.2)

We have already examined this passage in chapter 14, where we distinguished between the timeless truth (male headship) and its 1st century cultural application (head coverings). Another contextual factor that needs to be incorporated, however, is the precise meaning of "man" and "woman" in this passage.

....

[Principle: LEXICAL CONTEXT]

One factor to consider is that the Greek word in this passage for *"man"* can also be translated *"husband"*. Similarly, the Greek word for *"woman"* can also be translated *"wife"*. Thus, in this passage, the issue being discussed may not be man's generic headship over woman in the church, but a husband's headship over the wife in the home. If this is the case, then the Bible is simply urging wives not to feel that they can lord it over their husbands, even though some wives may have "greater" gifts for public Christian ministry than their husbands.

....

[Principle: INTERPRET SCRIPTURE WITH SCRIPTURE]

Another clue to the puzzle is found in 1 Timothy 2:12, where, as we have already seen, Paul only prohibits a woman's use of domineering or usurping authority. Women can minister alongside men in any area, provided they do not seek to lord it over men. They may (and did in the Bible) minister authoritatively, providing they do not do so domineeringly.

This kind of harmonious sharing of ministry is evidenced by Priscilla and Aquilla always being mentioned as ministering together, and by Junia being mentioned alongside Andronicus as Apostles. It is also evidenced in this passage on headship, in verse 11:

> "In the Lord, however, woman is not independent of man, nor is man independent of woman"

One may ask: Why the need for any kind of headship at all? The answer is found in 1 Corinthians 11. God is a God of order. Just as there is a certain order of function within the Godhead, so he has ordained a functional order in mankind (v.3). In practice, such a functional order does not necessarily preclude a woman from any particular ministry activity, as long as it does not result in her seeking to dominate her husband (if she is married) or her male counterparts within the church leadership. If a woman is willing to respect what appears to be a timeless principle of male headship, there are no biblical grounds for excluding her from any Christian ministry, including being part of an eldership or paid ministry team of a church, as well as exercising a preaching ministry.

CONCLUSION

There is strong evidence within the Bible of God gifting and calling women into teaching and leadership roles within his church. It is not unequivocal evidence, but it seems to me that negating these scriptural examples requires major hermeneutical gymnastics. Paul's seemingly prohibitive injunctions cannot, therefore, be interpreted as universal, timeless prohibitions, but must be regarded as relating to particular precipitating local and cultural factors within the churches to which they were addressed.

The ongoing divergent and hotly debated interpretations of Paul's injunctions, however, highlight the difficulty of distinguishing timeless truths from cultural particularity in the Bible.

Reflection Questions 17

1. What new insights have you gained from reading this chapter?

2. What have you found challenging or difficult in this chapter?

3. Read Acts 21:7-9, which refers to four women prophets in the church at Caesarea. Then read 1 Corinthians 12:29 where prophecy is ranked higher than teaching. Then read 1 Corinthians 14:31 where Paul states that through prophecy the church may "learn". What kind of picture does this build of the role of women in the church gatherings of the first century?

4. Read Judges 4:1-10. How would you describe Deborah's role? Does this passage portray her as exercising leadership and authority? Do you regard this as an exception or a norm? Do you regard this as irrelevant because it was in the old covenant?

5. Compare 1 Corinthians 14:33-35 with 1 Corinthians 11:5. How can you explain the apparent contradiction? Note again, Acts 21:7-9.

6. Read 1 Corinthians 11:2-3 and 7-12. How do you regard this teaching about the relationship between man and woman? Is there a God-ordained hierarchical order? Does the idea of male headship still apply today? How does this relationship play out in marriage? How does it play out within the ministries of the church?

CHAPTER 18

READING THE BIBLE WITH DISCERNMENT

If one thing has become obvious by now, it is that the Bible is a complex book. Its complexity is a result of several factors:

- It was written over a period of 1600 years by over 40 different authors. No other book in history comes close to this diversity of authorship and impressive time-span. The diversity of authorship presents unique challenges to those wanting to understand its message, due to the necessity to understand the unique perspective of each author.

- It is an ancient book, over 2000 years old, separated from our modern world by a vast cultural and historical gulf. Many of the concepts within the Bible are deeply bedded in a culture that is very different to ours. Consequently, there are many points where the Bible's message will only become clear once we have developed an understanding of life in ancient times.

- It contains a broad range of literary styles; poetry, songs, laments, historical narrative, prophecy and doctrinal dogma, each of which require a different interpretive approach.

The principles of biblical interpretation (hermeneutics) that we have explored in this book are all essential tools for those desiring to interpret the Bible accurately. The practical examples in each chapter have, hopefully, "put legs" on each of these principles and revealed their importance. There are countless other passages and doctrines within the Bible that require equally stringent application of these principles, the lack of which can easily lead to misinterpretation and misapplication.

As we reach the end of our exploratory journey into understanding and interpreting the Bible, I want to offer some practical guidelines for ordinary Bible readers who want to improve their interpretive skills. Here are my top tips for reading the Bible with discernment.

1. UNDERSTAND THE DIFFERENCE BETWEEN THE TWO COVENANTS

Three whole chapters of this book have been devoted to explaining the crucial distinction between the two covenants. The Old Testament blessings and curses, rewards and punishments, belong to a covenant that is now obsolete, and cannot be applied to Christians. This fundamental truth must be foremost in your mind as you read the Old Testament. Failure to understand the obsolete nature of the old covenant is one of the most common causes of biblical misinterpretation and false teaching within Christianity today.

2. READ EVERYTHING IN CONTEXT

Context is King! No verse of the Bible exists as an isolated, independent precept. Each verse must be read in the context of its immediate passage, the theme and flow of the whole book, its literary genre, its place in covenantal history, its cultural context, its lexical context, and the context of any specific historical precipitating events that might have given rise to that statement. Taking all these contextual factors into account, however, can be quite complex, requiring a comprehensive understanding of the Bible and its cultural and historical background. It is a daunting task for the ordinary Bible reader who is not a biblical scholar. This brings me to my next tip.

3. USE A RELIABLE STUDY BIBLE

A Study Bible is an essential tool for the serious Bible reader. For the average person who does not wish to spend a fortune on Bible commentaries, a Study Bible is an inexpensive tool that provides essential insights from some of the world's most respected Bible scholars. In particular, a Study Bible provides:

- Introductions to books of the Bible, including the purpose, occasion and theme of the book, any precipitating historical events, as well as any other distinctive characteristics.

- Explanatory footnotes. While these are not as comprehensive as a dedicated Bible commentary, they provide a succinct explanation of the meaning of key verses and outline any relevant cultural or historical context.

- Textual footnotes. These will indicate the presence of any textual variants that may have an impact on the meaning of the text.

- Cross referencing. This allows you to easily check other textual locations where the same theme or topic is addressed. The importance of checking cross-referencing cannot be over-estimated, as other Bible passages will often have a moderating influence on the interpretation of the original verse, and will allow the reader to build a comprehensive and balanced understanding of the topic.

- Maps and timelines. These occasional visual aids can be a valuable tool in providing context and overview.

4. USE A BIBLE APP

I can't recommend this highly enough. A decent Bible app will open up a whole new world of resources for the serious Bible reader. These include:

- Multiple translations to compare alternate readings. Most apps will allow you to have multiple translations open simultaneously.

- Greek / Hebrew meanings of words. In most apps, simply by highlighting a word in the Bible text, a secondary window will open, providing you with the original Greek or Hebrew word, together with its concise dictionary definition and a link to other passages where the same word is used.

- A range of free online commentaries (usually quite old but still helpful). These can provide valuable assistance in explaining difficult passages.

- Contemporary Bible commentaries that can be purchased through the app, at a fraction of their hard copy price.

- A search and cross-referencing system that enables you to quickly jump to other similar passages with the touch of a finger or the click of a mouse.

A Bible app is a convenient means of tapping into a world of scholarly resources. Some apps are free, but the better ones will require a small expenditure. In my opinion, it is the best money you will ever spend! I happen to use Olive Tree Bible App, but there are plenty of other very good apps out there.

5. READ THE WHOLE BIBLE

There is no better way of developing a contextual understanding of biblical truth than reading the whole book. I am amazed at how many Christians have never actually read the whole Bible. They may have read dozens of novels, read hundreds of blogs, listened to hundreds of podcasts, but never bothered to read the whole of God's Word at least once. One of the reasons is that it seems a daunting task, but if it is broken down into daily portions it is very achievable.

I used to do an interesting class activity, when I was a Biblical Studies teacher. I got all the students to read a single chapter of the Bible, and timed how long it took them, reading at a comfortable pace. The average time was 2 minutes 30 seconds. I rounded that up to 3 minutes to be generous. I then explained to the class that the Bible contains 1,189 chapters. We calculated that reading the whole Bible would take: 3 minutes x 1,189 = 3,567 minutes. Therefore, to read the whole Bible in one year would take 3,567 minutes divided by 365 days = 9.7 minutes per day.

Just 10 minutes per day would enable you to read the entire Bible in one year! Most people spend much more than 10 minutes each day on social media or watching TV. How important is God's Word to you? The more you read it, and the more familiar you become with the flow of its story, the better you will be able to interpret its message contextually.

Charles Spurgeon, the great preacher of the 19th century, once commented,

> *"Why is it that some Christians, although they hear many sermons, make but slow advances in the divine life? Because they neglect their closets, and do not thoughtfully meditate on God's Word. They love the wheat, but they do not grind it; they would have the corn, but they will not go forth into the fields to gather it; the fruit hangs upon the tree, but they will not pluck it; the*

water flows at their feet, but they will not stoop to drink it. From such folly deliver us, O Lord."

6. JOIN A BIBLE STUDY GROUP

The insight and perspective of other Christians can be extremely helpful in broadening your own understanding. Christians aren't meant to fly solo. We need each other. The wisdom of God's Spirit is more clearly manifest when we meet together than when we sit at home trying to read the Bible on our own. This is why the writer to Hebrews exhorts us, *"Do not give up meeting together, as some are in the habit of doing" (Heb 10:25)*. Often the meaning of a passage that is difficult for you will become much clearer when others contribute their insights.

7. READ PRAYERFULLY

In the end, the Bible is a spiritual book, that requires spiritual insight. It is the Holy Spirit who brings the words of this book to life, enlightening our minds, convicting our hearts and inspiring our spirits. Without his illuminating work within us, the Bible is simply a collection of words. We need to read the Bible with a prayerful heart, trusting in the Holy Spirit to open our hearts and minds to God's message, so that we might discern and apply God's truth to our lives. All the hermeneutical principles in the world cannot do this. As helpful and important as they are as interpretive tools, they can only take us so far. We need the Holy Spirit to breathe life into the words that we read, so that their message penetrates our hearts and transforms us from within.

CONCLUSION

We have reached the end of our journey of discovery regarding this unique book that we call "the Bible". Along the way we have:

- Examined the fascinating journey from autographic texts to final translations.

- Seen the complex task facing textual critics as they scrutinise the thousands of textual variants in order to reconstruct an accepted version of the original text.

- Highlighted the difficulties faced by translators in dealing with lexical uncertainty and grammatical incompatibility as they seek to produce an accurate and meaningful rendering in our receptor language.

- Noted the hundreds of minor internal inconsistencies within the Bible that result from unresolved textual variants between parallel historical narratives.

- Developed a more sophisticated, mature understanding of the nature and extent of the Bible's inspiration and inerrancy.

- Examined the fundamental theological differences between the old and new covenants, and extrapolated some vital principles for interpreting the Old Testament.

- Highlighted the importance of reading the Bible Christologically, because the whole Bible, including the Old Testament, is ultimately pointing us to Christ.

- Investigated the crucial hermeneutical principles that must be constantly employed as we read the Bible, to ensure that the message we receive is the message that was originally intended.

- Analysed many practical examples of Bible passages and doctrines that are commonly misinterpreted due to ignorance of fundamental hermeneutic principles.

It is my hope and prayer that your understanding of the Bible is now clearer, your faith in its inspiration is more mature, and your ability to interpret its message is more refined.

Thomas Carlyle, the 19th century Scottish philosopher, once wrote,

> *"The Bible is the truest utterance that ever came by alphabetic letters from the soul of man, through which, as through a window divinely opened, all people can look into the stillness of eternity, and discern in glimpses their far-distant, long-forgotten home."*

May you find within the Bible's pages an ever-clearer window into eternity and an increasingly surer glimpse of your not-so-distant, not-so-forgotten true home.

Reflection Questions 18

1. Reflect upon the many topics that you have studied in the course of reading this book. What have been some of the highlights for you?

2. What have been the most difficult or challenging aspects of the topics that the book has examined?

3. How have your views changed or been modified as a result of the topics you have studied in this book?

4. What are the biggest challenges for you in becoming a regular reader of the Bible? What practical steps can you take to make Bible reading a more regular component of your life?

AUTHOR BIO

Kevin Simington (B.Th. Dip. Min.) is a theologian, apologist and social commentator. He spent 31 years in Christian ministry, as a church pastor and a Christian educator. He is now a full time author and speaker. His website, SmartFaith.net, and his Facebook page, "Reflections on Faith and Life", provide valuable resources for defending the Christian faith and equipping Christians. Kevin's weekly blog, available through his website, provides incisive commentary on social issues, theology, apologetics and ethics.

OTHER TITLES BY KEVIN SIMINGTON

FINDING GOD WHEN HE SEEMS TO BE HIDING:

Intelligent Answers to Profound Questions

This book provides intelligent answers to the 12 most common objections that are raised against Christianity. Questions such as: What evidence is there for God's existence? If God wants people to believe in him, why doesn't he make Himself more obvious? If God is so good, why is there so much suffering in the world? Hasn't science and evolution disproved God? God-ordained killing in the Bible, and throughout the ages, makes Christians no better than terrorists! What sort of narcissistic God eternally tortures people for not loving him? Is the Bible reliable? Has it changed over time? Is the life of Jesus a myth? What evidence is there for his resurrection? How can God permit abuse and religious violence?

This book is highly recommended for anyone who is struggling to believe in God and in the truth of Christianity. It addresses these difficult issues with remarkable clarity, insight and wit. It proposes meaningful answers that will challenge the most hardened of sceptics, and will strengthen the faith of those who already believe.

"Finding God When He Seems To Be Hiding" is available in print or as an eBook from SmartFaith.net and from all major retailers.

NO MORE MONKEY BUSINESS:

EVOLUTION IN CRISIS

"The shocking truth behind a failed theory!"

"No More Monkey Business" is a concise, easy-to-read summary of the overwhelming and rapidly accumulating scientific evidence against evolution. Written with wit, and using simple layman's language, yet brimming with incontestable scientific evidence, this book highlights the huge problems now facing Darwin's original theory. Each chapter is full of fascinating scientific facts and discoveries which now directly contradict Darwin's naïvely simplistic theory proposed more than a century ago. *"No More Monkey Business"* documents the abandonment of the theory of evolution by a growing tide of the world's leading scientists, as well as the startling declaration by several recent scientific conferences that the theory of evolution can no longer be considered to be scientifically tenable. This book will challenge those who have unthinkingly assumed evolution to be a proven fact, and will enable Christians to defend their faith with confidence.

"No More Monkey Business" will be available in late 2019 in print or as an eBook from SmartFaith.net and from all major retailers.

CONNECT WITH KEVIN SIMINGTON

Visit Kevin Simington's website:

https://smartfaith.net

SmartFaith.net contains a large repository of helpful resources in the areas of apologetics, theology and philosophy.

Visit Kevin's facebook page, "Reflections on Faith and Life" at https://www.facebook.com/ReflectionsKev/

Subscribe to Kevin's weekly blog at https://smartfaith.net/blog/

TOPICAL INDEX

Evidence for The Inspiration of The Bible 7
Apparent Contradictions in The Bible 10
Manuscripts and Variants 19
God's Miraculous Protection of Manuscripts 39
The Transmission of The Old Testament 49
The Nature of The Bible's Divine Inspiration 60
Challenges Faced By Translators 67
Types of Bible Translations 72
Interpreting The Old Testament 87
The Two Covenants 101
Obsolescence of The Old Covenant 103
A Brand New Covenant 103
The Old Testament as Pre-Christian 131
Harsh Punishments in The Old Testament 140
God's Discipline of Christians 149
Progressive Revelation in The Old Testament 155
The Trinity in the Old Testament 161
Prophecies Concerning The Messiah 164
Eternal Life in The Old Testament 169
Marriage and Polygamy in The Old Testament 173
Progressive Revelation in The New Testament 185
Church Leadership in The New Testament 190

Typology 205

Principles For Interpreting Historical Narratives 222

The Gift of Tongues 228

Alcohol 232

Interpreting The Book of Revelation 241

Women's Head Covering 250

Male Headship 253

Prosperity Doctrine 261

Salvation: What Must I Do To Be Saved? 272

Conditions For Answered Prayer 274

Healing 278

Women in Church Leadership 289

General Principles For Interpreting The Bible 307

www.ingramcontent.com/pod-product-compliance
Lightning Source LLC
Chambersburg PA
CBHW071855290426
44110CB00013B/1161